Managing Healthy
Sports Fields

Managing Healthy Sports Fields

A Guide to Using Organic Materials
for Low-Maintenance and Chemical-Free
Playing Fields

Paul D. Sachs

WILEY

John Wiley & Sons, Inc.

To
M. Robin Barone
and
George Wightman Williams
The special teachers in my life

This book is printed on acid-free paper.

Copyright © 2004 by John Wiley & Sons, Inc. All rights reserved

Published by John Wiley & Sons, Inc., Hoboken, New Jersey
Published simultaneously in Canada

No part of this publication may be reproduced, stored in a retrieval system, or transmitted in any form or by any means, electronic, mechanical, photocopying, recording, scanning, or otherwise, except as permitted under Section 107 or 108 of the 1976 United States Copyright Act, without either the prior written permission of the Publisher, or authorization through payment of the appropriate per-copy fee to the Copyright Clearance Center, Inc., 222 Rosewood Drive, Danvers, MA 01923, (978) 750-8400, fax (978) 750-4470, or on the web at www.copyright.com. Requests to the Publisher for permission should be addressed to the Permissions Department, John Wiley & Sons, Inc., 111 River Street, Hoboken, NJ 07030, (201) 748-6011, fax (201) 748-6008, e-mail: permcoordinatorwiley.com.

Limit of Liability/Disclaimer of Warranty: While the publisher and author have used their best efforts in preparing this book, they make no representations or warranties with respect to the accuracy or completeness of the contents of this book and specifically disclaim any implied warranties of merchantability or fitness for a particular purpose. No warranty may be created or extended by sales representatives or written sales materials. The advice and strategies contained herein may not be suitable for your situation. You should consult with a professional where appropriate. Neither the publisher nor author shall be liable for any loss of profit or any other commercial damages, including but not limited to special, incidental, consequential, or other damages.

For general information on our other products and services or for technical support, please contact our Customer Care Department within the United States at 800-762-2974, outside the United States at (317) 572-3993 or fax (317) 572-4002.

Wiley also publishes its books in a variety of electronic formats. Some content that appears in print may not be available in electronic books.

Library of Congress Cataloging-in-Publication Data:
Sachs, Paul D.
    Managing healthy sports fields : a guide to using organic materials for low-maintenance and chemical-free playing fields / Paul Sachs.
        p. cm.
Includes bibliographical references and index.
    ISBN 0-471-47269-7 (Cloth)
    1. Turf management. 2. Athletic fields—Maintenance and repair. I. Title.
SB433 .S233 2004
635.9'642—dc22   2003021221

Printed in the United States of America

10 9 8 7 6 5 4 3 2 1

CONTENTS

ACKNOWLEDGMENTS

Appreciation is due to Rob Baken, David Bergquist, Herman Blanchette, Will Brinton, Paul Chu, Peter Cookingham, Alan Eaton, John Evans, Jeff Frank, David Friedman, Beat Hauenstein, Don Houston, Bob Labbance, George Leidig, Richard Luff, David Mattocks, Mike Mueller, Bill Quarles, James Ricci, Frank Rossi, Peter Russell, Roy Tamir, Jim Snow, Patricia Vittum, Paul Wagner, and David Wieprecht for sharing their knowledge and experience with me.

Special thanks to George Brothers, Randy Brown, and Bob Thebodo at the Dartmouth College Maintenance Department, Elaine Ingham of Soil Food Web, Inc., Bob Norsen at GroundUP LLC, and Bruce Richards for the time and effort they contributed for this book.

INTRODUCTION

The grounds supervisor works in a climate-controlled cubicle high above the stadium floor. He watches as robotic mowers, programmed to cut in specific patterns, scurry about the field. Within an hour, the job is done. The mowers are followed by laser-guided topdressing machines that create a surface more true than a glass tabletop. The topdressers are equipped with ArthroTraks™, a device that scans for insect larvae and adults with a combination of resonance spectroscopy and carbon dioxide (CO_2) detectors as the machine moves slowly across the field. When the location of a larva is determined, it is automatically extracted with a tweezers-like device, identified, and conveyed to an incineration chamber. The location, depth, identification, size, and instar stage are logged in an onboard computer that reports its findings at the end of the operation. The machine is programmed to ignore any arthropod determined to be beneficial or neutral.

The topdressing machine is also armed with an electronic de-weeder that locates unwanted plant cultivars by infrared biotelemetry. Detection immediately triggers a probe that kills and incinerates the weed with a short but powerful and incredibly precise pulse of electrical current. When the topdressers are done, hovering Pathopods™ begin scanning the field for signs of disease. The Pathopods, using magnetic resonance and gas spectrometry, can detect not only active mycelium but also dormant spores. Minimum detection limits are microscopic in size. The Pathopods treat afflicted areas with specific bio-antagonists and antigens that boost the turf plant's immune system. They are also equipped with infrared scanners that measure the chlorophyll content of plant leaves. Measurements outside a given range indicate plants that are stressed and thus susceptible to infection. Prophylactic treatments with biostimulants and antigens are immediately initiated.

Aeration is an operation that has been obsolete for decades. Whenever needed, soil decompression is accomplished with sonic pulses generated from 12 inches beneath the surface. Low-frequency, inaudible blasts move through the soil, vibrating compacted particles apart. Surface disruption is nominal. Radar penetrometers mounted on each mower monitor soil compaction daily and send the data to the central control unit, which determines when, where, and if sonic pulsing is necessary. Everything is automatic.

Irrigation also originates beneath the surface. Underground tubing supplies pressure-regulated emitters that typically release a special highly oxygenated, bio-inoculated liquid. The dissolved oxygen feeds roots and aerobic organisms that colonize the rhizosphere. These organisms establish symbiotic relationships that both feed and protect the turf. The central computer can control each individual emitter. The emitters do not release any water until each active one has an exact amount of back-pressure, ensuring that every cubic inch of soil receives exactly the right amount of moisture. Computers that monitor evapotranspiration, soil moisture, and leaf tissue temperature control the amount of water injected into the soil. Doses are automatically delivered when and where needed. The emitters can also perform as siphon heads if too much moisture is detected in the soil. The system can create negative pressure with vacuum pumps and extract superfluous water from the soil. Each emitter can be controlled individually so only the areas that need it are treated.

Soil temperature is also controlled with this system. The special tubing can carry either heated or cooled water through the system and can raise or lower the soil temperature. The removal of heat from the soil during the hot summer months mitigates stress so significantly that heat-related problems rarely develop. Warming the soil as the weather cools keeps turf growing vigorously and even melts the occasional snow that falls during the football season.

Turbulence is an important component of natural growing systems from which stadium turf is sheltered, especially in arenas with roofs, retractable or not. Immense blowers were used as a substitute for natural turbulence until macrowave-induced turbulence (MWIT) was discovered. MWIT works in much the same manner as microwaves in that individual plant cells of the plants are vibrated. Unlike microwaves, however, macrowaves do not create friction and, consequently, heat. Macrowaves massage the plant cells and strengthen their walls much as turbulence would. The grounds superintendent is alerted when routine tissue analysis reveals weakened cell walls, and macrowave generators are engaged for a predetermined amount of time.

Chemical fungicides, insecticides, and herbicides have been obsolete for nearly half a century. The only pesticide manufactures that survived the dawn of the ecological era were those involved with the development of botanical or biological pest controls. Pest control has been nearly 100 percent, 100 percent of the time since 2052, far more effective than chemical controls ever were. The old pesticide factories have been taken over by pharmaceutical companies. The only damage sports turf incurs these days is from the players. Even this, however, is mitigated by deep-rooted, healthy, resilient turf plants that better tolerate traffic damage.

Occasionally, turf damage does have to be repaired. Special topdressing machines are dispatched to scan for surface disruption and implement repair. They carry a blend of mature, bio-inoculated compost, medium-coarse sand, seed, and natural plant growth regulators that trigger quick germination and root establishment. The special raking/topdressing mechanism is automatically engaged if sensors detect any surface anomalies.

Sometimes the damage is extensive enough that sod must be replaced. Laser-guided sod cutters are used to extirpate the damaged areas. The areas where they work are recorded with a geopositioning system, and the machines that lay down new sod duplicate the sod cutter's path to within a thousandth of an inch. Three position sensors, located high in the stadium light frames, triangulate the sod machines' movements. Natural rooting hormones are injected through the irrigation system to ensure rapid establishment. All sod is scanned for insects and disease before it is shipped, so the chance of importing pests is remote; those that manage to get through are quickly discovered and dispatched during routine maintenance. Mowers can reestablish patterns within hours of the completed sodding operation.

Excessive thatch is another obsolete problem. Biological fertility management has balanced plant needs with availability, and saprophytic (decay) organisms are introduced regularly. Natural extracts from compost, seaweed, humates, and rock dusts are automatically delivered through the irrigation system when the main computer calls for it. Fertility is determined through near-infrared leaf tissue analysis performed on clippings collected during mowing. Earthworm cocoons are seeded once per year, and castings are swept daily with a hovering power whip that covers the field in less than 15 minutes. The power whip resembles a twentieth-century floor polisher but, instead of a polishing pad, it has four flexible carbon-fiber tentacles that rotate and sweep the turf canopy. Earthworms and saprophytes can control the accumulation of thatch but sometimes overmanage it. The system engineers understand that some thatch provides mechanical protection for both players and turf. Biomass measurements are used to balance populations of decay organisms with fertilization and thatch production.

The result of all these advances in field maintenance is a nearly flawless natural turf playing surface. The environment these plants grow in is as close to heaven as any earthly organism may ever experience. The marriage of technology and biological stewardship began in the twenty-first century and evolved into what is currently referred to as *Applied Ecological Growth Idealization Science*, or AEGIS. The main premise of AEGIS is that no ecosystem can be stable without a complex diversity of organisms. Practitioners of AEGIS do not pretend to know enough about the intricacies of the ecosystem to micromanage it, but they understand that biological diversity is crucial to the stability and functionality of a turf ecosystem.

Because turf is a monoculture, diversity is a challenging proposition, but the lack of plant diversity is offset by the infusion of resources for soil organisms. Carbohydrates, proteins, fibers, and other foods are used to feed a vast diversity of organisms from bacteria to arthropods. The proliferation of these organisms feeds predators, parasites, and many other members of the soil food web. Maintaining this diversity is the key to a stable ecosystem. Even on low-budget fields where expensive automated equipment is beyond fiscal reach, AEGIS is still employed as the best management technique. Regular applications of resources to promote biological diversity are introduced to the soil and plant surfaces. Botanical and biological controls are used more often where detection equipment is unaffordable.

The change from chemical management techniques to AEGIS came about slowly. Rachel Carson began the environmental movement in the mid-twentieth century, but her views and those of her followers were not taken seriously for more than half a century. When research began to connect pesticides with health issues, controversy erupted, as did the resistance of the chemical industry, especially pesticide manufacturers. The evidence was disputed for decades. In 2001, the Lymphoma Foundation of America released a comprehensive report indicting many pesticides as causal agents of non-Hodgkin's lymphoma. The report, an analysis of 117 studies from well-respected sources, was reviewed by a committee of 12 eminent scientists. Soon after, many more scientific papers began to emerge supporting the findings of the Lymphoma Foundation. The issue of liability began to grow, and it was only a matter of time before pesticide manufacturers fell prey to the same fate as tobacco companies at the turn of the twenty-first century.

As a result, new management techniques quickly developed. Now, the thought of releasing synthetic pesticides into the ecosystem is as absurd to a turf manager as bloodletting is to a doctor. Nearly 100 years after Rachel Carson's revealing work, the use of chemical pest controls is obsolete, but after 150 years of release, it may be a millennium or more before all traces of them are gone. Indeed, some of these toxic concoctions may be with us for the rest of time.

Although the preceding description is fiction—except for the Lymphoma Foundation of America's report—it's not unreasonable to believe that many of these ideas may become reality, especially when one considers how dubious managers a century ago might have been on reading a description of our contemporary tools or management methods. Many turf managers already practice the concept of AEGIS, and some of the tools mentioned above are either in use or being researched. The Prescription Athletic Turf (PAT) system, for example, can pump water out of or into the soil when it becomes saturated or dry. Super-accurate mowers that cut with laser beams were introduced in 2000 and, although impractical for large expanses of turf, robotic mower technology has been around for years (Friendly Robotics). Near-infrared leaf tissue analysis is currently available (Spectrum), and geopositioning is an existing technology that just hasn't been applied to turf maintenance yet. Underground capillary irrigation has been available since 1999 (see Chapter 6, p. 209); underground pans are used to collect drainwater, which is then naturally wicked upward through the soil to the plant roots (ECS).

The experienced manager knows, however, that high-technology innovations are usually exciting but not always ideal. As much as we might like the practice of AEGIS to be universal, pragmatic, inexpensive, and always effective, it may be a while before *Applied Ecological Growth Idealization Science* is as widely recognized as *Integrated Pest Management* (IPM). Indeed, this fictitious acronym (AEGIS) may never acquire any notable recognition.

With or without AEGIS, today's sports field managers face difficult challenges. First and foremost, they must provide a safe environment for athletes of all ages that also looks good. Given the amount of abuse turf endures from athletic activities—often combined with the stress of maintenance and sometimes severe environmental conditions—it is easy to understand how turf health problems can develop.

Health problems weaken turf and present opportunities for pathogens, insects, and weeds to succeed. Horticultural scientists usually recommend symptom relievers (pesticides) to deal with these problems, but as more and more of these products are applied, a chemical dependence is often established. What many of us involved in turf maintenance fail to embrace is that disease, weeds, and insects are not the cause of unhealthy turf—they result from it.

In the old world of turfgrass maintenance, before an extensive chemical arsenal was available, keeping the grass as healthy as possible was the first line of defense against problems. Much attention was paid to soil fertility and structure, and organic matter was considered essential. Most of what is published about turf maintenance, no matter how long ago it was written, proclaims plant health as an important aspect of preventing pest problems. Many books and articles, however, especially those written in the 1950s and 1960s, recommended the application of the newest and most powerful pesticide at the slightest hint of a problem. Indeed, many advocated the use of pesticides in anticipation of problems that did not yet exist.

Now the green industry has come full circle. Our huge chemical arsenal is slowly but steadily being restricted by local, regional, state, and federal regulation as well as outright banning. The green industry is fighting hard to retain the right to use these chemicals, but the trend is against them. The chemical industry is responding with stronger active ingredients to reduce application rates and with less environmental persistence to mitigate long-term ecological impact and shorten reentry periods. Unfortunately, if the effect of these bioicides is ephemeral, it's inevitable that they will have to be used more often. Realistically speaking, most pest controls don't solve problems; they just mitigate or eradicate symptoms. What is becoming clear to more and more turf managers is that as the level of stress increases and the tolerance threshold for pests decreases, biological diversity, complexity, and stability in a turfgrass ecosystem become increasingly more important. Unfortunately, the use of many chemical biocides can reduce the stability of this system.

This book proposes to partially or perhaps completely liberate the modern turf manager from this chemical dependence by suggesting methods that don't adversely affect the game or the appearance of the playing field but nevertheless dramatically reduce the need for pesticides and other chemicals. The political battle against the systematic reduction of chemical choices may only postpone the inevitable. Moreover, learning alternative and ecological methods of sports field management can be an intriguing pursuit with tremendous rewards. But ecological management techniques are as much an art as they are a science. An art is a skill gained from experience, observation, or both. It cannot always be replicated or proven by the unskilled, inexperienced, or unobservant. Techniques that work for one manager but not for another are not necessarily invalid; they are either specific to the site where they are successful or they require a degree of skill and finesse not being applied elsewhere.

The information in this book does not constitute formula for every sports field on earth. The book presents alternatives and information that will enable the turf manager to consider or even invent new ways of solving problems; the new approaches may include botanical or biological biocides, changing cultural practices, or just cultivating a healthier and more biologically active ecosystem. Ecological turf maintenance calls for the manager to consider *all* of the organisms in the turf ecosystem, because most of them are allies. It also means expectations may have to be adjusted to a more realistic and practical threshold where a natural equilibrium can be maintained. It does *not* mean that the natural beauty of a thick, lush turf or the level of play must be sacrificed.

ABOUT THE AUTHOR

Paul Sachs is the founder and owner of North Country Organics, a Bradford, Vermont–based manufacturer and supplier of natural fertilizers, soil amendments, and environmentally compatible pest controls.

Paul has studied natural soil system dynamics for over 18 years and is considered one of the foremost authorities in the United States on organic land care. He has written four books and hundreds of trade journal articles, and he speaks regularly at association conferences for professionals in agriculture and horticulture. He has served as a member of the Technical Advisory Panel for the National Organics Standards Board of the U.S. Department of Agriculture. He also works as a consultant for a highly diversified group of clients. In 1993, he completed work on his first book, entitled *EDAPHOS: Dynamics of a Natural Soil System*; in 1996, he finished his second book, entitled *Handbook of $uccessful Ecological Lawn Care*; in 1999, he completed a second edition of *EDAPHOS*; and in 2002, he coauthored a book with Richard Luff entitled *Ecological Golf Course Management*.

Chapter 1

THE SOIL ECOSYSTEM

If one were to imagine the soil ecosystem as a machine, it would have billions of functioning parts. It would be such a complex mechanism that, were it to break, no repairman on earth would be capable of fixing it. Fortunately, in its exquisite design, the soil also contains its own repair mechanism and, even in cases of extreme damage, it can almost always repair itself. The time it takes to recover, however, depends on both the extent of the damage and the conditions that regulate the renewal of life, as it is the soil's biological component that facilitates its ability to heal.

In 1980, the volcano Mount Saint Helens exploded and destroyed the surrounding 234-square-mile area. The soil disappeared under a thick blanket of volcanic ash and rock. Soil life—all life—was annihilated. The devastation from extremely hot ash, pyroclastic flows, blowdowns, and mudflows was severe and seemingly irreparable—but slowly, over the decades, life has begun to reestablish itself. The repair is an ongoing and joint effort of teams of plants, soil organisms, insects and other arthropods, amphibians, birds, and mammals, some of whom work around the clock, 365 days a year.

Restoration probably began by photosynthesizing (autotrophic) bacteria that extracted energy from the sun, combined it with carbon dioxide from the atmosphere and terrestrial minerals, and produced the organic materials necessary for proliferation. As these pioneers of life grew in number, some predator organisms were able to subsist and they, in turn, fed others on the next link of the food chain. Eventually, more and more kinds of organisms began to colonize the devastated area, and organic residues from their activities and expired bodies began to accumulate. Before long, plants were able to acquire the necessities for life. Wildflowers, especially prairie lupines and fireweed, were probably the first to reappear. (The prairie lupine survives and thrives in nutrient-poor soils and, because it's a legume, it works with rhizobacteria to fix nitrogen from the atmosphere for itself and to share with other organisms.) As more and more plants appeared, wildlife began to graze again. Gophers and mice were among the first mammals to migrate into the devastation, and their burrowing activities, through the ash to the soil below, began mixing the horizons. The spread and proliferation of life begun by autotrophic bacteria have brought significant change to an area that, a relatively short time ago, resembled the surface of the moon more than anything on this planet. As more and more life inhabits the devastated soil, it becomes more inhabitable for other organisms, including forest plants. The essential interdependence of life in a functioning ecosystem is an important lesson to learn from Mount Saint Helens, and one that applies everywhere (see Figure 1-1).

The chemical, biological, and physical reactions that make soil functional need air, water, minerals, energy from the sun, and time. The scenic beauty of natural landscapes was not created from a grand plan engineered by a landscape architect and constructed by people in a single season. It evolved over thousands of millennia from organisms in stiff competition that nevertheless created symbiotic alliances. It is that competition and those alliances that must be better understood to engage the soil ecosystem in the creation of a sustainable recreational landscape.

The soil machine can be nudged perhaps, but it cannot be controlled, which is fortunate, because no one really understands the complexities of the soil system well

FIGURE 1-1   Mt. Saint Helens devastated almost 250 square miles of the Pacific Northwest. Photo courtesy U.S. Geological Survey.

enough to govern it. When control is attempted, a part of the machine may be altered or damaged and cease to function properly. In a simple machine, like an automobile engine, malfunctioning parts are noticed almost immediately. But in a complex system, like the soil, dysfunction can go unnoticed for years, decades, or perhaps even centuries. Because the machine is so complex, the cause of a symptom can easily be misunderstood.

SOIL CREATION

To get a sense of how the soil functions—and it will be a superficial sense at best—let's first take a look at how the soil, as we know it, was formed.

Before there was soil, there was rock—perhaps one extremely large chunk called Earth. Eventually, tectonic movement, volcanoes, and other natural forces created pieces of rock, some of which were large and some mere particles of dust (see Figure 1-2). This process of rock size reduction is called *weathering*, and many forces contribute to it. The typical analysis of a well-developed loam (see Figure 1-6) shows that half of the soil's volume is pore space that is (ideally) filled with equal parts of air and water. Most soil solids are minerals derived from rock.

Water, especially when it freezes, is a bull in a china shop when it comes to weathering. In a river, stream, or brook, water constantly washes away surface particles from rocks in its path as it cascades over, under, around, and sometimes through the parent material (see Figures 1-3a and 1-3b). What may seem gentle to the observer is an unrelenting torrent of force to particles clinging to rock surfaces. Those particles snatched by the water's will become unwitting accomplices in tasks downstream, abrasively

FIGURE 1-2   Rock is soil's main ingredient. Over time, natural forces reduce rock size from majestic to sometimes microscopic soil particles.

FIGURE 1-3A   Flowing water is constantly wearing down rock surfaces and carries liberated particles away.

betraying brethren particles. When gravity's assistance wanes, the water slows, and many of the suspended particles settle to the bottom. Over time, the bottom is built up from these deposits and the water finds a new path, leaving behind beds of sediment—the foundation of a riparian soil.

When the temperature drops below freezing, water changes from liquid to solid and expands with a force few natural materials can contain (see Figure 1-4). One hundred fifty tons of expansive force per square foot can compromise the structure of nearly any rock that allows moisture to enter through cracks, fissures, or pores. If the force of frost separates a boulder from its mother mountain, gravity can assist in the process of weathering as the accelerating rock smashes itself and the surface against which it falls into smaller and smaller pieces.

Wind is another persuasive natural force that not only can coax small particles of rock away from the parent surface but also spread it to areas far and wide. As these pieces ride the wind, they too become unwitting accomplices, blasting free other particles with which they collide. Glaciers, earthquakes,

FIGURE 1-3B   As the flow of water slows, suspended rock particles settle and form the basis of riparian soil.

and volcanic eruptions are other forces that produce weathered rock particles.

As powerful and persuasive as these physical forces can be, yet another type of weathering also makes significant contributions to the formation of soil. Surprisingly, the largest facility on earth where chemical reactions occur is the natural environment. Naturally occurring elements react with each other regularly to form compounds, many of which then react with other compounds or elements. This con-stant manufacture and disintegration of chemicals in nature is an integral part of terrestrial functions. One of the effects of this natural chemical activity is an advanced stage of weathering rock into soil.

FIGURE 1-4   Water that finds its way into rock expands with a force of 150 tons per square foot when it freezes.

Water is chemically expressed as H_2O. Its two constituent elements (hydrogen and oxygen) can react chemically with many other elements in nature. The entire water molecule can react in a process called *hydration*. Rock minerals that bond with one or more water molecules become hydrated and are more easily dissolved into a soil sys-tem. *Hydrolysis* occurs when a hydrogen atom in water bonds with natural elements, often forming acids that contribute to weathering rock surfaces. Chemical chain reac-tions, initiated by either the hydrogen or the oxygen in water, can change the original composition of rock; the resulting mineral compounds can have completely different structures and reactive characteristics within the soil.

The formation of inorganic acids, such as sulfuric acid and hydrochloric acid, occurs naturally through reactions between soil chemicals. These acids are extremely effective at separating and dissolving rock components. Carbonic acid, a powerful weathering agent, is formed from the combination of carbon dioxide and water, two relatively abundant substances in the soil.

The different types of parent material determine the rate at which rock is weath-ered and, to a large extent, the size of the resulting particles found in the soil. Lime-stone, for example, is a rock that is easily weathered and can eventually dissolve so completely that few particles can be found. Quartz, on the other hand, weathers slowly; because of its structure, it is difficult for nature to completely weather it into its molecular components.

Another factor that influences weathering is surface area. The greater the surface area exposed to soil acids, the faster rock particles can be dissolved. A fist-sized stone may have several square inches of surface area when intact, but when it is ground into a fine powder, the overall surface area increases to several *acres*. The amount of time it takes for nature to weather the material is measured in years for the powder, compared to centuries for the intact stone.

Rocks composed predominately of aluminum, potassium, or magnesium silicates (generally insoluble compounds) are commonly weathered into tiny (<0.002-inch diameter) platelike particles classified as *clay*. Because of complex substitutions of ele-

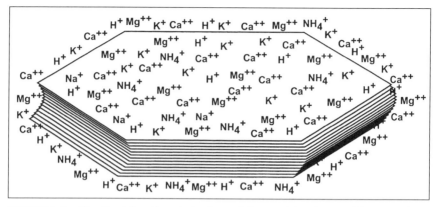

FIGURE 1-5   Clay Particles. Negatively charged clay particles shown with a typical platelike appearance and swarm of adsorbed cations.

ments within their molecular structure, many clay particles inherently have a negative electromagnetic (anionic) charge that enables them to adsorb positively charged ions (cations) such as potassium (K), calcium (Ca), and magnesium (Mg) (see Figure 1-5). This magnetic ability is described as *colloidal* (from the Greek *koll*, meaning "glue," and *oid*, meaning "like") and is inherent in humus particles as well. Colloidal particles play a crucial role in the soil system. Soil environments devoid of either clay or humus—like pure sand fields—have a greatly diminished capacity to hold plant nutrients and, consequently, do not naturally support an abundance of plants or other biological life.

Soils formed from rock are called *mineral soils*; this is the most common type of soil on earth. An analysis of a well-developed mineral soil might reveal around 90 percent rock particles on a dry basis (see Figure 1-6). Volumetrically, 50 percent of this type of soil is made up of air and water. In a rich, healthy soil, an average of only 5 percent is organic matter. Natural levels of organic matter vary considerably.

There are about 90 naturally occurring elements on earth; most are found, at least in trace amounts, nearly everywhere. The most common elements found in the min-

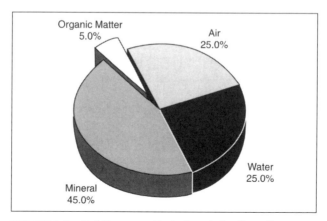

FIGURE 1-6   Soil Structure. Typical analysis of a well developed loam.

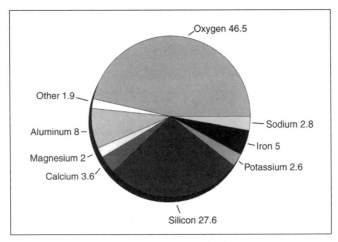

FIGURE 1-7   Mineral Components. Eight elements comprise 98% of soil mineral.

eral component of soil, however, are oxygen, silicon, aluminum, calcium, sodium, iron, potassium, and magnesium (see Figure 1-7). The oxygen that exists in soil minerals is part of the chemical structure and is not in a gaseous state. Many elements exist in a naturally formed molecule with oxygen.

All of these weathering forces, both physical and chemical, combine to form soil particles from rock that are better known as *sand*, *silt*, and *clay*. These particles are defined by size, as shown in Table 1-1. Most soils have a combination of all three sizes of particles and are classified depending on the percentage of each (see Chapter 4, under "Texture Analysis").

TABLE 1-1
USDA Soil Particle Classification

Clay	≤ 0.002 mm
Silt	> 0.002 mm ≤ 0.05 mm
Sand	< 0.05 mm ≤ 2.0 mm
Gravel	> 2.0 mm

The concept of weathering isn't difficult to grasp and seems to give a clear picture of how soil is formed, but the result is not soil yet—just dirt. Weathering simply provides a picture of how soil texture is formed.

BIOLOGICAL CONTRIBUTION

Dirt needs something else before it can become soil, and that is life—and also death. Life and death in the soil are vital phenomena of an ecosystem that perpetually generates energy for the biosphere. Here is where the soil and its system of cycles become more complex. Magdoff and van Es (2000) classify the organic fraction of the soil into three categories: the living, the dead, and the very dead. The soil's living component includes the biomass—that group of organisms from the single-celled bacillus to macro-organisms such as earthworms, arthropods, and mammals that live in the soil. But all organisms, including plants and humans, are connected to the soil in many ways. They are affected by and have effects on the soil. So all terrestrial life should be included in this category.

Leaves that fall from trees, grass clippings, animals that burrow into or just trespass on the soil leave residues that contribute to the system of cycles (see Figure 1-8). Most of these residues fall into the dead category. They not only provide energy and sustenance for numerous organisms but also contribute to the development of humus— the very dead.

HUMUS

Humus is a byproduct and end product manufactured by organisms during decay processes. Humus is a dark, inconsistently shaped substance that is biologically resistant to decay and makes up the major portion of organic matter in most soils. A vital component of soil, humus provides a cornucopia of benefits.

Humus may be crucial to the existence of every living thing on earth, but it is not a sexy topic of discussion. It constantly contributes to the mechanisms of life but can't carry on an engaging conversation or take out the garbage (but it has some friends that can break down food waste into a soil-like substance). It can't keep you warm at night unless you belong to a family of thermophilic or mesophilic bacteria, and, although all material wealth in the world is linked either directly or indirectly to humus, it can't buy

FIGURE 1-8   Organic residues in different stages of decay.

you a new car or anything else. It is important, however, to understand the role humus plays in the soil ecosystem. So put the kids to bed, grab a cup of strong coffee, and turn off the TV. This section may be as boring as the Department of Motor Vehicles driver education booklet, but you needed to get your driver's license and you need to know this too. This information is, without a doubt, more interesting than the stuff one has to read to get (and keep) a pesticide applicator's license.

The following discussion covers two distinct forms of humus. The first is young or *labile* humus, and the second is *stable* humus. Labile humus is like compost; it has a wealth

FIGURE 1-9   Even when mature, compost is still undergoing physical, chemical, and biological changes. It cannot be considered stable humus.

of resources available for soil organisms but is fragile and relatively ephemeral (see Figure 1-9). Labile humus is still undergoing humification, and very little of it may ever become stable humus; its future depends on the chemical structures of its organic contents and environmental conditions. Stable humus, compared with labile humus, has fewer available resources for soil organisms but makes greater contributions to soil structure and cation exchange capacity (CEC). Both types contribute to the soil's capacity to hold water and air—two essential constituents for most soil organisms (including turf plants). Both can increase a soil's resistance to compaction. In fact, humus is an amazing soil conditioner—a mere 3 to 5 percent humus can transform almost lifeless sand into a relatively rich soil. Humus can both bind sand and flocculate clay. Plants tend to produce more microscopic root hairs when growing in a soil environment that contains adequate amounts of humus. These tiny root hairs have significantly more surface area than the coarse roots that typically grow in sandy soils and can absorb more water and nutrients than an equal mass of larger roots.

In sandy soils—those often prescribed for sports field construction—plant and microbial mucilage from humus can reduce the size of the pore space between sand particles, increasing the moisture-holding capacity of the soil and reducing the leaching of soil solution with all the dissolved nutrients it carries. As moisture-holding capacity increases, more plants and soil organisms can inhabit the environment. This, eventually, creates more humus. Under ideal conditions, the advancement of humus in sand can develop the preferred type of soil for plant production. Many sports field designers and builders, however, will tell you that the accumulation of organic matter is one of the last things a manager wants. A common belief is that, left unchecked, organic matter will accumulate to monstrous levels that arrest drainage and weaken turf. In a biologically impoverished environment where only undecomposed organic residues can accumulate, this may very well happen, but in a biologically active environment where residues are constantly being consumed by soil organisms, it rarely does.

Conditions for the development of humus in sand, however, are seldom ideal. In tropical and subtropical environments, for example, where moisture, temperature, and the duration of the warm season are optimum for populations of bacteria, fungi, and other saprophytic (decay) organisms, organic matter is quickly assimilated back into the biomass. This rapid assimilation, coupled with the abundance of oxygen in porous sand, makes it extremely difficult, if not impossible, for humus to accumulate to an adequate, let alone an extreme level. Unlike a rain forest, a playing field situated in a tropical or subtropical environment has little chance of maintaining adequate levels of humus mainly because little organic debris is contributed to the soil. The types of debris that contribute to thatch are not at issue here. These tough, fibrous residues may eventually contribute to the formation of humus, but they must be balanced with residues containing sugars, starches, and proteins such as clippings, organic fertilizers, and mature compost. Without this balance, not only is there little chance of soil improvement from humus accumulation but also less carbon dioxide can be recycled back to the grass plants for the production of photosynthesized materials (see Chapter 2, under "Carbon"). Many sports field architects recommend sand-based fields for their water-draining characteristics; however, this near obsession with drainage obscures the view of other necessary components of the plant-growing system. This approach is a little like washing and waxing a car twice a week but never changing the oil.

In clay soil, humus forms an alliance with clay particles because both humus and clay particles are colloidal, possessing an electronegative charge capable of attracting and holding cation nutrients. These complexes not only increase the soil's overall cation exchange capacity (CEC—a good thing; see following paragraph) but also lessen the cohesive nature of clay by causing granulation; they also increase the decay resistance of humus, giving it a longer life span. Clay is considered an even more taboo soil component than organic matter. An abundance of clay is, without argument, a less than ideal medium on the field, but does that mean there should be no clay in the soil? We know arsenic can be lethal, but we also know that a little is essential to human health. The common assumption among most turf managers is that clay is not added to soil mixes because of compaction and drainage problems. The real reason clay is not commonly used anymore is cost. The addition of clay to soil mixes results in superb physical properties.

The term *colloidal* refers to the attraction certain soil particles have for ions of mineral nutrients. Whether organic (humus) or mineral (clay), the colloid is a tiny soil particle, often referred to as a *micelle* (meaning "microcell"), and it carries a negative electromagnetic charge that can hold positively charged ion nutrients (cations), such as calcium, magnesium, ammonium, and potassium, in a manner that allows plant roots access to them. This phenomenon is called *cation exchange*. The quantity of clay and humus in a given soil is usually relative to the amount of cations the soil can retain, but the type of clay and the age of the humus are also factors. Different types of clay have varying abilities to hold cation nutrients, as does humus at different stages of its development. The combined competence of clay and humus quantitatively determine the soil's capacity to hold cations, which is measured as CEC. Clay is not a material often used in sports field construction; however, many experiments have shown that small additions of clay materials like bentonite, montmorillonite, and zeolite significantly benefit the dynamics of a soil ecosystem. Not only do they increase CEC but also they can improve plant performance.

Humus accumulates more easily in a soil containing some clay than in sand because the clay soil's environmental conditions tend not to support decay bacteria. Pore space in clay soils can often reach the point where the oxygen needed by aerobic life is restricted. Soil water can also act as a buffer for temperature changes, which often suppresses the warmth needed for biological activity. In addition, the evaporation of moisture from the surface has a cooling effect on the soil (just as the evaporation of perspiration from the skin cools the body). Clay can also assist in the stabilization of humus. The clay-humus complexes formed in the soil can further inhibit rampant bacterial decomposition and can increase the life span of humus to over a thousand years. Soil scientists calculate that in Allophanic soil (a type of volcanic clay soil) the residence time of humus can range from 2,000 to 5,000 years. This clay-humus complex may form in old fields built with native soils but is rare in a field constructed predominantly with sand.

The formation of humus begins when residues from plants and animals come in contact with decay organisms (saprophytes) in an average soil. Many of the carbon compounds contained in those residues are proteins, carbohydrates, and other organic materials that supply energy to soil bacteria, fungi, actinomycetes, nematodes, earthworms, protozoa, and other organisms involved directly or indirectly in the decay process. Aerobic saprophytes are the most adept at decomposing organic matter. To live and be active, they need an environment containing an adequate amount of free oxygen. The degree to which free oxygen exists in the soil plays a major role in regulating the conditions under which humus is formed. The same is true for the amount of moisture, the soil temperature, and the carbon-to-nitrogen ratio of the residues being decomposed (see Chapter 3, under "Compost Production"). Where little or no free oxygen exists (for example, in stagnant water), anaerobic organisms contribute most to the decomposition of organic matter. The process is slower than that conducted by aerobic organisms but can, in the long run, produce a greater amount of humus (as muck, or organic soil).

OK! Turf is not an aquatic plant, but it's important to understand the whole picture, so hang in there. Many fields are constructed from native muck soil. Humus formed under water is slightly different than its aerobic counterpart, due as much to the nature of the residues from the two environments as to the process of aerobic versus anaerobic humification (see Figure 1-10). Most of the contributions of organic matter to organic soils are from water-dwelling insects and other organisms, which have a higher percentage of protein than do the plant residues commonly found in soil. Other components come from organic residues transported by wind and water currents to a location where they accumulate and settle. In fact, some of this translocated material may already be humus. Higher percentages of humus are found in soils formed anaerobically because conditions are both more favorable for humus accumulation and less favorable for its destruction.

At the other extreme is an environment containing too much oxygen. If moisture and soil temperature are at optimum levels, organic residues can be decomposed so quickly that little or no humus accumulates. We see this in tropical and subtropical environments, where high temperatures and moisture levels occur in predominantly sandy soils that naturally contain an abundance of air. Conditions such as these also

FIGURE 1-10   Humus formed under water is different than its aerobic cousin but is the basis for many organic soils.

occur on many sports fields, even in the more temperate regions of the world. If the soil is composed mainly of sand, the turf is mowed too low to protect the soil from the sun's heat, and irrigation provides precipitation like that of a tropical rain forest, then soil organic matter (humus) may never accumulate.

Soil temperature is an important controlling factor in the formation of humus. As the temperature of a soil increases, there is a corresponding increase in biological activity. Soils in warmer regions of the earth tend to have lower average levels of humus than soils in colder areas (see Figure 1-11). Figure 1-12 shows that at a soil temperature of 88° F (30° C), with adequate aeration, humus can no longer accumulate. When soil temperatures rise beyond a certain point, not only are the activities of decay organisms stimulated and prolonged but also plants often use more energy than they can create. This phenomenon significantly reduces the amount of plant residues contributed to the soil. If the height of cut (HOC) is unreasonably low, this scenario is likely to occur sooner rather than later on sports fields.

During humification of organic matter, saprophytes use most of the sugars, starches, proteins, cellulose, and other carbon compounds for their own metabolism. The assimilation of nutrients and energy from organic residues is the first stage in the process of creating humus. It is not precisely known to what degree the different residues contribute to the creation of humus. Some of the more easily digested components of the residues end up being used by many organisms and may never actually become humus. However, these components provide energy and protein for organisms involved in synthesizing humus. The components of the residues, which are more decay resistant, are not so much assimilated as they are biologically altered into humic substances. Soil organisms actively involved in the humification process produce substances that can also contribute to the components of humus.

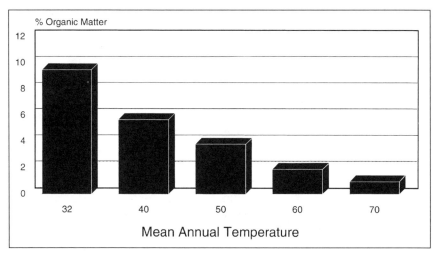

FIGURE 1-11   Influence of temperature on soil organic matter content. Adapted from Jenny, 1941.

The nutrients and energy assimilated into the bodies of soil organisms is normally reused by other organisms that are either predacious or saprophytic. Some is assimilated by the consumer, some is mineralized into plant nutrients, and some is changed into biologically resistant compounds that accumulate as components of humus. The cycles of soil life are implemented as more and more members of the biomass club participate in the festivities of eating, dying, and being eaten—dead or alive. Plants create organic residues that feed soil organisms that then transform the resources from the residues back into plant nutrients, into food for other organisms, and into humus.

Some of the components in organic residues are much more resistant to decay than others. Most carbohydrates, such as sugars and starches, decompose faster than mate-

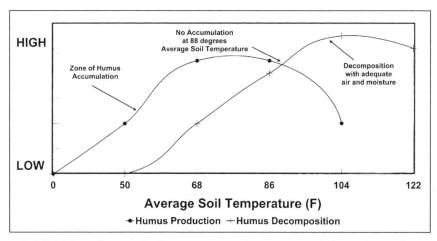

FIGURE 1-12   Influence of soil temperature on humus accumulation. Adapted from Waksman, 1936.

rials such as cellulose. Of all organic components, fats, waxes, and lignin are the most resistant to decay. Proteins vary in decay resistance: they are generally more resistant than sugars and starches but more easily decomposed than many other components.

Although many of these components exist in humus in a biologically altered form (see Figure 1-13), the degree to which they exist in the organic residues plays a role in the accumulation of humus. Materials that contain high percentages of easily decomposed components such as sugars, starches, and some proteins are, for the most part, assimilated back into the living biomass. Although the energy and protein provided by these residues help in the creation of humus, the ratio of their mass to the measure of humus produced is relatively wide (i.e., a small amount of humus is created).

Materials that contain a large percentage of lignin, cellulose, or other biologically resistant components have less recyclable nutrients to offer the soil food web but contribute significantly more to the formation of humus. Different plant residues have inherently different ratios of these organic components, but variance also appears in the same plants at different stages of their lives. Green leaves from deciduous trees, for example, contain a different ratio of proteins to other components than do their dry, fallen counterparts. These same differences would appear in grass plants if they were allowed to mature and produce seed. Constant mowing, however, produces a fairly consistent residue (clippings) throughout the growing season. At this young, succulent stage, grass clippings contribute far more recyclable nutrients and less of the substances needed for the accumulation of humus. However, much of the turf root system, which dies off periodically throughout the season, contributes many components needed for the production of humus. Thatch is also made up of components that can contribute to the accumulation of humus—but, for the most part, don't. Unlike roots, thatch has limited contact with the soil and the decay organisms therein. It also cannot sustain moist enough conditions to support abundant soil life. Additionally, thatch residues may lack sufficient sugars, starches, and proteins for relatively rapid decay.

Biological processing structurally and chemically changes decay-resistant components such as lignin, fats, and waxes into other biologically resistant byproducts, and

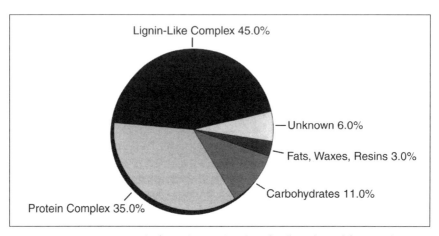

FIGURE 1-13   Humus. Typical consistency in mineral soils. Adapted from Waksman, 1936.

these decay resistant compounds are what make up humus. This is not to say that humus is immune from further decay, but its resistance to decomposition enables it to exist for decades, if not centuries, as a soil conditioner, a habitat for soil life, and a vast reservoir of moisture and dissolved nutrients for plants and many groups of soil organisms. The three main components of humus—fulvic acid, humic acid, and humins—all decay slowly, but at different rates. Fulvic acid is the most ephemeral, lasting only 15 to 20 years. Humic acid compounds can last several hundred years and humins, over 1,000 years.

The digestion of organic matter in the soil is analogous to digestion in mammals. Mammals ingest food and derive nutrients from it. The nutrients are diffused into the body and used for energy to function and to produce new cells. Byproducts, such as urea, water, carbon dioxide, and other simple compounds, are given off. The indigestible portion of the food is excreted as feces.

In the soil, organisms assimilate organic residues, using the nutrients and energy for their own metabolism. Their activities convert some of the organically bound nutrients back to a mineral form, which is usable by plants and other soil organisms. The indigestible portions of the residues accumulate as humus. However, humus is not completely immune to decomposition. Soil organisms eventually recycle all the elements in humus, even if it takes a millennium (or longer).

Humus, plant residues, and other components of soil organic matter are like storage batteries containing energy originally derived from the sun. Researchers in England calculated that an acre of topsoil (6–7 inches deep) with 4 percent organic matter contains as much energy as 20 to 25 tons of anthracite coal. A researcher in Maine equated the energy in the same amount of organic matter to 4,000 gallons of number 2 fuel oil. Most of this organic energy was originally derived from the sun by plants, but only about 1 percent of the sun's energy that reaches plant leaves is used to produce photosynthates. During its life, a plant uses most of the energy it absorbs from the sun for growth, foliage production, flowering, seed production, and other functions. About 10 percent of the absorbed energy is left in the plant tissue for a consumer (e.g., an organism that eats and digests the plant). This leftover energy is called *net primary production*. Like the plant, the herbivore uses most of the energy it consumes for functions such as growth and sustenance, and it offers about 10 percent of the energy it derived from the plant to the next consumer in the food chain.

Subsequent digestions through the food chain continue the rapid depletion of available energy from one link to the next. Often, the final consumers of this energy reside in the soil. In Figure 1-14, an arbitrary quantity of energy is used as an example to show its flow and use. In this case, a figure of 1,000,000 calories of energy offered by the sun is reduced to 1 calorie of available energy by the time it flows through the food chain to soil saprophytes. During the season when plants are active, however, up to half of their photosynthesized nutrients are released through the roots into the soil. Organisms living near, on, or within the root surface then use these compounds for sustenance. One might consider plants rather inefficient organisms for allowing half of their photosynthetic production to leak from their root systems, but nature has a good reason for this design. This phenomenon provides a direct and constant flow of

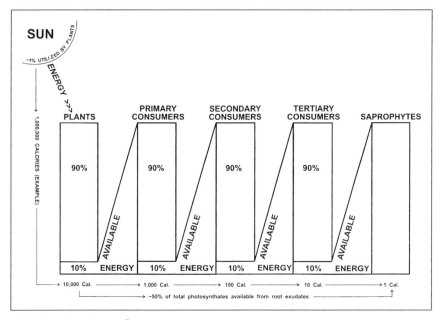

FIGURE 1-14   Energy flow.

plant-synthesized energy for many groups of beneficial soil organisms. The substrate exuded from the plant roots provides sustenance for huge populations of organisms that, among other jobs, make mineral nutrients available to the plants, protect the plants from pathogens and other pest organisms, and produce carbon dioxide that plants need to conduct more photosynthesis.

The amount of available energy in plant residues, in the remains of herbivores, and what is left over from carnivores is significantly different. The various energy levels of these different residues can stimulate different populations of soil organisms that can perform different functions in the soil. These populations are often controlled by the amount and type of residues introduced into the soil, which, in turn, controls the quantity and characteristics of humus.

THE CARBON CYCLE

Throughout this process of digestion and assimilation, from the first consumption of the sun's energy to the decomposition of all residues in the soil, carbon is released back into the atmosphere as carbon dioxide through a process called *respiration*. The evolution of carbon dioxide from the decay of organic residues is an integral part of the life cycle. Figure 1-15 shows how carbon from the atmosphere cycles through the food chain and back into the atmosphere. Plants need atmospheric carbon dioxide to live. If carbon dioxide were not evolved, it would not be available to plants, and the accumulation of humus and other organic materials would bury the planet. Life, as we know it, could not exist.

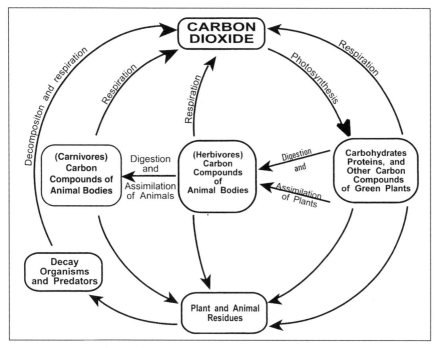

FIGURE 1-15   Carbon cycle.

Over a one-year period and under average conditions, about 60 to 70 percent of the carbon in fresh organic residues is recycled back to the atmosphere as carbon dioxide. Five to 10 percent is assimilated into the biomass, and the rest resides in labile humus. Labile humus is not stable humus, however. It can take decades for humus to develop the biological resistances necessary to be considered stable.

We can see from the carbon cycle that it is necessary for humus to not only accumulate but to be destroyed as well, so carbon dioxide can be returned to the atmosphere where plants can access it. In an uncultivated, natural environment, humus accumulates in accordance with the favorable and unfavorable conditions of the region. Unless global or regional conditions change, the level of humus accumulation reaches equilibrium with the factors that destroy it. The level of humus then becomes a relatively fixed component of that environment so long as the quantity and source of the organic residues being contributed to the soil remain relatively constant.

In cultivated environments, both labile and stable humus are important assets that, like most assets, are easier to maintain than replace. Unfortunately, the value of humus is too often overlooked until it is severely depleted and its benefits are no longer available. Even then, deficient levels of organic matter are rarely recognized as a possible cause of problems that inevitably arise. The importance of soil organic matter and the populations of organisms that it supports should rank very high on the manager's priority list. The first step toward preserving and maintaining this resource is to understand its value.

Old, stable humus is biologically resistant. Depending on the environmental conditions under which it exists, humus can sit in the soil for centuries, even millennia, with a minimal amount of decomposition. But however slight, decay still occurs, and even old humus eventually cycles back from where it came. The formation of new humus, which requires a constant source of organic residues, is critical to maintaining a stable presence of this asset.

Figure 1-16 shows the typical fate of organic matter introduced into the soil. It is important to note that even under the best conditions, a relatively small amount of humus is created in comparison to the level of organic residues initially introduced. If conditions exist that further accelerate the decomposition of organic matter, even less humus may eventually be created. In extremes, such as tropical or subtropical environments where moisture, heat, and soil oxygen are abundant, a great amount of carbon dioxide may be evolved but little humus is produced.

SOIL MINERALS

Organisms that create humus and that prosper in soil enriched with organic matter also contribute to the phenomenon of soil formation and the availability of plant nutrients. Populations of soil organisms facilitate chemical weathering by creating organic acids—corrosive materials formed in nature by plants, animals, and soil organisms. These include citric, acetic, amino, lactic, salicylic, tannic, nucleic, and humic acid, to name only a few. All of these acids have varying abilities to react with rock surfaces and liberate minerals from parent material.

Soil organisms dissolve minerals from rock through three basic functions: *assimilation*, the creation of *organic acids*, and the creation of *inorganic acids*.

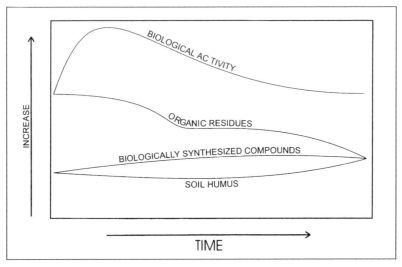

FIGURE 1-16   Humification.

Assimilation is the direct absorption of nutrients by organisms. Most soil organisms work to free nutrients from organic and inorganic matter for their own metabolism. Saprophytes primarily feed on dead residues of plants and animals but also can absorb essential minerals from inorganic sources in the soil. Predators feed on saprophytes and other organisms (including other predators), and much of what becomes available to plants is released during predation. Some organisms work together symbiotically to secure their nutrition. Lichens, for example, are symbiotic combinations of fungi and algae that attach themselves to various surfaces (often rocks) and dislocate minerals for their own nutrition. The hyphae (microscopic tubing) of the fungal component can penetrate the finest hairline cracks in rock, releasing enzymes and acids powerful enough to liberate mineral ions from surrounding surfaces. Eventually, the minerals assimilated by the lichen are recycled through the agency of other organisms that either feed on lichen or decompose their remains after death. After mineral nutrients are incorporated into the body of an organism, however, the nutrients are bound in organic compounds, which are easier for nature to process. Unless these elements are removed from a given area (by cropping, erosion, or other means), they tend to accumulate over time and increase fertility for both plants and other indigenous organisms.

Most organisms create enzymes and organic acids during assimilation, or the acids are byproducts of their metabolism. Regardless of their origin, these acids and enzymes contribute to the formation of soil and to the availability of many essential plant nutrients. Figure 1-17 shows the influence of azotobacter bacteria's organic acids on the mineral content in soil solutions. These beneficial organisms also fix nitrogen from the atmosphere.

Inorganic acids, such as sulfuric and nitric acid, are formed in the soil as an indirect result of biological activity. Specific organisms such as sulfur bacteria and nitrify-

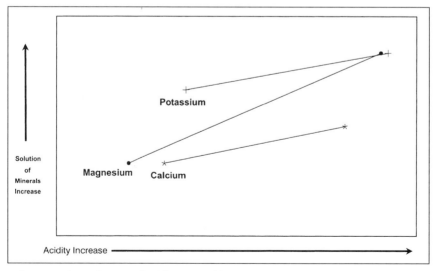

FIGURE 1-17   Influence of acidity created by azatobacter on solutions of Ca, Mg, and K in the soil.

ing bacteria oxidize (combine with oxygen) sulfur and nitrogen respectively and can then combine with soil hydrogen to form strong inorganic acids. The chemical reaction between rock surfaces and strong acids changes both substances. Part of the rock dissolves, and the acid can then become a mineral salt, which is more soluble and, once dissolved, more easily assimilated by plants and other soil organisms.

Mycorrhiza is a family of fungi that can dissolve mineral nutrients from rock surfaces. These organisms work under the soil's surface in a symbiotic relationship with perennial plant roots. The fungi attach themselves to roots and, in exchange for a small amount of carbohydrate supplied by the plant, provide water and mineral nutrients to the plant. They retrieve and transport the water and mineral nutrients via their hyphae from regions of the soil beyond the reach of the plant roots.

The chemical weathering effect of roots comes from several sources. Carbon dioxide given off by root hairs can combine with water to form carbonic acid. Research has shown significant mineral release from carbon dioxide when dissolved in water. This process is known as *carbonation* and involves the attachment of mineral ions, such as potassium, magnesium, or calcium, to a carbonate ion, thus forming other mineral salts. Plant roots indirectly participate in the formation of organic acids through their relationship with soil organisms. The population of organisms within the rhizosphere (the soil region immediately surrounding the root hair) is always significantly higher than in other parts of the soil. The production of organic acids and enzymes that are destructive to rock is directly proportional to the level of biological activity. Up to 50 percent of the carbon that plants fix from atmospheric carbon dioxide is released through their roots as carbohydrates, most of which are consumed by soil organisms that constantly produce organic acids.

PLANTS

Plants are the link between the atmosphere (heaven) and the pedosphere (earth). Their remains make rich soil from weathered rock particles, and they provide nutrients and energy for most other living things on the planet. They complete the cycles of water, nutrients, and energy. Plants are producers; they combine energy from the sun, carbon dioxide in the atmosphere, and mineral nutrients in the soil to synthesize sustenance, directly or indirectly, for almost every other living thing on earth. Almost all of the protein, energy, and carbohydrates that humans need comes from plants or from animals raised on plants.

Plant life slowly began to appear as prehistoric soils evolved. The meager amount of available nutrients, coupled with what was probably a harsh environment, at first permitted only small, perhaps microscopic, plants to grow. As time went on, the accumulation of organic residues from the remains of countless generations of microplant life slowly enriched the soil, creating an environment that could support a larger and more diverse population of soil organisms. The cycle snowballed for a time, creating a richer soil with each successive increase in vegetative establishment, until an ecological equilibrium was reached—that is, the production of organic matter by plants was roughly equal to the environmental factors that destroyed it.

Plants stabilized much of the volatility in the ecosystem. In a sense, plants bottled the energy of the sun and made it available to other living things. The evolution of plants and other photosynthetic organisms changed the ecosystem of the planet dramatically. Prior to autotrophs (photosynthesizing organisms), life existed on available energy. When the energy was depleted, the organisms often became extinct, and new organisms evolved to recycle the energy left behind by their predecessors. The renewability of energy on earth enabled many species of consumers (heterotrophs, such as mammals) to exist for many generations without depleting their food supply. This phenomenon allowed for the systematic evolution of different species into present-day life forms.

Most plants are composed of two fundamentally different parts: the root system, which anchors the plant and absorbs water and mineral nutrients; and the shoot system, which consists of the plant's trunk, branches, shoots, stems, and leaves. Those parts of the plant that connect the roots to the leaves provide structural support as well as transport passageways for water and nutrients. Leaf surfaces contain pores, called *stomata* or *stomates*, that function as gas exchangers and as part of the plant's ventilation system.

The plant's link to the atmosphere is through its use of carbon dioxide gas, with which it creates almost all the organic carbon compounds that exist on earth. Without carbon dioxide, plants could not live, and neither could any of the organisms that depend on the nutrients plants provide. The balance of carbon dioxide with other gases in the atmosphere depends largely on plants—or, more accurately, on the use of energy stored in plants. Whenever energy is extracted from plant tissue (or animal tissue), whether by animals, insects, or soil organisms, carbon dioxide is given off. Plants capture some carbon dioxide as it wafts from the soil's surface into the atmosphere and transform it into plant tissue. The more carbon dioxide generated by organisms under the plant, the more likely it is that adequate amounts are captured by plant stomates located on the underside of the leaves.

Plant roots make the organic-inorganic connection in the soil. The fine root hairs combine so well with the earth that it is difficult to tell exactly where the soil ends and the root begins. Not only are many root segments microscopic, but they are also so numerous that a single mature grass plant can produce almost 400 miles of roots. In fact, a square foot of thick turf can be connected to over 325,000 miles of roots (13½ times around the world). The roots of plants depend on the shoot system for nourishment. Throughout the plant's life, carbohydrates and other organic nutrients flow to the root system from the leaves, where energy from the sun, carbon dioxide from the atmosphere, and minerals drawn from the soil combine in a complex process called *photosynthesis*.

The root system and plant tops act like different organisms living together symbiotically. The leaves are autotrophic, using carbon dioxide from the atmosphere to manufacture organic carbon compounds and giving off oxygen as a waste product. The root system acts like a heterotrophic organism, dependent on the sugars and other compounds produced in the leaves and using oxygen from the soil while giving off carbon dioxide.

The roots of plants are more than just anchors and siphon tubes extracting water and nutrients from the soil. The rhizosphere is teeming with life in the form of billions of microorganisms. Up to half of the nutrients photosynthesized in plant leaves is released from the roots into the rhizosphere, supplying nourishment for most of these organisms, whose activities help the plant in numerous ways. They can mineralize organic nutrients, compete antagonistically with pathogens, weather parent material, regulate nutrient availability, decay plant residues, return carbon dioxide to the atmosphere, and mobilize water and nutrients (e.g., via mycorrhizae). Some organisms in the rhizosphere can also fix nitrogen from the atmosphere, solubilize phosphorus, and produce growth hormones that increase the plant's resistance to environmental and other types of stress.

Plants also affect soil factors that in turn influence plant growth. Environments like prairies and forests are formed initially by factors such as climate, parent material, and topography, but the establishment of certain types of plants soon becomes another factor acting on the environment. The plant factor can influence the establishment of soil organisms, change the effects of topography, and even create subtle differences in the atmosphere that may affect climate. Turf affects its environment too. Turf plants complete the cycles of nutrients, water, and soil life, providing environmental stability. Most environments are still evolving, but plants act like a sea anchor, stabilizing and often removing much of the volatility from the evolutionary process.

Soils are subject to eventual ruination by the same forces that created them. The inherent mineral content of any soil may be vast, but it is also finite and can eventually be depleted by weathering. At some point, perhaps a billion years from the time of a soil's creation, leaching, erosion, or both can fully deplete the mineral resources crucial to the existence of living organisms. As the availability of minerals and organic residues wanes, so does the biomass that sustains the level of native organic matter that structurally protects the soil from erosion and stores much of the moisture and nutrients necessary for biotic development. As depletion continues, only the most weather-resistant particles of quartz and other mineral compounds remain. A rich soil can eventually evolve into a habitat that sustains only the hardiest of organisms.

Erosion, one of the forces that weathers rock and carries particles of parent material to deposits called soil, can also carry soil away. Often, soil is carried all the way to an ocean, where tremendous pressures for long periods can transform the mineral particles back into sedimentary rock. Perhaps, a million years from now, a broad tectonic event will lift the recreated rock into a mountain, and the process can begin all over again. A crucial component of the soil ecosystem that retards weathering and erosion is plant life and the diverse population of soil organisms it supports. Gluelike substances created by many soil organisms, aggregate soil particles and protect them from erosion and other weathering forces.

Plants also protect the soil environment in a number of ways. They provide shade and slow the evaporation of precious moisture needed for their own lives and the lives of other soil organisms. The shade they provide reduces soil temperature, which can increase net primary production (i.e., the production of energy beyond the plant's own needs). The extra energy produced feeds soil organisms that also participate in soil conservation. Plants also control erosion with their root systems and the organic matter they produce. The adhesive qualities of humus hold soil particles together and provide greater absorption of water through an increase in soil porosity. This increase in water absorption provides a relative decrease in surface runoff.

The mechanism by which plants produce the proteins, sugars, starches, fat, and fiber needed by the consuming species of the world is chemically complex. A plant's ability to use the endless energy from the sun and the small percentage of carbon dioxide in the earth's atmosphere to produce all of these organic nutrients is nothing short of a miracle. In simple terms, the stomates on the underside of the plant's leaves allow the transference of gas and moisture into and out of the plant. Plant leaves intercept carbon dioxide, much of it generated by the biological decay of organic residues, as it escapes the soil. Plant cells that contain chlorophyll are excited by the energy of the sun and conduct chemical reactions within the leaves. These reactions combine the carbon and some of the oxygen from carbon dioxide with hydrogen from water, nitrogen, phosphorus, sulfur, and other minerals from the soil to form the complex organic compounds that give life and growth to the plant, to its roots, and to every other organism that depends either directly or indirectly on plants for sustenance. The six elements mentioned above—carbon, oxygen, hydrogen, nitrogen, phosphorus, and sulfur—make up 99 percent of all living matter.

Other nutrients considered essential to plants are calcium, molybdenum, magnesium, boron, copper, iron, zinc, chlorine, potassium, and manganese. It is important to note that elements not considered essential for plant tissue development may be of vital importance to other soil-dwelling organisms, which play their own crucial roles in the dynamics of the plant growing system (see Chapter 2, under "Trace Elements").

All of the carbon plants use is derived from the atmosphere. Oxygen comes to the plant from the atmosphere (as carbon dioxide and free oxygen) and from water (H_2O), which also delivers hydrogen. These three elements—carbon, hydrogen, and oxygen—constitute the basic building blocks of all organic compounds and comprise approximately 95 percent of a plant's diet. The remaining 5 percent is in mineral form and derived from the soil (see Figure 1-18).

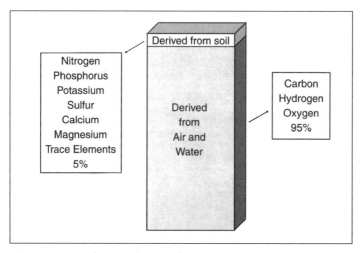

FIGURE 1-18   Plant nutrient needs.

HOLISTIC VIEW

Weathering forces, soil organisms, climate, plants, and animals (including humans) have had, and continue to have, a profound effect, both direct and indirect, on the soil's evolution. The existence of almost all life is both controlled by, and controls, the biological, physical, and chemical diversity in the soil. Managers certainly belongs in this equation, so it is important that they have a basic understanding of the soil ecosystem. The overview presented here is painted with a broad brush. Volumes of information—some of it conflicting—have been published about the soil, and only a brief scan of that material is included in this chapter. But all the currently available information on soil probably represents only a fraction of what has yet to be discovered. The soil is a complex ecosystem whose biological health and vitality appear to be inextricably linked to the vigor and resilience of turf. Recognizing the living component of the soil system as the most ideal barometer of soil health may be the extent of what we need to understand. It's possible that all we have to learn now are the best ways to care for it.

POINTS TO REMEMBER

- Soil was not created overnight. Weathering forces and biological organisms are continually shaping the texture and properties of soil.
- The basal energy that fuels the soil's living component is extracted from organic material.
- Carbon dioxide—a plant nutrient needed in greater quantities than all soil-borne nutrients combined—is generated in the soil by biological respiration.
- Trace minerals in the soil are as essential to plants and soil organisms as water—just in smaller quantities.
- Plants act like two distinctly different organisms—the root systems and the plant tops—living together symbiotically.
- Roots release up to half of the photosynthesized carbohydrates they receive to feed large populations of soil organisms that live in the rhizosphere.
- Plant growth and health are not linked solely to fertilizer, irrigation, and occasional aeration, but also to the physical, chemical, and biological diversity in the soil.

Chapter 2

FERTILITY

Before discussing the appropriate diet for turf, it might be worth examining how plants managed to survive before humans intervened. There's no argument that turf needs fertilizer, but surprisingly, the nitrogen, phosphorus, potassium, calcium, magnesium, sulfur, and trace elements managers apply account for only 5 percent of the plant's total diet. The other 95 percent comes from the atmosphere and from water. As relatively minor as their mineral requirements may seem, the question remains, how does the plant acquire the nutrients it needs if no one is there to apply them? Obviously, plants have been surviving on their own for millions of years, well before humans or any other beings with fertilizer spreaders appeared on earth.

Carbon and oxygen from carbon dioxide in the air and hydrogen from water combine to make the building blocks of all the organic compounds produced by photosynthesis. All of the other necessary nutrients are digested from organic and mineral sources in the soil and made available to plants by many groups of soil organisms. Proteins, carbohydrates, fats, waxes, cellulose, and other organic compounds found in plant and animal residues, in soil organic matter, and in the soil's biomass, and minerals contained in inorganic soil particles all contribute essential nutrients to plants. But soil organisms must first digest and transform these nutrients into an available form; you might say these organisms function as the plants' digestive system. Much of the carbon dioxide in the atmosphere is generated in the soil from biological activity. Just as humans and animals release carbon dioxide as a respiratory waste, so do soil organisms, and the grass plants' best opportunity to absorb carbon dioxide is when it first emerges from the soil's surface—before atmospheric turbulence can dilute it with other gases. This delivery system has, over the millennia, proved effective, efficient, and difficult to improve upon.

Unfortunately, this system is not functioning at or even near peak performance on most areas of many sports fields. Typically, the soil contains little organic matter, which limits the population of soil organisms and the creation of biomass, and not much in the way of organic residues is ever applied. If grass clippings are removed from the field, the situation worsens. Soil organisms have limited resources, which limits their ability to make nutrients available to plants, and their production of carbon dioxide is relative to their level of activity. Realistically, when speaking of fertility, we should consider the needs of the entire plant growing system—including soil organisms.

Normally, fertilizers are chosen based on the N-P-K analysis, which is the percentage, by weight, of total nitrogen, available phosphate, and soluble potash. Managers may also apply secondary macronutrients—calcium, magnesium, sulfur, trace elements—if a soil test or leaf tissue analysis indicates a deficiency. It is the rare steward who seeks a fertilizer that provides digestible carbon for soil organisms and even rarer the one who asks whether or not the carbonaceous fertilizer will favor populations of bacteria or fungi. These are, however, important questions to ask. The right balance of organisms living in the soil provides turf plants with both sustenance and protection, and, as carbonaceous residues are digested, these organisms also generate carbon dioxide that grass plants can capture as it passes through the soil's surface. Adequate populations of these organisms cannot be sustained unless the proper resources are available.

Weed, insect, and disease problems and poor turfgrass performance are often symptoms of an incomplete or deficient soil system. Pests are typically kept in check with pesticides, and poor turfgrass performance is normally dealt with by adding chemical nutrients. But the underlying problem may well be biological. On sports fields, biological imbalances are generally less problematic than inadequate levels of biological activity.

CARBON

Carbon in the soil is found in the living biomass, organic residues, labile humus, and stable humus. These sources provide energy for most soil organisms. Soil carbon is produced by autotrophic organisms such as plants and algae that can combine carbon from the atmosphere with energy from the sun to produce organic stuff. The carbon compounds produced by autotrophs eventually become part of the vast warehouse of energy and protein known as *soil organic matter*. This warehouse functions beneficially in hundreds of ways; two essential purposes are to provide energy for soil life and carbon dioxide for plants.

When fresh organic residues come in contact with the soil, decay begins almost immediately—at least during the seasons in which soil organisms are active. Temperature, moisture, air, and the balance of carbon and nitrogen in the residues determine the speed at which organic residues are decomposed. The carbon-to-nitrogen ratio (C:N) is always measured as x parts carbon to 1 part nitrogen. If the C:N ratio is wide (i.e., high carbon), as it is with straw and wood chips, decomposition occurs slowly. Furthermore, soil organisms must commandeer available nitrogen from the soil as they digest the carbon because their diets demand a narrower C:N range. This usurpation temporarily overrides the nitrogen needs of plants. If the original organic litter has a narrow C:N ratio, as with grass clippings, food wastes, and animal wastes, decomposition is likely to occur more rapidly, making nitrogen available to plants and other organisms. Each time saprophytes (decay organisms) digest components of organic residues or organisms are consumed by predators, some energy is used and carbon is oxidized into carbon dioxide, which is then released into the soil atmosphere.

Turf is healthiest in a biologically balanced soil—one in which bacteria accounts for slightly more than half of the biomass. Bacteria thrive in soils that contain residues high in carbohydrates—that is, sugars and starches. Vegetable and animal meals and compost made from food waste, manure, or biosolids contain the carbohydrates necessary to sustain a bacteria-dominated soil. Yard waste often contains more cellulose and lignin, which can favor fungal domination. Yard waste compost is a good soil conditioner but may not be ideal for turf, where a more even balance between bacteria and fungi is preferred. According to Cornell University research, yard waste compost does not offer as much disease suppression as composts made with less woody ingredients. However, procedures can be undertaken to change the balance of bacteria and fungi in a yard waste compost pile (see Chapter 3).

Feed the soil. We have all heard this axiom before—sometimes from people who have an organic garden, a woodstove, and a composting toilet. Whatever your opinion of the messenger, the philosophy is sound, and it describes the basic needs of a functioning soil ecosystem. We usually pick fertilizers based on the guaranteed analysis, which tells us the total nitrogen, available phosphate, and soluble potash. Sometimes magnesium or trace minerals like iron or manganese are added. If we are to feed the soil, we must apply food such as carbohydrates and proteins—ingredients that are difficult, if not impossible, to find on fertilizer labels. The essential nutrients we apply are important, but without a healthy, functioning ecosystem, they may be utilized inefficiently.

NITROGEN

Nitrogen (N) is a great example of this. Plants use nitrogen for many functions. Without nitrogen, plants cannot manufacture peptides, amino acids, proteins, enzymes, chlorophyll, or nucleic acids (the building blocks of DNA and RNA). These components are essential for plants to grow and function properly. The reactions that occur during photosynthesis require a lot of nitrogen. If nitrogen is deficient during photosynthesis, less chlorophyll is produced, and plants begin to lose their green color (chlorosis). Turf responds to many stress conditions by producing special proteins and other metabolites that are rich in nitrogen. Inadequate access to nitrogen renders plants more susceptible to stress-related problems. Plants also produce special enzymes to combat pathogen infection and even insect attack. Enzymes, like protein, need nitrogen.

On the other hand, excessive applications of nitrogen can also contribute to problems. Plants respond to abundant nitrogen by increasing top growth and arresting root growth. Free amino acids often accumulate in the leaves and invite both foraging insects and disease pathogens. In addition, a guttation fluid that is rich in nitrogen and other nutrients can exude from the leaf tips—a phenomenon analogous to raising a banner that reads "EAT AT JOE'S." When the guttation fluid dries, the remaining salts can burn the leaf tips. Another potential problem is that when plant growth is pushed with excess nitrogen, the production of defense compounds is often suppressed. Water use increases as the level of nitrogen increases, and the plant is less able to control moisture loss because the stomates cannot close as quickly or tightly with too much nitrogen in the plant. Consequently, wilting occurs sooner under dry conditions. In fact, there is a linear relationship between wilting and levels of nitrogen in the plant.

Applying just the right amount of nitrogen is not only extremely important but almost impossible because conditions that determine the amount a plant needs at a given time are constantly varying. Air and soil temperature, moisture, height of cut (HOC), the angle and intensity of the sun, biological production of carbon dioxide, and the variety of grass all affect the rate at which turf plants use nitrogen. The optimal amount of nitrogen today could be excessive or inadequate tomorrow. Plants can respond to both deficient and excess nitrogen, but the response is not always enough to overcome the problem. When nitrogen is inadequate, plants produce sugars in the leaves that are quickly transported into the roots. These sugars feed roots and enable them to grow farther into the soil in search of more nitrogen. If too much nitrogen is available, the leaves produce amino acids, which increase shoot growth. Sugar production is all but arrested, and root growth is suppressed. This slows nitrogen absorption through the roots.

Plants don't understand the difference between nitrogen biologically released from organic sources and the soluble kind applied by modern turf managers. To plants, nitrogen is nitrogen. But they also have a hard time understanding and adapting to the rags-to-riches scenario associated with many chemical feeding programs. During periods when nitrogen is inadequate, plants respond by elongating roots. When a tidal wave of nitrogen becomes available from an application of soluble nitrogen and an extradiffusive root system absorbs more than the plant needs, serious side effects— including disease susceptibility, insect attraction, and burning—can occur. In a healthy soil ecosystem, however, mechanisms exist to buffer and regulate the amount of nitrogen available to plants.

Many soil organisms need nitrogen more than plants do, but they need it balanced with a certain amount of carbon. This balance occurs in proteins that reside in organic residues, labile humus, and in the prey on which many soil organisms feed. In fact, one of the main ways in which organisms make nitrogen available to plants is through predation of other organisms. Predators such as bacteria-feeding nematodes, for example, don't need or want the amount of nitrogen inherent in their prey and release the excess as ammonium, which is then biologically converted into nitrate, which turf roots can absorb. Applications of compost or natural organic fertilizers complement the functions of soil organisms, and they, in turn, regulate the amount of nitrogen available to plants. This is not to say that soluble nitrogen should never be used, but if it is the *only* source of nitrogen applied, biological activity is likely to be suppressed to a point where nutrient regulation is inadequate. Digestible carbon must be available if soil organisms are to regulate applied nitrogen.

If the turf ecosystem is healthy and functioning properly, judicious applications of soluble nitrogen can be regulated by soil organisms. Soluble nitrogen can be used by many soil organisms—which, in turn, moderates the amount available to plants. As predation and other biological activities occur, more nitrogen is released for turf roots to absorb. Coincidentally, the activity level of the organisms that release nitrogen and other available nutrients respond to many of the same conditions that stimulate plant activity, so the availability of nutrients is often synchronized with need. Spoon-feeding soluble nitrogen is rarely as ideal.

If large doses of soluble nitrogen are applied, both plants and organisms can be overwhelmed. High-salt fertilizers can act like a dry sponge, drawing moisture away from the surrounding area. This can cause osmotic shock, killing organisms in close proximity. Eventually, as the salt is dissipated within a greater solution, the dissolved nutrients change from harmful to helpful and can be assimilated by some soil organisms. Once absorbed into a living organism, the nutrient is somewhat stable until the organism dies or is preyed upon. If it dies, nitrogen may or may not be released, depending on the saprophyte that consumes the remains. If the saprophyte requires less nitrogen than the amount available from its food source, some will be released; however, if it requires more, then nitrogen may be immobilized from other sources. In a turf soil, the former scenario is more likely. If a predator eats the organism, there is almost always a release of nitrogen in a form available to plants. Not only can this system increase nitrogen efficiency but it can also sustain nitrogen release for a longer period.

Unfortunately, little of this biological regulation can occur on a field constructed of sand, topdressed with sand, and fertilized purely with soluble salts. A healthy, active, well-fed, and diverse population of soil organisms is essential, yet this is nearly impossible to achieve or maintain in an environment without adequate resources. The sand-based environment on many fields serves as an almost inert medium that provides mechanical support for the turf plants. It is rarely cultivated as a habitat for soil life.

Developing a program that addresses the biological needs of the soil is a logical step toward improving fertility. The use of compost in the topdress mixture, compost tea in the irrigation system, and natural organic fertilizers in the spreader can not only reduce the need for soluble nitrogen but increase its efficiency as well. In other words, less soluble nitrogen can accomplish more. Applications of compost during spring and fall core cultivation incorporates valuable resources for a diversity of soil organisms. The addition of compost tea and natural organic fertilizers provides more nutrients and even some inoculation. If soluble nitrogen is still needed, small doses can react synergistically with biological functions that increase overall nitrogen efficiency. It may not be needed, however. Well-made, mature compost can contain anywhere from 0.5 to 3 percent nitrogen, depending on the feed stock from which it was made and on the moisture content. Nitrogen content in compost is usually measured on a dry basis and the value found is a percentage of the material's weight, so if a dry compost contains 1 percent nitrogen but its as-is moisture is 50 percent (of its weight), then the actual nitrogen content is 0.5 percent. If a topdress layer consisting of 50 percent sand and 50 percent compost is applied at a thickness of $\frac{1}{4}$ inch, then almost 0.8 cubic yards of material (~0.4 yd^3 sand and ~0.4 yd^3 compost) has been applied per 1,000 square feet. If the weight of the compost per cubic yard is 1,500 pounds and it contains 0.5 percent of nitrogen (on an as-is basis), then almost 3 pounds of nitrogen have been applied per 1,000 square feet. Don't expect a great flush of growth, however. The release of nitrogen from compost is slow and sustained and depends on factors such as temperature and moisture. If turf is growing in a cold soil, where biological activiy is suppressed, some soluble nitrogen may be necessary to fulfill the plants' needs until the soil warms up.

Natural organic nitrogen is synonymous with protein. The main reason it is more expensive than its chemical cousin is that it has a greater value in animal feed and pet food markets than it does as fertilizer. Protein is not an available nutrient for plants. The chemical structure of protein is too large and complex to be assimilated directly through plant roots. Protein, however, can be assimilated by soil organisms. When proteinaceous materials come in contact with the soil, organisms begin dismantling it into amino acids and peptides. Most of the nitrogen and carbon is consumed and temporarily immobilized, but some is released and mineralized by other organisms into simple nitrogen ions that plant roots can absorb. The population of saprophytes that consume the protein grows exponentially, which results in a relative increase in the number of predator organisms that feed on them. The result of this increased predation is an increase in available nitrogen for plant roots, but the release is steady and sustained—unlike the tsunami of pabulum that is typical of soluble fertilizers. An additional advantage to using proteinaceous nitrogen is that it is extremely efficient. Little, if any, is lost to leaching, volatilization, or denitrification, and the corresponding increase in biological activity can often reduce plant susceptibility to disease infection and attractiveness to foraging insects. Taking into consideration its efficiency and its ability to nurture an active soil food web (which can lead to significant savings elsewhere), the value of natural organic nitrogen is easily worth the extra price.

Researchers have found that soil where unfertilized turf is growing contains more soluble nitrates during the late summer. It would not be unreasonable to assume that applications of soluble nitrogen at this time of the season are more prone to leaching. Natural organic nitrogen may be a much more appropriate material to use at this time of year.

Natural sources of nitrogen include blood meal, feather meal, meat and bone meal, hoof and horn meal, whey solids, leather meal, compost, cocoa meal, soybean meal, cotton seed meal, manure, biosolids, crab meal, fish meal, grass clippings, castor pomace, coffee grounds, alfalfa meal, and peanut meal. In fact, most organic residues from plants or animals contain some nitrogen, but sometimes not enough to be valuable as a nitrogen source. Manure is not a recommended amendment for application anywhere on a sports field. The only appropriate exception is the nearest compost pile. It would be an unusual raw manure that doesn't contain a cornucopia of weed seeds.

Constant and excessive infusions of soluble nitrate or ammoniated fertilizers not only can do more harm than good in the soil but also can pollute shallow groundwater as well. Moreover, a significant amount of money may be wasted on the percentage of these materials that never reaches the plant. Consequences of excess nitrogen for turf include higher susceptibility to disease and insect pests; excessive thatch development; decreased tolerance of environmental stress conditions such as heat, drought, and cold; poor root and lateral shoot development; and reduced production and reserves of plant carbohydrates.

In addition to improving the efficiency at which plants use nitrogen, a diverse and prosperous soil food web can also bring free nitrogen down from heaven. Free-living, nitrogen-fixing bacteria—those not associated with the roots of legumes—can consume atmospheric nitrogen for the production of proteins, enzymes, etc. When they die or are consumed by predators, that nitrogen is cycled through the soil ecosystem and eventually becomes available to plants. Measurements taken in the 1960s show fixation of between 20 and 100 pounds of nitrogen per acre per year by nonsymbiotic bacteria. The research also found a corresponding relationship between the amount of organic residues returned to the soil and the amount of nitrogen gained from free-living, nitrogen-fixing bacteria. The more residues made available to soil organisms, the more nitrogen fixation occurred. Interestingly, the study found that the highest level of nitrogen-fixation occurred in a bluegrass sod. There were no details in the reference (Brady 1974) about how the sod was cared for or its ultimate use, but the findings suggest great potential for turf to feed a prolific web of soil organisms.

Even though sports field conditions are found nowhere in nature, contemporary fertilization practices do not in any way resemble natural feeding phenomena. The use of soluble, available nutrients bypasses the digestive system of plants—that is, the living biomass in the soil. A fertility program that ignores the needs of these organisms is, in a sense, repudiating their value and importance. The assumption that these soil organisms have little or no worth may be the main reason why managers in both agriculture and horticulture have become dependent on chemicals.

PHOSPHORUS

The availability of most other plant nutrients also has direct and indirect relationships with biological activity in the soil. Phosphorus, for example, is a nutrient plant roots can have a hard time finding without the help of soil organisms. Most turfgrass experts will tell you that established grass does not need a lot of phosphorus because it is needed mainly for germination, flowering, seed production, and initial root development—unnecessary or unwanted activities for a mature stand of turf. In fact, applications of phosphorus in excess of turf needs may serve only to increase the germination of annual weed seeds. Phosphorus is, however, an extremely important element for turf plants and all other living organisms. Adenosine triphosphate (ATP) is a component involved in reactions that transfer energy throughout the plant. The genetic information components, DNA and RNA, also contain phosphorus. Phospholipids form the basic structure of cell membranes and play a role in the selective movement of nutrients and other materials into and out of the cell.

The activities of soil organisms make phosphorus available to plant roots in many ways. Phosphorus that is tightly fixed with other elements can be released when the acids, enzymes, or chelates produced by biological activity make contact. Humates produced by soil organisms can prevent phosphorus from fixing with other elements by forming complexes with phosphate ions, by interrupting the sites where fixation might occur, or both. The production of carbonic acid that results from biomass respiration can also free fixed phosphate ions. The introduction of fresh residues often stimulates the decomposition of humus containing phosphorus. Additionally, the abundance of root hairs that are typical in biologically rich soils have significantly greater opportunity to encounter phosphate ions. The likelihood of these scenarios occurring, however, is relative to the amount of resources the soil holds for members of the food web. In a biologically inactive soil, it is often necessary to apply phosphorus in higher quantities than actually needed to compensate for what will be immediately fixed to other soil ions. In fact, plants may receive as little as 10 percent of a phosphate application. Some of the ions—such as iron, calcium, or magnesium—that bond with phosphorus are also rendered unavailable to turf roots. In a calcareous soil, the availability of calcium is rarely affected because of its abundance, but the availability of phosphorus is significantly reduced.

Most of the phosphorus used in fertilizers is refined from phosphate rock. Phosphate rock is a mined marine deposit that typically contains ~30 percent total phosphate, but only 3 to 8 percent is considered available, depending on the method used for analysis. The amount of available phosphate from phosphate rock is generally higher when it is introduced into a biologically active soil. Eventually, over a period of three to ten years, most, if not all, of the phosphate contained in phosphate rock is likely to be released. The advantage to this slow, long-term release is that the phosphorus need not be reapplied more often than every half-decade (if at all). Conventional fertilizers contain refined derivatives of phosphate rock that dissolve easily and move quickly into the soil solution. The availability of phosphate from these materials is much higher, and, consequently, what plants can't use can quickly fix with other elements or compounds in the soil and become unavailable. Soil reactions that release phosphate from phosphate rock do so slowly, and over time plant roots receive small but consistent doses of this essential element. If needed, phosphate rock can be applied alone or as a component of a topdress mixture.

When phosphate ore is first mined, it is washed to remove impurities (mostly clay). The effluent from this operation is deposited in lagoons, where its moisture evaporates in the sun. The remaining material is almost as rich in phosphate—2 to 5 percent available, 18 percent total—as the washed phosphate rock, but it also contains colloidal clay. The clay is called colloidal because it can bind coarse soil particles together and increase the soil's cation exchange capacity (CEC). It is unusual for a turf manager to use colloidal rock phosphate (a.k.a. soft rock phosphate), especially on sand-based fields, but a few managers put a small amount in their topdress mixture to conserve water use and increase the CEC.

Compost usually contains a small amount of phosphorus (<1 percent) but, again, the volume usually applied more than makes up for the low analysis. The phosphorus in compost is organically bound and biologically released. The activity that makes phosphorus from compost available to plants is normally synchronized with plant need, so efficiency is increased. The resources in compost also stimulate the release of phosphorus from inorganic sources and can reduce the level of phosphorus fixation with other elements.

Most soils contain adequate levels of phosphate for plants, but little may be available if soil organisms are relatively inactive. Research has shown that the availability of phosphorus—along with many other elements—increases when organic residues (food for soil organisms) are introduced into the soil and that the increase exceeds the amount of phosphorus contained in the residues. Additionally, mycorrhizal relationships are often established with roots growing in a biologically active soil. Mycorrhizae are great retrievers of phosphorus (and other nutrients) from the soil. Not only do their hyphae explore far greater regions of the soil than roots do but also they secrete powerful acids and enzymes that solubilize phosphorus from fixed locations.

The beauty of this system is that mycorrhizae can deliver phosphorus only to the roots to which they are attached. They do not supply phosphorus to germinating weed seeds and do not normally colonize annual weed roots. The organic fraction of the soil, which includes stable and labile humus, plant and animal residues, and the biomass, contains a significant amount of phosphorus in a form more easily mineralized than most of the tightly bound inorganic sources. Soil organisms continually cycle this phosphorus through the soil ecosystem—that is, if they are active enough. Earthworms increase phosphorus availability by 500 to 1,000 percent, and by increasing the soil region to which turf roots have access (through earthworm tunnels), plant roots have greater opportunities to find phosphorus-containing sites.

POTASSIUM

Like phosphorus, potassium (K) is regulated, to a large degree, by soil organisms. Potassium is an extremely important nutrient for turf, especially if the plants have to endure the rigors of most sports—both the games and the maintenance. Potassium gives plants the strength to stand upright and better endure both natural and man-made stress. Disease resistance is often credited to adequate levels of potassium, as is the stress tolerance to traffic, drought, and salinity.

Unlike phosphorus and nitrogen, potassium doesn't combine with other elements or compounds in the plant to form proteins, carbohydrates, or other products of photosynthesis. It lives by itself in the plant fluids and is responsible for maintaining the correct hydraulic pressure within plant cells and assisting with the accumulation and translocation of photosynthesized materials. Without adequate potassium, nitrogen cannot be used efficiently by the plant. In fact, some of the detrimental effects of excessive nitrogen are regulated by potassium. Potassium helps increase translocation of nitrogen to the shoots of the plant, where it can be processed into amino acids and proteins. Adequate potassium also enables stomates to function properly and reduces evapotranspiration during dry periods. Research has found that winter injury is often significantly reduced when potassium levels are optimal (Beard 2002). Turf roots, especially those growing in sand, become more fibrous and diffusive in response to potassium.

Unfortunately, soil conditions on many fields are not ideal for holding a good supply of potassium. Available potassium usually resides in the soil solution and on colloidal exchange sites (see Chapter 1). Colloidal exchange sites are (negatively) charged particles of certain types of clay or stable humus, neither of which are abundant in sand-based fields. Potassium in soil solution is susceptible to leaching out of the root zone, especially in soils designed to drain rapidly. Liming can help slow the loss from leaching but can also reduce the amount of potassium available to plant roots. Potassium is also contained in the cells of soil organisms, and their life cycles make some available to plants.

Most mineral soils contain a tremendous amount of naturally occurring potassium, but the vast majority is unavailable to plants. Some of this bound potassium can be released through the activities of soil organisms. Secretions of their acids and chelates can release potassium from insoluble mineral sources. These biologically freed potassium ions are generally assimilated into the biomass, but some inevitably become available to plants. Abundant potassium is also fixed between layers of certain types of clay. These ions are less tightly bound than the insoluble mineral sources but are much less available than potassium ions attached to soil colloids or in soil solution.

Sandy soil typically contains little clay or humus. Even if there were an abundance of fixed potassium in the soil, biological activity would probably be inadequate to release substantial amounts of it. Soil organisms do more than just release fixed sources of potassium; they create humus that can magnetically hold potassium ions in an available form and encourage plants to grow finer, more abundant root hairs. Finer roots have greater surface area and can absorb potassium and other nutrients more efficiently. The production of stable soil humus can only be accomplished by soil organisms. It is not commercially available and, if it were, moving and handling it would destroy most of its beneficial properties. Many products on the market contain clinoptilolite (see Chapter 6) that claim to raise the cation exchange capacity (CEC) and increase the soil's capacity to hold cation nutrients like potassium. Research is generally positive, but these products are relatively expensive to use, and there is evidence that a few of them can inhibit the diffusion of water through the soil. Humus is the quintessential colloidal particle. Adequate levels of humus in the soil do not inhibit drainage beyond an acceptable threshold but offer tremendous benefits to the soil ecosystem. The only way to introduce humus to the soil is to add organic residues to the biological, humus-manufacturing machine on a regular basis.

As the pH of a soil increases, so does the capacity of humus particles to hold cations. At optimum pH for turf, the CEC of humus is often at least twice that of clay particles. A near neutral pH normally reduces both the amount of potassium in the soil solution and the potential for leaching, but it can also reduce the amount of potassium available to turf roots. A soil that is rich in humus, however, encourages diffusive and abundant rooting accompanied by a prolific biomass congregating in the rhizosphere. The greater root surface area gives turf plants better access to potassium in the soil solution and attached to humus particles, and the biological activity in the area immediately surrounding the roots lowers the pH in the rhizosphere and increases the availability of potassium. It is difficult to improve upon this natural system.

Potassium moves by diffusion—that is, it moves from areas of high to areas of low concentration. If the amount of potassium in the soil solution wanes, potassium ions quickly move from the exchange sites into soil solution, or vice versa. If, however, the CEC of a soil is extremely low (typical in sandy soil), storage sites are inadequate, and movement of potassium is normally from the fertilizer spreader to soil solution. From there, roots absorb some and the rest moves away from the root zone as the soil solution percolates downward. Capillary activity can move some soil solution back up to the root zone, but irrigation can disrupt upward mass flow. In sandy soils, water films that surround soil particles are thinner and the distance around sand particles is greater, so diffusion in sand is more difficult. Adequate moisture in the soil is crucial for diffusion to occur, but excessive water decreases utilization if oxygen levels fall below a certain threshold. As oxygen levels in the soil decrease, roots become stressed and overall nutrient uptake is reduced; potassium absorption is affected more than that of any other nutrient.

Plants are like most dogs in that they will consume far more than they need, at least with respect to potassium. This presents an efficiency problem for turf growing in sandy soil. Consumption beyond the optimum doesn't improve quality, but the turf plants have little choice. Since colloidal particles are scarce in sand, applied soluble potassium can reside only in the soil solution, and because of the superfluous drainage through sand, plants are faced with a use-it-or-lose-it situation. Turf plants do not contemplate their choices, of course, but they seem unable to regulate the amount of potassium they consume. The excess potassium roots absorb is not stored and used when needed; it is essentially wasted. A higher CEC from the presence of stable humus and a greater population of soil organisms better regulates the availability of potassium and allows plants more efficient access.

Soils that contain an abundance of clay can hold a tremendous amount of potassium—that is, if the clay is colloidal. Most clays are but some are not, and these do not contribute much to the soil's cation-holding capacity. Clayey soils with high CECs can hold large reserves of potassium and other cations and require less frequent applications; however, when potassium *is* needed, larger amounts are usually appropriate.

The most common sources of potassium are mineral salts such as potassium chloride, potassium sulfate, and magnesium/potassium sulfate, all of which are considered soluble. Once dissolved, the potassium enters the soil solution and is absorbed by turf roots, is adsorbed onto exchange sites (if they exist), or remains in solution and eventually leaches out of the root zone. Insoluble sources of potassium include greensand and other rock dusts, but these materials are slow to break down, and they are unlikely to meet turf's immediate potassium requirements, especially in an environment where biological activity is indigent. Some managers add these rock powders or ashes of wood or seed hulls to their compost pile, where biological activity is abundant.

Compost typically contains 0.2 to 1.0 percent potassium on a dry weight basis, which doesn't seem like a lot, but given the average compost application can add up. A ¼-inch topdress application consisting of 50 percent compost may deliver 1 pound or more of potash per 1,000 square feet. The potassium in compost is located in the biomass and is chelated to organic molecules of protein, fatty acids, lipids, and others. These ions are released biologically. Not only is this delivery system more efficient than applications of soluble salts but also the compost can eventually contribute to the CEC of the soil and increase the efficiency of applied potassium salts over time.

CALCIUM AND MAGNESIUM

Calcium (Ca) and magnesium (Mg), like potassium, are cations, and they reside in soil solution and on colloidal exchange sites. Both calcium and magnesium move through the soil by diffusion like potassium, but they can also move with the flow of water through the soil. Balancing calcium, magnesium, and potassium in the soil is important because they compete for space on exchange sites; the abundance of one can cause the deficiency of another (see Chapter 4, under "Base Saturation"). Potassium, the biggest ion, can displace calcium or magnesium; excess potassium is likely to result in a magnesium deficiency first. An ideal ratio of calcium, magnesium, and potassium for turf is ~80:11:3, but this is not to say that one cannot have a healthy stand of grass at a slightly different ratio. Since magnesium is the weakest of the three cations—in terms of exchange site competition—many believe that an overage of magnesium in the soil will not create any problems. Anecdotal evidence, however, indicates the important of maintaining the correct ratio, especially between calcium and magnesium. Many agronomists believe that a Ca:Mg ratio that is narrower than 7:1 (but not wider than 10:1) can result in an eclectic but indirectly related group of symptoms that include compaction, disease susceptibility, insect attraction, and stress intolerance.

A narrow Ca:Mg ratio (<7:1) is often caused by overuse of dolomitic lime. Most plants consume significantly more calcium than they do magnesium and reduce the soil's inventory of calcium at a faster rate. Dolomitic lime has a Ca:Mg ratio of ~2:1—which, over time, can cause a buildup of magnesium. The opposite (too wide a Ca:Mg ratio) can occur from high calcareous sand content in the soil. Calcium buildup from this type of sand can create shortages of magnesium, potassium, or both. In this situation, the use of either calcitic or dolomitic lime is unwarranted, and applications of potassium/magnesium sulfate, potassium sulfate, or magnesium sulfate may be necessary to improve the Ca:Mg:K ratio.

Calcium helps give plants structural rigidity, which is extremely important for recreational turf. It also regulates root and shoot growth and the development of several important enzymes. Magnesium functions as crucial component of chlorophyll, activates many essential enzymes, and plays a role in protein synthesis and in the production of ATP. Consistent availability of calcium and magnesium is crucial to the health of turf plants. As with potassium, however, the storage facility in some soils is less than ideal.

Unlike potassium, calcium and magnesium can be supplied by liming, which naturally releases ions into the soil solution at a relatively slow and sustained rate. This release rate is typically more effective and efficient in a biologically active soil environment. The system of exchange that nature created protects plants from deficiencies of vital cation nutrients. Without adequate storage capabilities in the soil, periodic shortages of cations can occur that may trigger symptoms not necessarily indicative of a nutrient deficiency. If, for example, a short-term deficiency of calcium suppressed root development enough to stress the plant but not enough to show symptoms of a calcium deficiency, the result may be disease susceptibility, drought intolerance, or just general decline. Having a constant and adequate supply of nutrients available to turf plants is important and difficult to accomplish without sufficient exchange capacity in the soil. Regular applications of compost in the topdress mixture can slowly build an adequate exchange mechanism in the soil without jeopardizing drainage.

Sources of calcium include gypsum (calcium sulfate), phosphate rock (tricalcium phosphate), super and triple-super phosphate (dicalcium phosphate), calcium nitrate, calcium oxide, and lime (calcium carbonate). Dolomitic lime (calcium/magnesium carbonate) also contains magnesium, as do Epsom salts (magnesium sulfate), potassium/magnesium sulfate, and magnesium oxide. There are occasions when calcium or magnesium may be needed but raising the pH is not necessary or desirable. Gypsum, Epsom salts, and potassium/magnesium sulfate can add these cations without altering pH. The application to the soil of any of these three also adds sulfur, which, in some areas, may be deficient. Calcium phosphates, calcium nitrate, calcium oxide, and magnesium oxide can raise the soil's pH, but application rates designed to fertilize are usually not large enough to significantly alter pH. The use of phosphates or nitrates where only calcium is needed may introduce excessive phosphorus or nitrogen.

SULFUR

Sulfur (S) is a plant nutrient that receives less attention than it should. Sulfur is available to plants from many sources. Organic matter contains sulfur, as does the mineral component of some soils, but, surprisingly, most of the available sulfur has, in the recent past, come from air pollution. Sulfur dioxide in the atmosphere is a byproduct of burning fossil fuels, especially coal, and can settle to earth in significant quantities. The deposition of sulfur from air pollution is usually greater closer to the source of pollution; it ranges from less than 4 pounds per acre in rural areas to as much as 175 pounds per acre close to industrial sites. Sulfur has also been used in the formulation of many pesticides and is a component of fertilizers such as potassium, ammonium, calcium, and magnesium sulfate. Deficiencies of sulfur are relatively rare and, because of their infrequency, the symptoms are often difficult to recognize. In recent years the release of sulfur dioxide into the atmosphere has been abated and the use of sulfate fertilizers and sulfurous pesticides has also decreased significantly. Add to these phenomena the relatively rare use of compost or organic fertilizer on most sports fields, and the possibility of sulfur deficiencies for turf plants significantly increases.

Sulfur is a component of many important amino acids without which some vital proteins cannot form. It also is a constituent of some essential vitamins and important enzymes that mediate crucial plant transformations. Some of these enzymes play a major role in photosynthesis. Sulfur deficiencies in soil can result in chlorosis in plant leaves from suppressed photosynthesis. Without sulfur, plants cannot produce chlorophyll, lignin, pectin, and other important components.

Most of the sulfur in soil resides in soil organic matter. Mineral soils rich in pyrite also contain sulfur reserves, but ample quantities of either pyrite or organic matter are found in few athletic field soils. Like nitrogen, sulfur is largely stored and regulated by biological activity. Depending on circumstances, soil organisms either release sulfur for plants or immobilize it. This phenomenon is usually controlled by fluctuating ratios of carbon to sulfur (C:S) in the soil. When the C:S ratio is greater than 400:1, organisms generally immobilize more sulfur than they make available to plants. As the ratio decreases from 400:1 to 200:1, there is a relative increase in the release of sulfur and a decrease of sulfur immobilization. Below 200:1, organisms release significantly more sulfur in a plant-usable form than they immobilize.

The ratio of C:S in soil organic matter varies but averages ~250:1. The variation of C:S ratios in organic residues not yet decomposed is also wide and that range would be relative in compost. Analysis of compost samples, however, reveals an average C:S ratio of ~200:1, which would not only provide for the release of sulfur from itself but would narrow the overall ratio in the soil (depending on how much and how often it is applied) for more sustained release. The adequate availability of sulfur for plants depends on several factors, including temperature, moisture, carbon-sulfur ratio, and pH, but the most influential factor is biological activity, which is stimulated by regular contributions of organic residues to the soil. It is nearly impossible to calculate the C:S ratio from the data of a soil analysis. Digestible carbon would never appear on a standard soil analysis, and if sulfur were measured, it would be as available—not total.

Plants absorb sulfur as sulfate (SO_4). Like potassium, sulfate moves through the soil by diffusion and, like magnesium and calcium, it also moves by mass flow (i.e., the movement of water through the soil). Unlike potassium, magnesium, and calcium, sulfate is not a cation—a positively charged ion—that can cling to colloidal exchange sites. Sulfate is therefore at much greater risk of leaching than potassium, magnesium, or calcium. Even in a sandy soil with a relatively low CEC, sulfate ions have a better chance of leaching than do cations. Sulfates leaching through the soil can contribute to micronutrient deficiencies because they often bond with trace mineral ions.

Microorganisms create sulfate by oxidizing reduced forms of sulfur such as sulfur dioxide, various sulfides, and elemental sulfur, and by mineralization/oxidation of organic sulfur sources. As sulfur is oxidized by microbes into sulfate, some enters the soil solution, where it is most available to plant roots. Unfortunately, given the way fields are designed to drain, the mass flow of soil solution is usually down and away from the root zone. Additionally, if the field is constructed of calcareous sand, the abundance of calcium ions can bind with sulfate to create gypsum, a relatively insoluble mineral. Turf plants growing in a sandy soil—depending on less than 1 percent organic matter to deliver adequate sulfur without other direct or indirect sources—may eventually suffer a deficiency. Symptoms of a sulfur deficiency include chlorosis, stunted growth, and underdeveloped shoots. The reduction of photosynthesis from a sulfur deficiency may also suppress root development, decreasing drought tolerance.

Even when the sulfur in the soil is ample, if the field is compacted there may not be enough available air in the soil for microbial oxidation of reduced sulfur forms into sulfate. As bacteria and a few other organisms create sulfate ions, they consume oxygen from the soil. If oxygen levels are inadequate, fewer sulfate ions can be created—and other problems may arise too. The consumption of oxygen where little is available can lead to anaerobic soil conditions and not only produce phytotoxic substances but also stress plants and suppress vital biological functions. Anaerobic conditions may also lead to denitrification of available nitrate dissolved in the soil solution and the reduction of sulfate into hydrogen sulfide, which easily combines with metal ions and forms what is commonly known as *black layer*.

Many managers use elemental sulfur to lower the soil's pH, especially on fields where they are trying to provide optimum conditions for specific varieties of turf. This practice provides more than adequate resources for sulfur-oxidizing bacteria but may be futile for adjusting pH. Fields built and constantly topdressed with calcareous sand may require impractical amounts of elemental sulfur to substantially lower the soil's pH. Calcareous sand can contain more than 20 percent calcium carbonate, which means that a single inch of sand contains the equivalent of nearly a ton of pure lime per 1,000 square feet. Multiply that by the depth of sand in the root zone to see how difficult pH reduction will be. The amount of elemental sulfur needed to effectively lower the soil pH would likely cause many more problems than it solves.

A rich soil containing both labile and stable humus naturally buffers extremes in pH. It also provides storage for organic forms of sulfur and provides habitat for the organisms needed to transform it into plant-usable sulfate. Biological activity in a rich soil aggregates soil particles, forming quasipermanent pore space that can protect the soil from anaerobiosis. Soil organisms do this more for their own survival than for the welfare of plants. Earthworms make passages through which air, water, and plant roots can travel. Their tunnels connect and widen the interface between soil and atmosphere, ensuring adequate release of carbon dioxide for plants and ample absorption of oxygen for roots and soil organisms. Regular contributions of well-made, well-aged compost can provide the soil not only organically bound sulfur but also an army of organisms that efficiently regulate its availability. This is yet another example of how well the natural ecosystem can function if ample resources are available.

TRACE ELEMENTS

Nitrogen, phosphorus, potassium, calcium, magnesium, and sulfur are categorized as macronutrients because plants use them in much greater quantities than the seven other soil-borne elements considered essential. These other elements are aptly called trace elements, trace minerals, or micronutrients because of the small amounts plants need to survive. In fact, doses greater than trace amounts can be toxic to plants.

When scientists began testing nutrients to determine which are essential for plants and which are not, they found that plants could not survive if one of 16 elements were missing. These elements are carbon, oxygen, hydrogen, nitrogen, phosphorus, potassium, calcium, magnesium, sulfur, iron, manganese, copper, zinc, molybdenum, boron, and chlorine. Logically, they concluded that these elements are the only nutrients essential to the plant's survival. However, other elements may be vital to plant health. Experiments have shown that many elements enhance plant growth or vigor, but because the plant can survive in their absence, they are not considered essential (Jones 1998). In fact, plants can substitute some nonessential elements for essential ones when the need arises. Sodium, for example, can function like potassium in plants and, in the absence of potassium, plants are able to survive using sodium instead. A similar substitution has been observed of vanadium for molybdenum.

Chemical analysis of plant tissue specimens revealed 26 such elements: antimony, arsenic, barium, beryllium, bismuth, bromine, cadmium, cerium, cesium, chromium, fluorine, gallium, gold, iodine, lead, mercury, nickel, selenium, silver, strontium, thallium, tin, titanium, tungsten, uranium, and vanadium. Whether any of these extra elements contribute to the plant's welfare has not been determined, but it is reasonable to assume that if the plant absorbs them, then they play some role in one or more of the plant's functions. Some of the elements on this list, although they seem downright lethal, in trace amounts can be functional and beneficial. Deficiencies of one or more of these obscure minerals may result in symptoms that make the problem impossible to detect. The underlying cause of many turfgrass problems may simply be that the plant's defense system is functioning below its potential. This theory is unsubstantiated by research and might be difficult to prove but beg these questions:

- If even traces of almost half the naturally occurring elements on earth are found in plant tissue, is it reasonable to assume that the majority do not contribute to the functionality of the plant just because we are unable to determine how?
- Is it possible that other beneficial elements are also in plant tissue but in such slight amounts that they are below the detection limits of our lab equipment?
- Is it likely that other naturally occurring elements would be found in plant tissue if they existed in the soil and were available to the plant's roots?

Silicon, for example, does not appear on the list above, but there is plenty of evidence that it benefits some plants. Rice is a crop that responds favorably where silicon is available. Not only does the plant stand more erect but also it appears to have measurably greater disease resistance and tolerance to iron and aluminum toxicity. Some researchers believe turf plants absorb silicon (as silicic acid) and that it accumulates in the walls of epidermal cells, creating a barrier that strengthens tissue, reduces transpiration, and protects against pathogen infection.

At one time in earth's history, these obscure elements were much more available in the soil than they are today mainly because countless generations of agricultural plants have extracted them from the soil, and they have not been replaced. The fact that crops absorbed these elements from the soil suggests they were either required or desired. Some managers believe soils should periodically be enriched with materials containing a broad diversity of natural elements. Seaweed, kelp (Acadian, North American Kelp), and many rock dusts from volcanic deposits (Peak Minerals, Summa Minerals, Morningstar Minerals) contain such a range of natural elements in trace amounts. These products can be mixed with topdressing materials or compost or be applied alone.

The consistency of dried seaweed may be too coarse for direct application to some fields. Mowing without the baggers will chop it into finer particles but, if there is any sand in the seaweed, the mower blades (especially reel mower blades) can be dulled or damaged. A more practical method is adding the seaweed to the compost pile, where biological activity will reduce its particle size. Clean, dried, and pulverized seaweed can be added to the topdress mixture. Sports fields in littoral regions may have free access to this resource. Many shorelines are littered with seaweed detritus, especially after a storm, and some municipalities go to great expense to remove it from their beaches. Generally, it is not difficult to obtain the permits necessary for harvesting seaweed that has washed ashore. Some municipalities may prefer to deliver seaweed from beaches directly to the field rather than pay tipping fees at the local landfill. A golf superintendent I know used to send his crew to the beach with a dump truck for two or three loads of seaweed once or twice a year. Upon their return, the seaweed was incorporated into the most active compost piles with a bucket loader. Now the town delivers seaweed to them free to save on landfill fees.

Rock powders from volcanic deposits are normally a dusty consistency and can easily be worked or watered through a turf canopy, but they can be difficult to apply through conventional equipment. Drop spreaders are more practical than broadcast spreaders, which often create clouds of dust. This swarm of suspended particles can drift away from the area where the application is needed. A drop spreader, however, is a laborious way to cover large areas of turf, and any moisture picked up from the turf can quickly gum the works.

Most rock powders and seaweeds are easiest to manage if used to enrich compost or other topdress material. Some manufacturers produce a soluble extract from seaweed that is applied as a liquid. Seaweed extract is compatible with most other sprays and can counter the stressful effects of some pesticides. It can also be used through the irrigation system, if one exists. The soluble extract contains just as diverse an inventory of elements as the dried algal remains and, because the contents are dissolved, utilization is often significantly greater.

Applications of organic fertilizers, compost, or both may indirectly increase the availability of some obscure elements by increasing biological activity in the soil. Most soils contain more than adequate amounts of trace elements in tightly bound mineral formations, and the acids, enzymes, and chelates created by soil organisms can dissolve the bonds enough for some elements to become available. Iron, for example, is abundant in a typical mineral soil, but its availability depends on organisms that can free it from its insoluble relationship with the parent material. Some organisms in the root zone can produce a scavenging chemical molecule (called *hydroxamate siderophore*) that finds and secures iron ions for plants. Many other organisms produce chelates that easily complex with iron and increase its availability to plant roots. Some strains of mycorrhizae produce this molecule and retrieve iron for the roots to which they are attached. This process is unlikely to occur to a great degree in a sandy soil, as the diversity of minerals in sand is relatively low and the degree to which they are insoluble and unavailable is relatively high. Researchers have found that as the level of organic matter increases in soil, so does the availability of iron, manganese, zinc, copper, boron, and many other nutrients (Brady 1974, Stevenson 1986).

Organic matter also plays a major role in the storage and availability of micronutrients. Its ability to establish complexes with metal ions is well known. The elements in these complexes are more easily accessed by the actions of organisms and even plant roots, to a certain extent. Contributions of organic residues from compost, clippings, and organic fertilizers can increase the production of humic and fulvic acids. These acids not only can dissolve micronutrients from their parent particles but also maintain many of them in soil solution, where they are most available to plant roots. Humic, fulvic, and other molecules often complex with metal ions, forming chelates that prevent the reestablishment of mineral bonds but allow plant and microbial access to the nutrients. It is important to note that well-decomposed organic matter (humus) has less ability to chelate micronutrients and can even fix some elements, rendering them unavailable to plants. Periodic applications of less decomposed organic matter, such as well-aged compost, is likely to increase availability of these nutrients.

Sand is not the ideal medium for biological management of micronutrients because its level of biological activity and inorganic sources of trace elements are usually lower. In calcareous sand, the abundance of free calcium carbonates can fix many micronutrients through a series of chemical reactions. The release of these nutrients is often difficult under conventional management practices, and foliar applications may be the only way to effectively increase availability. Regular contributions of organic matter, however, may stimulate enough biological activity to release fixed sources of micronutrients.

If the health of soil organisms is directly related to the health of turf, then it is logical that nutrients important to them are also important to turf plants. Turf plants may not absorb some of these elements, which are therefore (mis)regarded as unimportant. But elements essential for the functions of beneficial soil organisms must also be regarded as important for turf. Soil scientists at the U.S. Department of Agriculture (USDA) recognize the fundamental importance of interactions between soil organisms for plant growth and health. Deficiencies of essential nutrients for any of these organisms could easily affect their ecological balance in the soil and their interactions. The list of nutrients considered essential for soil organisms is similar to the list for animals; however, the methods of measuring essentiality for plants and animals are different. As previously mentioned, nutrients considered essential for plants are those that enable plants to survive, whereas nutrients essential for animals may serve only to enhance growth or benefit functionality. The animal may be able to survive without them. Only one element, boron, is considered essential for plants but not for animals, but several are considered essential for animals but not necessarily for plants: chromium, cobalt, fluorine, iodine, nickel, selenium, sodium, tin, and vanadium. It stands to reason that if the growth and function of soil organisms are enhanced by any of these elements, then plants would also benefit. Cobalt, for example, is essential for symbiotic nitrogen-fixing bacteria. Without cobalt, these essential organisms would not be able to survive and colonize the roots of leguminous plants. Since cobalt is essential for the conversion of atmospheric nitrogen into protein, it is reasonable to assume that free-living, nitrogen-fixing bacteria need it too.

It is not being suggested that concentrated preparations of any trace element be arbitrarily applied to the soil. Unless a micronutrient deficiency is determined by a soil test or leaf tissue analysis, the threshold between helpful and harmful is too narrow for these types of amendments. Additionally, applications of a micronutrient beyond optimum can cause the deficiency of another. Seaweed, volcanic rock dusts, or both can, however, add a rich diversity of slowly released nutrients to the soil without increasing any one to a phytotoxic level. Decades of research on the use of both volcanic rock dusts and dried seaweed reveal not only the potential for benefits but also the improbability of harm.

Regardless of whether rock powders or seaweed is applied, the wealth of nutrients they contain may remain unavailable to plants if biological activity in the soil is inadequate to release it. Soil organisms release trace elements through the production of organic acids, enzymes, and chelating agents used to extract nutrients from decaying plant or animal residues and from inorganic mineral sources. Much of what they extract is assimilated and then released for plants when the organisms are preyed upon or when their dead bodies are consumed by saprophytes. There are times when soil organisms make trace elements less available by immobilization or oxidation. If deficiencies occur due to biological immobilization, it is unlikely that the pool of trace elements was adequate before bioconsumption. An affluence of biological activity may usurp the supply of trace elements in the soil but, normally, the problem would be ephemeral. The army of predators that commonly follow a bloom of decay organisms would invariably release ample amounts of consumed nutrients. Plant roots exude a wide variety of organic compounds that attract and feed a relatively diverse population of soil organisms. But plants have the ability to attract a more specific group of organisms that better serve the plants' needs. Shortages of a particular nutrient may induce the plant to release pabulum that attracts organisms suited to securing what the plant needs. Oxidation transforms some nutrients into plant-available forms and others into unavailable forms. Biological oxidation is balanced by biological reduction, which contributes to the system of storage, release, and availability of many nutrients.

ECOSYSTEM

Growing turf in a relatively inert medium such as sand is a little like caring for a newborn child. It can't tell you what it wants; it can only cry, and its needs are constant. The manager has to spoon-feed everything the child cannot—through a functioning soil ecosystem—provide itself. And those needs are erratic and inconsistent. This morning it was nitrogen, this afternoon, water. Yesterday it was iron, and the day before that it had a type of diaper rash called dollar spot. This is not to say that fertilizer is unnecessary on an ecologically maintained sports field, but the system of nutrient exchange and cycling, biological oxidation and reduction, and natural storage and release functions poorly in an environment where too many important components are missing. Unfortunately, adding only soluble nutrients to the baby's formula rarely helps the situation. This approach amounts to taking the bottle (or the breast) from the child and replacing it with an intravenous drip. Eventually, those unused digestive organs become dysfunctional and the baby's health begins to decline. Countless components of a whole ecosystem function spontaneously. To manually provide all the benefits of those chemical, biological, and physical interactions, using only symptoms as a guide, is a monumental task.

POINTS TO REMEMBER

- Carbon, hydrogen, and oxygen from water and the atmosphere constitute 95 percent of the nutrients plants need.
- Carbon is available to plants as carbon dioxide only and is absorbed through pores in the leaf blades called *stomates*.

- Nitrogen is an essential nutrient, but too much can contribute to serious problems.
- Established turf has a relatively low need for phosphorus, and it can easily extract an adequate supply from the soil.
- Potassium helps plants stand upright, tolerate natural and man-made stress, and use nitrogen efficiently—and plants depend on soil colloids like clay and humus to store it in an exchangeable, available form.
- Few field managers worry about sulfur deficiency, but the recent abatement of both sulfur emissions and the use of sulfur in fertilizers and pesticides has significantly decreased sulfur levels in some soils.
- Potassium, calcium, and magnesium need colloidal exchange sites (clay or humus particles) for adequate soil storage.
- Like most soil chemicals, trace elements are essential to both plants and soil organisms.
- A functioning soil ecosystem most likely needs more than nitrogen, phosphorus, and potassium. Applying a diversity of nutrients from raw materials is a good method of enabling (or reenabling) the soil ecosystem to manage itself.

Chapter 3

COMPOST

Managers may have a difficult time maintaining high-quality turf without chemical pesticides on sports fields where compost or compost tea cannot be used. Compost is an essential tool on any ecological field but, like any other tool, it must be well made to produce good results. There is compelling evidence that topdressing with mixtures of sand and compost or compost alone notably improves soil conditions and turf performance. If the compost is made well and aged correctly, it can also suppress disease organisms, reduce thatch, inhibit compaction, diminish palatability of plant tissue to herbivorous arthropods, reduce the soil's thermal conductivity, increase turf's stress tolerance, and decrease the field's water consumption, all to a significant degree. Because of its potential for inhibiting pathogens, compost is currently being examined as an alternative to methyl bromide (a soil fumigant facing regulatory extinction).

Compost not only contains many groups of beneficial organisms but provides resources for indigenous groups of organisms as well. The populations of these beneficial soil-dwelling creatures swell after compost is applied and, as their numbers increase, so do the beneficial tasks that they perform. They can regulate fertility (see Chapter 2), for example, and reduce the superfluity or deficiencies of nutrients often experienced with the use of conventional fertilizers. Their regulation of nitrogen reduces the level of free amino acids and nitrates in plant tissue that often attract insects and pathogens. Compost also provides fertility, which eventually may supplant the need for other fertilizers. In an ongoing study that began in 1997 at Rutgers, researchers found "the plots with some percentage of compost material have consistently been the top performers in the trial" (Rossi 2002[b]). For each of the hundreds—perhaps thousands—of benefits from compost that scientists now recognize, probably scores of advantages are yet to be discovered.

Making compost with waste materials generated on or near the field may be practical for some managers but not for others. There are many reasons why on-site composting may be unrealistic, but lacking the skills to make compost should not be one of them, as such skills can be acquired with practice and patience. The time, equipment, and materials needed to make quality compost may not be readily available or within the manager's budget. Local ordinances and the absence of a suitable location may also pose restrictions. Purchasing compost from private or municipal facilities may be the only alternative, but the manager must be able to judge the quality of the compost—or, more accurately, material that has the potential to become quality compost.

HISTORY

Using compost on sports fields is not new. The Turfgrass Information Database at Michigan State University has literally hundreds of articles written in the early part of the twentieth century about making, curing, storing, and applying compost to turf (see Figure 3-1). Managers back then understood the need for a healthy, functioning ecosystem without knowing nearly as many of its benefits as are known today. Many turf managers, for example, used compost to dormant-feed turf without knowing that it also offered protection against winter diseases. The use of compost was ubiquitous, even though relatively little was known about the subtle but important differences in processing and aging techniques. Although less information about making and using compost was available back then, most managers had a fair amount of experience with it.

During the chemical revolution that began after World War II, turf stewards began to lose touch with the composting skills they had acquired in the preceding decades. The ease with which modern pesticides could control symptoms lured many well-meaning managers away from the basic tenets of soil and plant health. Unfortunately, this new trend kept the old-school managers from passing on the wisdom of composting to subsequent generations of groundskeepers. Over the years, while few people were paying attention, the art of composting has been refined and a lot more discovered about its potential benefits. Much of this information was uncovered by accident during research aimed at solving solid waste disposal problems. Now managers are beginning to rediscover the benefits of compost and, at the same time, learning that well-made compost has much more to offer than their predecessors imagined.

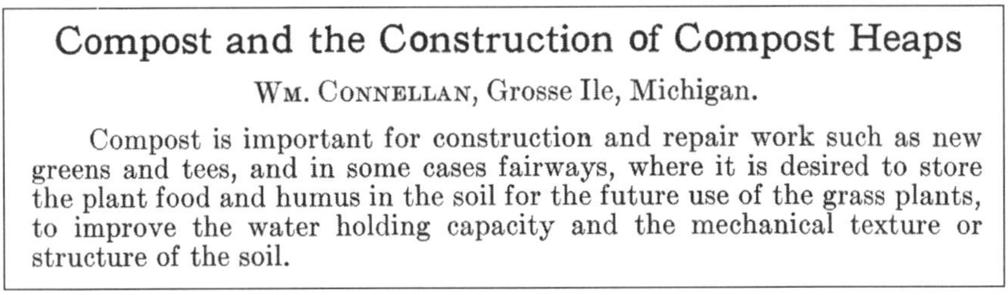

Compost and the Construction of Compost Heaps

WM. CONNELLAN, Grosse Ile, Michigan.

Compost is important for construction and repair work such as new greens and tees, and in some cases fairways, where it is desired to store the plant food and humus in the soil for the future use of the grass plants, to improve the water holding capacity and the mechanical texture or structure of the soil.

FIGURE 3-1   Compost used on turf in not new. This article appeared in the April 1921 issue of the USGA Green Section Bulletin. Photo courtesy USGA.

ORGANIC MATTER

Compost undergoes a complex transformation into many products as it is consumed and recycled by soil organisms; the end product is humus—the most stable component of soil organic matter. However, humus does not support the degree of biological activity compost does. Organic matter, as a whole, is an essential component of a natural soil system, and it would be hard to find an expert who disagrees. The term *organic matter* describes many materials from thatch to humus. It also includes senescent roots, shoots, and the bodies of soil organisms. Within each category of residue is an infinite number of decomposition stages, all with distinct characteristics. About the only thing these organic materials have in common is that they are all dead.

Every organic residue at all stages of decomposition has something to offer the soil ecosystem. Mature compost is a stage of decomposition that is relatively stable but, unlike humus, still offers a plentitude of resources for soil organisms. Soil organisms improve soil structure by binding organic matter together with clay and other soil particles, creating pores through which air, water, and roots travel more easily. Organisms aggregate clay by interrupting the bonds between particles. These bonds can be extremely tight and make the soil more prone to compaction and problems associated with air and water movement.

Soil organisms thrive in organic matter. It has everything they need to exist, including water, food, and air. Consequently, many varieties of microorganisms are constantly competing for those resources. This competition creates a biological equilibrium that, in the long and short term, can prevent or mitigate many insect, disease, and even nutrient imbalance problems that plague the turf manager. Carbon in organic matter is the source of energy for most soil organisms. The greater the available source of energy, the larger and more diverse their populations can be. Compost, however, has many more resources to offer to soil organisms than humus. As the humification process matures, fewer nutrients are available for soil organisms, so fresh material must be added regularly to maintain a high level of biological activity.

Organic matter, in almost any form, can absorb an amount of water many times its own weight. This property increases the soil's capacity to retain dissolved nutrients and decreases the likelihood of nutrients leaching away from the root zone. Humus itself is not porous, but its ability to hold as much water as it does can create porosity. Humus swells in order to accommodate as much as four to six times its own weight in water. This swelling causes a sort of heaving in the soil. When water is released during drier periods, organic matter contracts and leaves behind air spaces. Earthworms and other larger organisms that burrow through the soil looking for organic residues create even more porosity. This activity lightens the soil but does not necessarily create an excessively soft playing surface. Humus—the most mature and often the most abundant form of soil organic matter—is also a colloidal substance that can magnetically hold mineral nutrients such as potassium, magnesium, ammonium, and calcium ions. Nutrients such as nitrogen, phosphorus, and sulfur exist as proteins and other compounds in organic matter and can be mineralized into available nutrients by soil organisms at a slow, sustained, and efficient rate.

Organic matter is lighter than sand, silt, or clay, which benefits root growth. As roots travel through the soil, energy, manufactured by photosynthesis, is used. The more difficult the journey, the more energy the root uses to travel the same distance, and root growth is often stunted. The farther roots travel and branch out through the soil, the more access they gain to the nutrients and water needed for synthesizing more energy.

Mineral nutrients are made available in the soil from the activities of organisms on parent material (rock particles). The average acre of topsoil contains approximately 52,000 pounds of potash, 40,000 pounds of magnesium, 72,000 pounds of calcium, 3,000 pounds of phosphate, 3,000 pounds of sulfur, and 100,000 pounds of iron (see Figure 1-7). Albeit abundant, the vast majority of these nutrients are bound in mineral structures that are insoluble and therefore unavailable to plants. On the other hand, many organisms in nature can dissolve minerals into available nutrients for plants. Soil organisms release acids and chelates that free nutrients from the surface of soil particles. They produce corrosive exudates specifically to liberate mineral nutrients for their own metabolism. Once assimilated by an organism, the mineral is bound in an organic complex more readily available to other soil life after the organism dies or is consumed by a predator. The mineral can be recycled endlessly through all types of soil organisms, including plants. Organic matter, especially from mature compost, directly influences the existence and proliferation of organisms that can free minerals from the soil's vast reserve.

UNSOLVED MYSTERIES

Most scientists admit that for every known benefit from compost there are several that are unknown or unexplainable. Recently, a phenomenon referred to as *compost-induced systemic acquired resistance* was discovered—a fancy name for the inexplicable disease resistance systemically spread throughout a plant growing in a compost-based medium. Researchers using containerized plants infected half of the plants' roots—separated from the other half by an impenetrable divider—with disease pathogens. The infected roots were growing in a peat mix. The uninfected roots were growing in peat, soil, or a compost-based mix. The containers where the uninfected roots were growing in either peat or soil showed symptoms of the disease on the roots in both sides of the container and on the aboveground portion of the plant. The plants whose uninfected roots were growing in a compost mix showed disease suppression in all parts of the plant, including on the side of the container where the pathogens were introduced. Scientists could not explain the phenomenon, but they could clearly conclude that it occurred (Zhang, W., et al. 1996; see Figure 3-2).

CARBON DIOXIDE

Another important benefit of applying compost to turf is the generation of carbon dioxide, which cycles from the atmosphere into plants and other photosynthesizing (autotrophic) organisms. Proteins, carbohydrates (sugars and starches), fats, waxes,

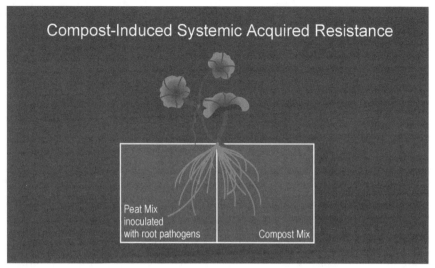

FIGURE 3-2   No one really knows how, but systemic acquired resistance is often induced by well-aged compost. Adapted from Zhang, W., et al.

lignin, cellulose, hemicellulose, and other carbon compounds produced by autotrophic organisms are food for almost all living things on earth, including soil organisms. Each time energy is extracted from these carbon-based foods, carbon dioxide is produced and released back into the atmosphere (see Figure 1-15). Plants "know" the value of biological activity on and around their root zone and release, through the roots, up to 50 percent of the photosynthesized foods they produce to feed soil organisms. In a perfect system, all the carbon dioxide produced by organisms existing on food released from roots is reabsorbed by plants. Unfortunately, perfection is unobtainable, and supplemental carbon dioxide is needed. The most likely source is from the decomposition of organic residues.

All of the nitrogen, phosphorus, potassium, calcium, magnesium, sulfur, and trace elements plants use constitute only 5 percent of their diet. The other 95 percent is from carbon, oxygen, and hydrogen. Plants derive carbon, hydrogen, and oxygen from carbon dioxide in the atmosphere and water. Organic residues decaying in the soil produce carbon dioxide that seeps up to the soil surface, where plants can absorb it. And even though concern is growing about the buildup of carbon dioxide in the atmosphere—and its relationship to global warming—its levels are often inadequate for plants.

In a natural system, the constant decay of plant and animal residues on or near the soil's surface produces a constant source of carbon dioxide for plants. The sand-based systems on many modern sports fields have few organic residues to offer decay organisms, and where the clippings are collected, even less. The inner atmosphere of the earth occupies about 100 miles of space over the planet, whereas grass plants often occupy less than an inch. It is difficult for the carbon dioxide produced elsewhere to settle on the earth's surface for any length of time. Although carbon dioxide is slightly heavier than air, forces such as convection currents, trade winds, prevailing winds, jet stream, pressure gradients, sea breezes, and land breezes tend to move it into portions of the atmosphere inaccessible to plant leaves. There are moments—usually in the early morning or evening—when air currents are relatively calm. These are the same moments when the plants' stomates (pores) are open, allowing for the exchange of gases. It's unlikely that these phenomena coincide accidentally.

If carbon dioxide is being generated in the soil, plants rooted there can absorb it as it seeps from the soil's surface. Compost offers many forms of food for soil organisms ranging from bacteria to earthworms, all of which derive energy and respire carbon dioxide that can be absorbed by plants.

The list of benefits from adding compost can go on for several hundred pages, and the expense of providing those benefits without regularly contributing this organic matter is staggering. It is important not only to add compost regularly but also to limit activities that deplete organic matter in the soil (see Chapter 6). Routine cultural practices performed by the grounds managers and their crews may inadvertently deplete soil organic matter content. When organic matter levels begin to drop, so do the corresponding benefits, including water- and nutrient-holding capacity and the production of carbon dioxide from respiring populations of soil organisms. This loss has a profound effect on the soil, creating an economic recession that affects the entire soil ecosystem. The only things that are often increased by lower levels of organic matter are bulk soil density and problems.

COMPOST PRODUCTION

Making high-quality compost is more an art than it is a science. Learning the most practical method takes effort and time but, as with any other endeavor, practice yields proficiency. Keep in mind that the decay of organic matter is a natural phenomenon that occurs with or without our help. All we are trying to do is speed the process, create heat to kill weed seeds and pathogens, and produce a material that not only improves the health and appearance of turf but protects it as well. It is important to understand, however, that all composts are *not* equal. The difference between high-quality and low-quality compost is comparable to the dissimilarities of a vintage Rolls Royce and a pile of scrap metal.

Five conditions must be met in order to accelerate the decay process and successfully produce compost in a reasonable amount of time. These conditions are adequate air and water, correct carbon-to-nitrogen ratio (C:N), initial ambient temperatures above freezing, and a pH range between 5.5 and 9.0.

The organisms that are most adept at breaking down organic residues are aerobic; they need oxygen to live. If a pile of material is wet and compressed, it will not contain enough air for the right type of organisms; instead, another type, the anaerobe, will process the pile. This condition can cause odor problems, will not create the heat necessary to kill weed seeds or pathogens, can produce phytotoxic compounds, and does not yield the same product—one that is capable of suppressing disease and feeding appropriate groups of soil organisms. In fact, poorly made compost can actually increase the severity of disease.

Turning and aerating the material several times increases the amount of oxygen in the pile and moderates the temperature. Many compost piles are set up on top of perforated pipes to ensure that plenty of air reaches the bottom of the pile (see Figure 3-3). There is a theory that proper mixing and a piped air infiltration system are all that is needed for proper aeration. The heat generated by the pile creates a chimney effect that draws fresh air in through the pipes. No turning or motor-driven blowers are necessary, but creating a porous mix to begin with is crucial. If the mix gets compressed by precipitation or just by gravity, air movement may be inhibited, and so will aerobic decay. If entrainment (air infiltration) loss is severe, the pile may become anaerobic. Additionally, all portions of a static pile may not heat adequately, and some weed seeds may persevere. During conventional composting, turning is a crucial component.

Knowing when and how often to turn a pile is the key to making compost quickly. Unfortunately, there is no set formula. The number and frequency of turns needed changes with the climate and the materials being decomposed. A good method of determining turning frequency is by using a thermometer with a 2- to 4-foot-long probe to monitor the temperature deep within the pile. When the pile is first mixed, the temperature should rise within one to three days to between 120° and 160°F. When the temperature drops 20°F below its peak is a often good time to turn the pile. Another good time to turn is if the pile gets too hot (>160°F). The hotter a pile gets, the more oxygen it is using and the more often it needs to be turned. Each time the pile is aerated, heat should increase again until the process is nearly completed. When the temperature remains relatively stable, the compost is probably ready to cure. Eventually, familiarity with the composting process can eliminate the need for a thermometer.

As mentioned earlier, compost happens whether we participate in the process or not. Many people who make compost don't have time to turn the pile regularly and, consequently, the process is retarded. But, eventually, compost is made, and it may possess the same characteristics as the compost that was pampered; it just takes longer.

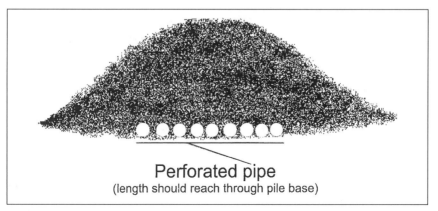

Perforated pipe
(length should reach through pile base)

FIGURE 3-3   Grass Pile—temporary storage. Allowing air entrainment to the bottom of the pile helps prevent anaerobiosis in its core.

Turning frequently at the early stages of the compost process ensures good aerobic decomposition, creates enough heat to kill weed seeds and pathogens, and shortens the amount of time needed for the pile to cure. Frequent turning during the early stages of composting is best, but a manager's time is often the limiting factor.

In some large composting operations, windrow turners are used to mix and aerate the pile. These machines are designed to add air to the windrows and circulate all materials into the core—the hottest part of the pile. For managers making just enough compost to satisfy their own needs, a bucket loader is usually a quick and efficient way to turn a pile. When turning the pile with a loader, scoop up the compost, raise the scoop to an elevated position, and allow the material to cascade slowly from the bucket. Generally, the pile is moved each time it is turned, so a site at least twice the size of the pile's footprint (plus maneuvering space) is ideal.

Surface area is another aspect of aeration to be considered. The smaller the particle of organic material, the more surface area is exposed to decay organisms and the faster it is decomposed. Sawdust decays faster than chips, which decompose considerably faster than whole branches. A proper mixture of coarse and fine materials encourages air infiltration. Material that is too fine can decrease air infiltration through the pile and retard aerobic decay or cause anaerobic conditions. The greater the amount of surface area, the faster the microbial consumption of oxygen and the more often turning is needed.

Moisture is an important consideration in the compost-making process. Living things need water to live, and the organisms that make compost are no different. A compost pile should contain somewhere between 40 and 60 percent moisture. A simple test to determine proper moisture content is to squeeze a handful of raw material. The material should feel damp to the touch, but no more than a couple of drops of water should be expelled. If the pile is too dry, reproduction of the composting organisms can be inhibited, which can slow the composting process. If the pile is too wet, it can easily become anaerobic.

During the composting process, the moisture level in the pile can vary. Heat and turning can drive off moisture, whereas excess precipitation can soak a pile and force out too much oxygen. Sometimes a pile can get too hot if there is inadequate moisture because the evaporation of water moderates the pile's temperature. Adding water to a pile is easy enough if it is needed, but extracting it is impractical. To correct excess moisture content, mix dry, bulky materials into the pile to absorb the water. Saw chips, sawdust, planer shavings, or shredded paper can be used. Paper products tend to mat when wet, so thorough mixing is necessary. Newspaper is more likely to mat and decomposes more slowly than other uncoated papers. Clay-coated papers used to produce glossy printing (such as magazines) are not recommended. Dry leaves are suitable if it is the season for them, and soil can also be used in a pinch. Many of these dry, bulky materials can alter the C:N ratio of the pile if too much is incorporated. If a wet pile fails to reheat after adding moisture absorbing material, the C:N ratio may have become too wide and feedstock with a narrow C:N ratio may have to be added. If no bulking materials are available, turning the pile can also help to dry it.

CARBON-TO-NITROGEN RATIO

The C:N ratio is important when combining materials for composting. The ideal C:N ratio for a compost pile is between 25 and 35 parts carbon to 1 part nitrogen (average 30:1). If the C:N ratio of the pile is too wide (i.e., high carbon, low nitrogen), composting will be slow because the amount of available nitrogen is too low for proper protein syntheses, and the reproduction of decay organisms is inhibited. Adding organisms or enzymes in the form of compost starters or inoculants will not correct this problem if the ratio is very wide. If the C:N ratio is too narrow (i.e., too much nitrogen, too little carbon), reproduction can be overstimulated, causing rapid oxygen depletion and, eventually, anaerobic conditions. If carbon is insufficient for microbial processing, excess nitrogen can be lost to leaching or volatilization. If the pile begins to generate unpleasant odors, chances are good that nitrogen is being lost through volatilization. Estimating how much of what material to add to the pile can be accomplished using the values in Table 3-1.

The values in Table 3-1 are in ranges because the C:N ratio of organic residues varies with age, variety, the source of the organic residues, and the nutrients they absorbed when they were living. The bulk density of these materials also varies greatly. Residues such as clippings, green leaves, garden wastes, food wastes, manure, and even soil generally have a comparatively narrow C:N ratio and are usually heavier—often because they contain more water. Residues such as dried leaves, wood chips, and straw usually have a wider C:N ratio and are lighter. C:N values are calculated on a dry matter (weight) basis, but compost feedstock is usually measured volumetrically.

Calculating exactly how much of each component to use must be done by dry weight. If, for example, equal (dry) weights of two materials are mixed together, one with a C:N ratio of 100:1 and the other with a ratio of 10:1, the resulting ratio is 110:2 or 55:1. To calculate this accurately, the moisture content must be determined first. This step seems both complex and impractical. Fortunately, it is also unnecessary. Table 3-1 gives a rough idea of what materials to use to raise or lower the C:N ratio of a pile. The ideal level for fast decomposition is around 30:1, so a combination of materials that have values above and below that level is a good starting place. A good beginning mix is approximately 3 parts of the lighter, more carbonaceous material to 1 part of the heavier, more nitrogenous residues (by volume). Depending on actual ingredients, particle sizes, and moisture content, adjustments may be necessary. Experience makes these adjustments easier to assess.

If the majority of available wastes have a wide C:N ratio (and a slow composting rate), organic or inorganic nitrogen fertilizer can be used to create a better balance. Fertilizer, however, should be used judiciously and mixed in thoroughly. Remember, if a little is good, more is not necessarily better. As soon as odors become evident, chances are that too much nitrogen has been applied. Carbonaceous additions and turning (oxygenation) are necessary to remedy the situation. It is also important to understand that decay organisms need more than just carbon, nitrogen, oxygen, and hydrogen. They, like plants and animals, need many other nutrients to thrive and proliferate. Deficiencies of any essential nutrients will limit population growth. Most

TABLE 3-1
Carbon-To-Nitrogen Ratios

Material	C:N Ratio	Material	C:N Ratio
Alfalfa meal	15	Newspaper	400–850
Animal tankage	7	Oat straw	50–100
Apple pomace	48	Paper	125–180
Aquatic plants	15–35	Paper fiber sludge	250
Blood meal	3	Paper mill sludge	55
Cardboard (corrugated)	560	Paper pulp	90
Castor pomace	8	Paunch manure	20–30
Cocoa shells	22	Pig manure	10–20
Coffee grounds	20	Potato tops	28
Compost	15–20	Potatoes (culled)	18
Corn silage	35–45	Poultry manure	5–15
Corn wastes	60–120	Rice hulls	110–130
Cottonseed meal	7	Sawdust	200–750
Cow manure	10–30	Sawmill waste	170
Crab/Lobster wastes	4–4.5	Seaweed	5–27
Cranberry wastes	30–60	Seed meals	7
Fish wastes	2.5–5.5	Sewage sludge	5–16
Food wastes	14–16	Sheep manure	13–20
Fruit wastes	20–50	Shrimp wastes	3.5
Garden wastes	5–55	Shrub trimmings	53
Grass clippings	9–25	Slaughterhouse wastes	2–4
Grass hay	32	Softwood bark	100–1000
Hardwood bark	100–400	Softwood chips, shavings, etc.	200–1300
Hardwood chips, shavings, etc.	450–800	Soil	12
Hoof and horm meal	3	Soybean meal	4–6
Horse manure	22–50	Tree trimmings	16
Leaves	40–80	Turkey litter	16
Legume hay	15–19	Vegetable wastes	11–19
Linseed meal	8	Wheat straw	100–150

residues contain a broad diversity of nutrients, but some materials, like wood chips and sawdust, contain mostly carbon.

Reducing the particle size of the waste by grinding or shredding can help speed the composting process in a pile that has a C:N ratio wider than 30:1. Smaller particles afford more overall surface area for composting organisms to decay. There is a limit, however, to how much this will help a pile heat if the C:N ratio gets too wide. There is also a limit to how small particle sizes should be. Piles of fine particles have less porosity and can contain too little oxygen for proper composting. If strong, unpleasant odors are evident each time the pile is turned, then the pile is probably using oxygen faster than it can be replaced.

DECAY ORGANISMS

Another important consideration with respect to compost ingredients is the groups of soil organisms the manager wants to proliferate in the soil. Most turf performs best in a soil that is slightly dominated by bacteria or has roughly an equivalent ratio of active bacteria and fungi. Composts made from mostly woody material, such as dry leaves and needles, bark, wood chips, and straw, are high in cellulose and lignin, which support fungal organisms more than bacterial. Even after these materials are completely decayed, the populations of fungi tend to outweigh the populations of bacteria. Compost that is ideal for turf can be made with some woody material, but a substantial amount of material high in carbohydrates and proteins—clippings, green leaves, food waste, manure—must be incorporated. Molasses, syrups, table sugar, plant extracts, or some other type of natural sugar can be added to increase populations of bacteria. (For a list of other suitable materials, see SFI 2000[b] in "Sources and Resources.") These materials ensure that good populations of beneficial bacteria are cultivated and that the compost, after proper heating, curing, and aging, will contain the highest level of disease-suppressive characteristics.

If turf managers are buying compost from an outside source, they should inquire from what feedstock the compost was made and avoid buying compost made exclusively from woody yard wastes. This is not to say that yard waste compost is detrimental or toxic to turf, but it may not be ideal for peak turf performance and disease suppression. If yard waste compost is the only kind available, mixing and curing it with one or more of the sugars mentioned above can significantly increase its potential for disease suppression. The material should be bioassayed, however, before it is used for disease prevention or control. Many producers of yard waste compost add ingredients such as grass clippings, manure, or garden wastes that significantly change the biological balance of the finished product. Bioanalysis can indicate its potential for disease suppression.

CURING

Curing compost may require turning the pile occasionally to see if it will heat again, but often the compost just has to sit. The time it takes to cure a pile is debatable. Research at Cornell University suggests that if disease-suppressive characteristics in compost are needed, the pile needs to cure for at least two years (Nelson 1997). The time it takes for compost to mature and become disease suppressive is not set in stone. Different combinations of feedstock, turning frequency, climate, and other factors play a role in the development of disease-suppressive organisms. Some compost may take far less time than others to mature and become disease suppressive.

But the manager must plan for the future, including calculating how much compost will be needed. The ratio of sand to compost in a topdressing mixture can be as rich as

1:1 (sand to compost), but less than 7:3 may be inadequate. Straight compost can be used on fields if it is mature and somehow incorporated into the soil profile (with aeration or similar equipment). Cornell University experimented with a $\frac{1}{2}$-inch layer of compost (200 pounds per 1,000 square feet) on golf course greens over the winter to successfully combat gray snow mold, but it had to be removed in the spring before the grass resumed growth. To cover an acre with a $\frac{1}{4}$-inch layer requires ~34 yards of a compost/sand mix. Calculating mixture ratio, coverage area, and application frequency gives the turf manager a rough idea of how much compost should be stockpiled.

HOW MUCH COMPOST IS NEEDED?

To calculate how much material is needed to cover a given area, multiply the thickness of the intended topdress layer by 3.086 for cubic yards per 1,000 square feet, or multiply by 134.44 for cubic yards per acre. For example, to topdress a $\frac{1}{4}$-inch layer of material,

$$3.086 \times 0.25 = 0.77 \text{ yd}^3 \text{ per } 1000 \text{ ft}^2, \text{ or}$$
$$134.44 \times 0.25 = 33.6 \text{ yd}^3 \text{ per acre.}$$

If the topdress mixture contains 50 percent compost, then 16.8 cubic yards of compost is needed per acre of turf per topdress application. (To convert fractions to decimals, divide the numerator by the denominator, e.g., $\frac{1}{4} = 1 \div 4 = 0.25$.)

PURCHASING COMPOST

Compost that is available from private or municipal compost-making facilities must be examined and tested before it is purchased. Two quick ways to test compost for quality is to feel it and smell it. Dig deep into the pile and pull out a sample. If it is hot, has objectionable odors, or both, it is probably still immature and needs more turning before it can begin curing. Managers must determine whether they have the time, space, and equipment to finish the process. It may be necessary to make accommodations for such an operation if a more finished product is not available elsewhere. Most commercial compost makers do not produce finished compost to the degree described here because the market absorbs most of it before it can age long enough. It is unlikely that commercially available compost that is sufficiently mature can be found, let alone compost that is made and cured carefully enough to provide disease suppression.

But commercial compost need not be written off entirely. Immature compost may be advantageous because the turf manager can control the final curing process. Some commercial producers begin the curing process too soon, and the compost pile can become anaerobic. Once this happens, the chemical and biological composition of the compost changes. Curing can reverse these changes only if the pile is porous enough for air to flow passively through it. If severe anaerobic conditions persist, phytotoxic compounds may be produced that not only can diminish turf performance but also may stress plants—increasing their susceptibility to disease, decreasing their competitiveness with weeds, and reducing their tolerance of herbivorous insects.

If compost becomes anaerobic, aerobic organisms must be reestablished by adding air to the pile. Frequent turning, and possibly the addition of carbonaceous residues, may be necessary to reverse the anaerobic process. A pile that is ready for curing does not reheat by an appreciable amount after it is turned. If immature compost is purchased, the new owner can continue turning the pile periodically until reheating ceases to occur. At this point, the manager can feel relatively confident that anaerobic conditions will not prevail and that the pile will cure adequately. Occasional turning (once every 2 to 4 weeks) during the curing process is often a good idea to ensure that an adequate supply of oxygen is always available to the compost organisms, but turning too often can disrupt the fungal growth necessary for suppressing some diseases (see Figure 3-4).

Each year the grounds manager must plan for future compost needs. It is best if more compost is acquired than needed because of shrinkage and because leftovers often come in handy. The volume of compost purchased can shrink as much as 30 percent, depending on the degree of its immaturity at delivery, and leftover compost, like a fine wine, gets better with age. Aging compost makes excellent compost tea that can be applied to turf areas afflicted with disease symptoms (see Chapter 5). The art of making good compost tea is another skill turf managers may have to master if they plan to part ways with pesticides.

COMPOST TEA

Compost tea has been used for centuries to enhance crop performance, but it is only recently that its strong disease-suppressive characteristics have been discovered. Apparently, most of the organisms delivered to plant leaf surfaces via compost tea parasitize, antagonize, or just plain steal food from disease organisms to the point where

FIGURE 3-4   Although endowed with great tools, commercial composters may not create the ideal turf product but with time and a little TLC, their product could become an excellent amendment.

they can no longer compete. Tea that seeps into the soil protects roots in much the same way. Making effective tea, however, requires as much attention and care as making good-quality compost. In fact, if the compost from which the tea is to be derived is not made from ingredients rich in carbohydrates with the correct C:N ratio, turned or aerated correctly, moisturized adequately, and cured correctly, there is little hope that the tea will display strong disease-suppressive characteristics. Unlike the tea that is served with crumpets, compost tea is not steeped in hot water until the color of the water darkens. Cool, nonchlorinated, and oxygenated water is used.

Commercial brewers are available to ensure the survival of aerobic organisms in the tea (Growing Solutions, Ground UP, Earth Tea Brewer, Northwest Irrigation, EPM). When compost is placed in a brewer, it cannot be packed too tightly or the water will not flow through it adequately and inadequate numbers of organisms will be extracted. If the compost is too wet at brewing time, the resulting tea will likely exhibit a microbial imbalance. The squeeze test—where you squeeze a handful of compost as hard as you can—should yield no more that a drop or two of water. The sniff test is important too. If you smell any foul or acidic odors, chances are good that the tea will be ineffective. These may not sound like highly analytical testing procedures, but it's truly amazing what experienced senses can perceive.

There should be a slight temperature increase (5° to 10°F) in the water during the brewing cycle. Reproducing organisms generate heat, but this is sometimes difficult to notice if ambient temperatures are too cold or too warm. Organisms also consume oxygen as they reproduce, so it is important that the compost tea brewer can diffuse enough air into the mix to sustain adequate numbers of beneficial organisms. If oxygen is consumed faster than it is added, aerobes begin to die off and anaerobes begin to grow. Oxygen levels are also affected by the ingredients added to the mixture—for example, materials rich in protein and amino acids like fish emulsion and fish hydrolysate. Too much can stimulate microbial reproduction to a point where oxygen is consumed faster than it is generated. An oxygen sensor is a valuable tool that can help ensure an aerobic tea, at least until one gains experience.

Unfortunately, not all brewers can generate enough air to ensure adequate amounts of dissolved oxygen for aerobes. Some brewers that work well in one region of the country (or world) may not in another because altitude, temperature, and humidity influence the density of the air and subsequently, the amount of oxygen dissolved into solution. Most manufacturers of compost tea brewers have bioassay data or dissolved oxygen data from different batches of tea made with their machines. It's a good idea to request a copy of those tests—preferably from a several regions of the country— before purchasing the unit. Make sure the data come from reputable independent labs such as Soil Food Web and BBC Labs (see "Sources and Resources" for contact information). Labs that conduct plate count analysis may not be able to provide adequate information (see Chapter 4, under "Biological Analysis").

When applying compost tea, back off on the pressure a little. Most organisms can withstand high pressure, but when they hit the leaf surface or ground at excessive velocities, it's a little like dropping a pumpkin from a second-story window.

At the moment, the thought of making good compost and effective compost tea may seem daunting, but keep in mind that so was tying shoes at one point. There's no doubt that anyone who's worn laced shoes for any length of time has gotten the hang of it by now. So it will be with the production of compost and compost tea (see Figures 3-5a, 3-5b, and 3-5c).

Good-quality compost tea is not likely to be commercially available. If it is not made with enough aeration in the container to ensure adequate oxygen levels in the water, the valuable aerobic organisms will be destroyed and the possibly destructive anaerobic organisms will be cultivated. Additionally, compost tea must be used as soon as possible after production, or the aerobic organisms will die and anaerobic organisms will grow. Ten to 20 pounds of compost can yield 50 gallons of tea and cover 2 to 10 acres. The ideal application of the tea is a fine mist with small droplets that adhere to the plant leaf surfaces; however, if this is impractical, the tea can be injected into an irrigation system and used as a drench. This method has also shown excellent disease suppression. Research on compost tea use on turf for disease suppression is in its beginning stages, and, since it's unlikely that compost tea will ever

Photo courtesy Ground UP, LLC.

FIGURES 3-5A, B, and C   Compost tea brewers come in different shapes and sizes but most have at least one thing in common...they infuse air into the water to proliferate aerobes.

become commercially available, little funding is available. However, many managers who have tried it can testify to its effectiveness, and many research papers offer positive evidence that compost tea can suppress disease on many types of plants (Ingham 2003).

If one has enough time, space, or resources for only a small compost pile (<1 ton of finished compost), then the best use of it would be as a tea. As noted above, a mere 10–20 pounds of compost can make enough tea to treat 2 to 10 acres. Remember, the compost and the tea have to be made right to be disease suppressive.

OTHER CONSIDERATIONS

Once a manager discovers the value of a mature, well-made compost, he will experience a compelling tendency to use more of it. This can present a supply problem, especially if the compost is being made or cured on-site. The availability of space or a suitable site may be a limiting factor. Local zoning regulations may also present a problem. If compost must be made on-site strictly from organic wastes generated on the property, available wastes may be inadequate.

Available space or suitable sites may seem difficult obstacles to overcome. Neighbors and fans may not appreciate conspicuously placed piles of organic debris. Add to these conflicts the bureaucratic hoops one may need to jump through to obtain necessary permits, and the idea of using compost becomes even more daunting. But! However difficult the situation may seem, the clear and immediately apparent benefits of using compost can strengthen a manager's resolve to overcome spatial and regulatory hurdles. In the face of growing intolerance to horticultural chemicals, most zoning or permitting agencies favor plans to reduce or eliminate their use, and there is plenty of scientific evidence that mature compost helps accomplish this goal. If compost is produced strictly from on-site residues, it is unlikely that permits are necessary.

Groves of trees can make ideal sites for compost piles. They are usually out of sight, and the shelter trees provide can protect the pile from the sun and wind. If there is enough low-growing brush around the outer edge of the grove, the compost pile may be almost invisible. The grove must have a center area with maneuvering space for a bucket loader so the piles can be turned. Some embankments are ideal for organic waste disposal but impractical for turning compost. On the other hand, if a loader can access the bottom level of the embankment, the site may be just fine.

Generating enough organic waste to produce ample compost may be a concern even if space, location, and permits are not. Grass clippings alone will not produce enough compost to treat the entire playing area. Thatch, leaves, harvested cores, and other miscellaneous wastes can increase the amount of compost produced, but chances are it still won't be enough. During the composting process, the mass of these residues can be reduced by 70 percent or more, so 100 cubic yards of waste may produce only 30 cubic yards of compost. A $1/4$-inch 50/50 (sand/compost) topdress layer covering a football field (playing area only) requires ~21 cubic yards of compost. Occasionally, a site improvement project may produce a windfall of waste, but if too much is woody, carbonaceous material, it probably won't produce ideal compost for turf; further, these projects don't usually occur annually. If available, kitchen wastes may contribute significantly to the production of good compost, but a sensible system must be devised to segregate the food waste from paper, plastic, glass, and other contaminants.

Accepting wastes from outside sources is generally not recommended unless one is very familiar with the source. The manager has little control over what is received, and so the risk of contamination is considerable. Additionally, as one enters the realm of commercial composting, special permits may be required. Some managers accept waste only from landscapers equipped with vacuum trucks. This equipment picks up only light material such as dry leaves and clippings and leaves glass, metal, and other contaminants behind.

In the event that the space, location, or regulatory obstacles cannot be overcome, off-site composting may be a viable alternative. Vendors who supply sand, topsoil, sod, plants, equipment, or even chemicals may have available yard space and equipment to produce quality compost. If they are offered some profit in the proposal, they may be more than willing to commit the space. For most managers, compost must be imported from a commercial or municipal producer.

CUSTOM PRODUCTION

Commercial compost producers located nearby may also be able to work with the turf manager. Most of the producers I have interviewed are willing to cure, according to the customer's specifications, enough compost for the entire area. Contracting with a commercial compost maker is a great way to avoid regulatory complications, but only if the producer is willing to commit the time and space required to produce well-aged, disease-suppressive compost. The compost maker must obtain a fair price that compensates for the extra time, effort, and monopolization of yard space, but chances are that a good relationship can be established between the turf manager and the compost producer. The customer should be willing to make a few inspection trips to the site while the compost is curing, and bioanalysis should be done before the finished product is delivered. Adding biostimulants, if necessary, should be done at the manufacturer's site, where the necessary mixing equipment and space is readily available.

ANALYSIS

Ensuring a good-quality, disease-suppressive compost requires a certain amount of analysis (at least until one gains ample experience) to determine if the material is within acceptable parameters. Tests can include measurements of organic matter, pH, conductivity, respiration, nitrate, nitrite, sulfide, ammonium, ammonia, C:N ratio, and biological activity. These tests have varying degrees of importance, and some negate the need for others. Disease-suppressive characteristics should be measured by a bioanalytical laboratory, where relevant organisms can be identified or actual disease suppression evaluated.

Respiration may be the only test an experienced compost maker needs to determine the stability of his compost. Simple on-site testers can measure the amount of carbon dioxide being generated from compost and determine the material's degree of maturity. Immature compost generates much higher levels of carbon dioxide than mature compost, and test kits like the Solvita® Compost Maturity Test (Woods End Research, see Figure 3-6) can measure how much is being generated. Maturity, however, is not necessarily an indicator of disease-suppressive characteristics. If a manager is relying on compost to suppress disease, it is important that a qualified laboratory performs a bioassay.

Conductivity determines the saltiness of compost and can be another indicator of maturity. Usually, values above 3 millimhos or siemens (1,920 mg/kg salt) indicate a less than mature compost. Conductivity can be measured with on-site equipment (Hach Company, Hanna Instruments, Spectrum, LaMotte, see Figure 3-7), or a sample of compost can be sent to a laboratory for analysis. Various factors influence both the respiration and conductivity tests, but as most of them differ for each test, each can offer confirmation of the other's outcome. The Solvita® Compost Maturity test actually measures both carbon dioxide and ammonia simultaneously, and the combined results factor into the interpretation of maturity. Woods End Research combined the two tests because a restriction of oxygen to decay organisms can reduce their ability to respire carbon dioxide—which, by itself, might indicate a mature compost. A compost approaching anaerobiosis, however, would produce relatively high levels of ammonia. Woods End Research recommends adequate moisture content before testing because neither carbon dioxide nor ammonia is produced in measurable quantities if moisture is deficient.

FIGURE 3-6   The Solvita compost test can determine the maturity of compost by measuring carbon dioxide production and ammonia content. Photo courtesy Woods End Research.

The Cress Test is an on-site maturity test where cress seed is germinated in a flat filled with compost or in absorbent material soaked with aqueous compost extract. Maturity is based on whether or not the seeds germinate and how much the plants grow in six days at 82.4°F (28°C). If the seeds do not germinate, the compost is most likely too young. The ideal growth range is 60 to 100 grams of plant mat-ter grown per 10 grams of seed in six days; 30

FIGURE 3-7   A conductivity meter can determine the saltiness of compost, another indicator of maturity. Photo courtesy Spectrum Technologies, Inc.

grams, however, is acceptable. This is generally an infallible test, but it requires a sensi-tive scale and six days of lead time to measure results. Some managers use grass or other types of seed. A good germination rate and plant health should be noticeable if the com-post is mature. Again, maturity is not a measurement of potential disease suppression.

Analyses of nitrate, nitrite, sulfide, ammonia, and ammonium are generally unnec-essary if a conductivity test has been performed. These compounds are some of the main contributors of salinity detected in a conductivity test. If analyzing for these compounds, however, the parameters are as follows:

- Nitrate–100 to 300 mg/kg (depending of ambient temperature)
- Nitrite or sulfide–Zero to trace amounts
- Ammonia, ammonium–0.2 to 2 mg/kg (3.0 mg/kg = critical limit)

The analytical instruments needed for on-site testing can be acquired from Hanna Instruments, LaMotte Company, or Hach Company, among others (see "Sources and Resources" for contact information).

Organic matter content is important to know, especially if compost is being pur-chased from an outside source. Standards set by the U.S. Compost Council require at least 60 percent organic matter on a dry basis for a material to be labeled compost. Some compost producers add sand or soil, or use an abundance of litter with low organic matter and high mineral content. Compost with a low level of organic matter can be a fine soil amendment and improve plant health, but it may not provide ade-quate disease suppression.

pH is another test that may be necessary only as one is gaining experience. If a compost pile is heating properly each time it is turned, chances are that the pH is within the range needed for active compost organisms. The ideal pH for compost materials is between 6.5 and 8.5, but materials with a pH of 5.5 to 9.0 can still create a hot and active pile. If the pH of the raw ingredients is too low or too high, the growth of composting organisms may be retarded and result in a pile that fails to heat prop-erly. It's important to remember, however, that organic residues *will* eventually rot despite their pH. Materials with a high pH, such as manure, can neutralize materials with a low pH, such as pine needles and oak leaves. Lime can be added if necessary, but decay organisms can usually alter the pH to a more favorable range for composting to occur. Additions of lime can volatilize nitrogen, a valuable component for both decay organisms and managers using the finished compost.

Nutrient testing is important because fertilizer programs usually need to be adjusted when compost is applied. Even though the analysis of compost is low, the amount normally applied can supply a significant quantity of nutrients. If, for example, compost containing 1 percent nitrogen is mixed 1:1 with sand and applied as a $\frac{1}{4}$-inch topdress, then half of ~0.77 cubic yards (the total volume of the mixture per 1,000 square feet) or ~0.39 cubic yards of compost is being applied per 1,000 square feet. If the compost weights 1,000 pounds per cubic yard and 1 percent of the weight is nitrogen, then ~3.9 pounds of N are being applied per 1,000 square feet. This may seem like a lot of nitrogen, but it is not soluble or immediately available so plants aren't overwhelmed. However, adding almost 4 pounds of nitrogen per 1,000 square feet to an already established fertilizer program could overdo the nitrogen to the point where other problems are created. Knowing the analysis of your compost could also save money on fertilizer bills. Some turf managers replace their normal fertilizer program with compost or compost tea. They keep the fertilizer in the shed but haven't had to use much since they began applying compost.

Bioanalysis is important if the grounds manager is going to rely on compost for disease suppression. Many laboratories can assay compost and either identify disease-suppressive organisms within the compost or introduce the compost to specific pathogens and measure the amount of inhibition. Laboratories such as Soil Food Web, Woods End Research, and BBC Laboratories can perform a microbial profile, pathogen inhibition assay, or both. They can also perform other compost tests such as compost maturity, compost stability, and VAM (mycorrhiza) analysis (see "Sources and Resources" for contact information).

COMPOST AMENDMENTS

A wide variety of materials can be added to compost that enhances its ability to grow healthy plants and suppress disease. In addition to locally available wastes, such as grass clippings, thatch, garden wastes, leaves, soil cores, pond muck, and other organic wastes, some managers add greensand, cottonseed meal, flower hull ash, seaweed, volcanic rock dusts, bentonite clay, alfalfa meal, basalt dust, wood ashes, or soybean meal. These additions all serve to encourage larger and more diverse populations of organisms in the compost.

Inoculants or enzymes are used occasionally to accelerate the composting process, but these sometimes fail to produce the desired results because the bacteria or enzymes are not matched correctly to the material in the compost pile. Indigenous decay organisms eventually inoculate the compost pile regardless of what inoculum is added, but introducing the right strains of organisms can decrease composting time and improve the balance of organisms in the final product. Using inoculants is the subject of considerable study and debate, but some experts believe they are essential. Many compost producers use soil as an inoculum. A healthy soil contains a broad diversity of indigenous organisms and can also narrow the pile's carbon-to-nitrogen ratio (the C:N ratio of soil is ~12:1).

Some managers are concerned with introducing clay or silt onto their soil and, depending on how it is made, compost can contain some of each in varying amounts. Physical analysis can determine the percentage of sand, silt, or clay in the compost, but it may be more revealing to test the topdress mixture rather than the compost alone. Keep in mind, however, that the biological response in topdress mixtures amended with high-quality compost can physically alter not only the topdress mixture's own texture but also the texture of adjacent soil particles into a more porous and less compacted environment. Clay or silt in small quantities shouldn't be a concern for most managers, especially if they are working with sandy soil.

CONTROLLED MICROBIAL COMPOSTING

For managers who need high-quality, disease-suppressive compost in a shorter period, controlled microbial composting (CMC) may be worth examining. CMC was developed by Austrian researchers, Siegfried and Uta Luebke. It is an intensely managed composting system that requires a special microbial inoculum, frequent turning, and additives such as clay loam, finished compost, and basalt rock dust. Monitoring equipment is also recommend that measures pH, oxygen, carbon dioxide, nitrate, nitrite, sulfide, and ammonium. Turning is required daily for the first week, six times in the second week, five times in the third week, four times in the fourth week, and twice weekly in the fifth and sixth weeks. Water added to the pile cannot be chlorinated. The initial pile is built in layers beginning with dry, carbonaceous materials and alternating with nitrogenous materials such as grass clippings, manure, and food wastes. Covering the pile with a fleece-type compost cover is also recommended. Although the process sounds complex, the result is finished and disease-suppressive compost in six to eight weeks. Companies marketing CMC technology and the special inoculum include Autrusa Compost Consulting, Herbert Ranch, Pike Lab Supplies, and Fresh Aire Implements. Sources of inoculum also include Josephine Porter Institute of Applied Biodynamics, Midwest Bio-Systems, and Petrik Laboratories (see "Sources and Resources" for contact information).

COLD COMPOSTING

Cold composting is another alternative to consider; however, no research could be found confirming its ability to suppress disease. Cold composting is accomplished by incorporating fresh clippings or other green wastes directly into the soil with a rototiller or rotovator. Chipped wood and autumn leaves can be incorporated also but, without a proper balance of green waste, they decompose slowly, temporarily immobilize nitrogen, and create fungal domination in the soil, which is not ideal for either turf or disease suppression. Cold composting eliminates the opportunity for odors to develop and may be appropriate in areas where adjacent neighbors might object to malodorous mistakes made by novice compost makers. Over time (the period depending on climate and other conditions), the soil becomes enriched with organic matter in the form of labile humus.

The size of plot needed depends on the amount of wastes generated and the equipment used to incorporate them into the soil. Two plots are ideal so one can age while the other is being used. As the process matures, some of the enriched soil can be excavated, screened, and mixed with sand for topdressing. Although, as noted, no research was found that substantiates disease-suppressive characteristics in this type of material, it is not unreasonable to assume that many of the organisms that would colonize such a rich habitat could suppress plant pathogens. A bioanalysis of the material would easily confirm this presumption. The special inoculum used to make CMC compost can also be used when grass clippings and other green wastes are being turned into the soil; however, inoculation and turning must occur simultaneously because even brief exposure to ultraviolet (UV) light can kill the beneficial organisms.

One of the problems associated with cold composting is the survival of weed seeds. If annual bluegrass or other weed seeds are collected along with clippings and incorporated deep enough into the soil, they will not germinate, but heat is not produced in this process that would kill the seed as it does in a conventional compost pile. Constant tillage will bring many seeds to the surface where they can germinate and be dispatched in the next tilling cycle, but it is likely that some viable seeds will remain. Clippings can be piled on perforated pipes and allowed to heat for a few weeks before incorporation into the soil (see Figure 3-1). This initial heating will kill most, if not all, of the seeds that may be combined with the clippings.

VERMICOMPOSTING

Cold composting eventually and undoubtedly involves the work of earthworms to varying degrees. Constant use of the tiller can suppress earthworm activities, but it will be hard for them to resist the organic residues being added to the soil. If cold composting is impractical, vermicomposting (worm composting) may be a manageable alternative. The conditions inside an earthworm are similar to those inside a well-made compost pile. Decay organisms flourish inside the worm and, it is believed, the worm extracts nourishment with the assistance of these organisms. Consequently, vermicompost is biologically active and disease suppressive. Unfortunately, like cold compost, vermicompost doesn't generate heat and cannot kill weed seeds. Brief, hot composting before vermicomposting, as before cold composting, may be a practical alternative.

Vermicomposting is usually done in bins so the earthworms do not escape into soil depths, but it can be done successfully on the ground or in sunken beds. As long as resources are abundant, it is unlikely that worms will venture far. Worms work from the bottom up, so fresh material is always added to the top of a vermicompost pile or windrow. Soil makes a good bottom layer and fresh clippings, garden wastes, thatch, and food wastes, can be layered over the top. Diversity of feedstock is important, but worms are unable to digest coarse woody material easily. Inoculating the pile or windrow with worms such as red worms (*Lumbricus rubellus*) or brandling worms (*Eisenia foetida*) that specialize in vermicomposting is a common practice. The usual addition is about 1 pound of worms per cubic foot of organic residues. Worms reproduce, so further inoculation is generally unnecessary.

When compost is needed, it must be excavated from the bottom of the pile. Since most of the worms are feeding in the top layer, where the freshest residues are, the top portion can be carefully removed and reused as the inoculum for another pile or replaced on the existing pile after the lower layers of compost are harvested. Vermicomposting should be done in a shady area without exposure to excessive wind. It is important to keep the pile moist. If the region is subjected to deep and sustained frost during the winter, bins cannot be used or the worms will probably perish. However, depending on the their size, bins can be moved indoors, where vermicomposting can continue through the winter.

Worm sources can be found online by typing the word *vermicompost* into a search engine. Some sources are yelmworms.com, happydranch.com, and vermico.com.

SITE SELECTION

Cold winters can freeze a compost pile if it is not actively heating or too small to generate and maintain high temperatures in a cold environment. Biologically active compost in a good-sized pile (>10 cubic yards) should be able to maintain internal warmth even in very cold ambient temperatures. Anaerobic piles often freeze solid. The outer layers of curing piles may freeze, depending on their stage of maturity, but it is unusual for them to freeze to the core. If compost will be needed in the early spring for topdressing or repairs, it is advisable to bring some indoors for the winter. It's important, however, not to let the material become excessively dry over the winter, or valuable organisms may be lost.

Site selection for producing compost is an important consideration. Shady areas conserve moisture and moderate pile temperature. Windy sites that could potentially dry out the pile should be avoided. A solid, well-drained pad composed of packed gravel or stay-mat is ideal for larger operations. Concrete pads are practical for smaller piles. In Europe, almost all farms, no matter the size, have a concrete compost pad consisting of a floor and back wall. Such sites are usually built into a hillside with a sloped parking area above the pad so that organic wastes can be easily unloaded from the bed of a truck or wagon onto the pad. Some pads have one or two side walls. Cement pads decrease the likelihood of picking up rocks or other large objects that must be screened out.

SCREENING

Screening is often a necessary step for compost used on playing fields, especially where the height of cut (HOC) is very low and the variety of grasses form a tight canopy. The longer compost cures (within reason), the less likely it is to contain chunks of partially decayed material. However, screening the material may still be necessary. Screen size is usually a personal preference. The smaller the mesh, the finer the finished product; on the other hand, screening through a fine mesh usually takes longer and produces more waste material. Waste material segregated by the screener should be returned to the unused portion of the compost pile. The longer it ages, the more of it will pass through the screener.

For most sports fields, $\frac{3}{8}$-inch mesh is a good compromise. Although time-consuming, double screening produces a more consistent material. Some managers mix their compost with sand first and then screen both together, and others screen just the compost and then mix it with sand. Premixing with sand often helps the material flow over the screens better; however, sand that clings to oversized compost particles is screened out.

Screening machines are relatively expensive, but they can last for decades. Some tool rental businesses may have screeners available. Companies that normally mix and screen topdress materials for golf courses or playing fields may be willing to provide the service. The manager may have to truck the compost to the screener unless the screening people also produce the compost. Most compost producers have screening equipment. Once the value of mature, well-made compost is discovered, the investment in related equipment is much easier to justify.

STAY TUNED

Much is still to be discovered about the benefits of compost as compared with the benefits of pesticides, for example. Pesticide manufacturers sell nearly $12 billion (yes, that's billion with a *b*) worth of products annually in the United States alone and, accordingly, can afford a significant amount of funding for research (especially research that makes these products look safe and effective). The compost industry, by comparison, despite its recent growth, has only a small amount of resources available for research. Most of the available funds are invested in solving solid waste disposal problems rather than dollar spot and brown patch.

Compost is used more widely in agriculture than in horticulture, and it follows that research done from the perspective of pedologic ecosystems will address crop concerns more than ornamental or, more specifically, sports turf concerns. Consequently, there are no real standards for compost made for turf. Many manufacturers produce compost from many organic residues, but relatively few produce it to the degree discussed in this chapter. In fact, it would be nearly impossible to find two different composts, regardless of quality, with exactly the same chemical, physical, and biological characteristics. The quality of compost turf managers need is not the commodity commonly being marketed.

The intent of this chapter is to familiarize the turf steward with the benefits and mechanisms of composting. However, the information is, without question, incomplete. Even if all that were known about compost were written here—which would take thousands of pages—it would still be incomplete. Given the almost infinite number of variables associated with all aspects of creating compost, what has been discovered thus far could easily be only the tip of the iceberg. The task and the rewards of discovery are, to a certain extent, left to the ingenuity of the groundskeeper.

POINTS TO REMEMBER

- Over the past 50 to 60 years, relatively easy chemical remedies replaced the compost approach. Unfortunately, widespread chemical use has begun to jeopardize the environment and the ecosystem.
- Recent discoveries that well-made, well-aged compost can improve turf's stress tolerance and suppress insect and disease problems has renewed attention to this important resource.
- An important but largely ignored function of decay organisms is the generation of carbon dioxide—an essential nutrient for plants.
- Making compost is more of an art than a science. Using the right combination of feedstock, maintaining proper aeration and moisture, and knowing when compost is at its ideal stage for use is critically important but not always scientifically measurable.
- When on-site production is impractical, the manager's ability to diagnose the quality of commercially available compost is extremely important.
- If the production or application of compost is impractical, compost tea may be a viable alternative, although research about it is still in its infancy

Chapter 4

ANALYSIS

Many turf managers tend to apply lime and fertilizers by instinct. They have developed a program that, over time, has become routine. This system can work for years, perhaps decades, but after a while, strange little problems may arise—problems that can eventually grow into bigger ones. What has changed? While we weren't looking, our program may have slowly changed the balance of fertility in the soil. Turf utilization of a particular nutrient may have exceeded the supply, or the buildup of one nutrient may have caused the deficiency of another. Many managers rely on fertilizer manufacturers for recommendations. Manufacturers usually have multistep programs that make the manager's job easier. However, we trust that the directions on the bag, box, or bottle of fertilizing material we are about to apply take into consideration all of the vagaries and idiosyncrasies of our soil. They don't. Standard fertilizer recommendations are made based on several broad assumptions:

- That climate (temperature, precipitation, etc.) are typical at every location,
- That all species of turf have the same nutritional requirements,
- That all soil types are basically the same, and finally
- That the existing fertility is already balanced.

These programs are not meant to correct imbalances. How could they? The fertilizer manufacturer has no idea of the soil conditions on every sports field. The only accurate way to determine those conditions is to perform a soil test.

Some of us fail to understand that the soil is not an inert medium where turf can be grown hydroponically. It is an ecosystem that functions in a symbiotic relationship with all plants. The best tools we have to follow the changes that occur in this system are analyses of soil (chemical and biological), plant tissue, and irrigation water. Leaf tissue analysis reveals the level of nutrients being absorbed into the plant. A nutrient may appear as adequate or optimal in a soil test, but plants may not be adequately absorbing it. Water analysis is important for any manager who uses irrigation. Many water supplies have nutrients, toxins, or inappropriate pH that adversely affect the growth or health of turf. Soil analysis tells us the chemical balance of nutrients (or toxins), the balance of soil organisms, and the physical structure of the soil. Unfortunately, the inherent weakness of analysis is extracting a sample that represents overall or average conditions.

SAMPLING

Imagine, if you will, Times Square in New York City on New Year's Eve. People are packed wall to wall, and every available place to stand is occupied. Now imagine an alien from another galaxy on a scientific expedition to gather information about humans. From his space vehicle, he focuses his scanner on one human, and his computer records important statistics such as height, weight, limb length and thickness, hair color, skin color, clothing, voice pattern, fingerprints, brainwaves, and cell analysis. The alien has his data and prepares for departure when, at the last minute, he decides to scan another person to make sure his equipment is working accurately. To his utter dismay, the data from the next scan is so completely different that he is unable to determine anything specific about humans. He checks his equipment and performs yet another scan. Again, the data fluctuate wildly. He does several more scans and cannot find any two subjects that are alike. After more than a hundred scans, all significantly different, the alien leaves in frustration. Eventually, the alien understands that the biological differences in humans are infinite and the best analysis he can make will come from averaging his data and determining typical statistics. After doing so, he can make these general observations: Humans like to stand outside in cold weather, drink beverages containing alcohol, make noise, and kiss other humans at the stroke of midnight.

It is rare to find two soil samples that produce the same test results, even when they are drawn a foot away from each other. The only way to effectively evaluate the soil in a given area is to draw many samples and mix them together. Then a single sample representing the characteristics of all samples can be drawn from the mixture. Random sampling can be done in a zigzag or a matrix pattern. The appropriate number of samples to take depends on the size of the area. Think of sampling this way: If you were in a room with two other people who represented the population of the United States and, after asking how many smokers were in the room, one raised his hand, the logical conclusion would be that 50 percent of the population smokes. If, however, 10,000 people were in the room, you might get a better representation of the U.S. population.

This is not to suggest that 10,000 soil samples should be drawn but that the more samples taken, the better the representation. Drawing samples from notably good or bad areas should be avoided (unless evaluation of a specific spot is needed). The conditions in these extreme areas can adulterate the average reading of the sample area as a whole. For obvious reasons, freshly fertilized or limed areas should also be avoided.

Very clean tools should be used for gathering soil samples. A small amount of rust on a shovel might indicate a promising location in which to start an iron mining operation. An example of an incident that gave misleading results from contaminated tools is the client who used the same shovel to draw samples that he normally used to remove ash from his woodstove. The results of the test were so far off they might as well have been from another planet.

It's unlikely that many turf managers use a shovel to draw samples. Stainless-steel or chrome-plated sampling tubes are the most efficient and accurate tools for drawing soil (see Figures 4-1a and 4-1b). They significantly increase the speed of the sampling procedure while decreasing labor costs and the chances of contaminating the sample. These tubes are durable, relatively inexpensive, and can be purchased from most horticultural suppliers. Even if sampling occurs only once a year, these tubes are worth the investment. Although these tools may leave core holes on a field that can disrupt some types of games, the holes will probably go unnoticed in most instances.

Sampling can be done in conjunction with a routine coring operation. In fact, if the manager is extracting cores 4 to 5 inches long, several can be gathered to represent the conditions of the soil. Most managers don't usually core that deeply, but the holes left from drawing cores with a sampling tube will be filled with topdress material after cultivation. If analysis is routinely done annually, biannually, or at other intervals, samples should be drawn during the same part of the season. The changes that naturally occur in the soil between spring and fall can give a false impression of progress (or the lack of it).

Wet or frozen samples are difficult to handle and test. The consistency of a soil sample for analysis should be moist but not soaking. Water should not drip from the sam-

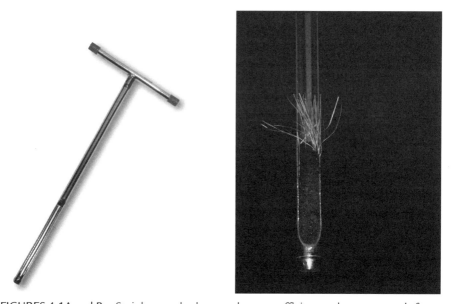

FIGURES 4-1A and B   Stainless steel tubes are the most efficient and accurate tools for drawing soil samples. Photo for Figure 4-1A courtesy AMS Inc.

ple when squeezed. Drying the sample is an acceptable procedure if necessary, but to preserve the original conditions of the soil, samples should be drawn when the soil is at a proper moisture level. If the soil in question is naturally sandy and dry, it is neither necessary nor advisable to moisten it.

The depth from which a soil sample should be drawn is normally about 4 to 5 inches for turf. The fertility of most soils increases nearer to the surface. Deeper samples tend to underrepresent the fertility of the root zone, and shallower sampling often overrepresents it. If testing is performed routinely for comparison purposes, it is important that samples be drawn from the same depth each time. Surface debris, such as sod, roots, and thatch, should be removed from the top of the sample. When enough samples from a given area are drawn, they should be mixed thoroughly in a clean container; a representative sample of approximately 1 cup can then be sent to a lab. The soil is a relatively dynamic substance and, if the sample is allowed to sit for an extended period, subtle changes may occur that, when magnified by the area it represents, may yield misleading results. Send the sample to the lab as soon as possible.

METHODOLOGY

Analytical laboratories are not obligated to use nationwide standard procedures for testing soil. Labs in a given area may employ regional methodologies, but they can opt to follow any procedures they want. *Methods of Soil Analysis*, published by the American Society of Agronomy, is the most widely accepted manual of testing procedures; still, the publication often describes many different yet valid ways to test for nutrients and other soil conditions. If several labs analyzed the same sample, each using a different methodology, the results may appear as though the samples were taken from several regions of the country. Additionally, the standard set of tests one lab does may be significantly different than another. Some labs, for example, calculate the cation exchange capacity (CEC) of the sample, while others calculate an effective cation exchange capacity (ECEC). The difference between the two (discussed later in this chapter) is significant. Some labs base lime recommendations on a buffer pH test, while others do so on a test for exchangeable aluminum. Because analyses from different labs often yield significantly different results, it is a good idea to choose a reliable lab and stick with it, especially if comparing tests with preceding or subsequent analyses. On a functional level, the most important service a lab can offer is an accurate, reasonably priced test delivered on a timely basis. It is also important to look at the kind of information offered by different labs. It is most cost-effective if all the necessary information is offered on the lab's standard test, since optional information can get expensive.

The American Association of Laboratory Accreditation (A2LA; see "Sources and Resources" for contact information) is an organization that accredits testing labs in many fields. A2LA recognizes many types of laboratories, many of which have nothing to do with soil, plants, or irrigation water. Physical analysis is important for fields built using U.S. Golf Association (USGA) specifications. The USGA recognizes eight labs as competent to perform physical analysis; however, other accredited labs may offer more specialized information for ecological management (see www.A2LA.org for more information). The USGA list includes Brookside Laboratories, European Turfgrass Laboratories, ISTRC New Mix Lab, Links Analytical, N.W. Hummel, Thomas Turf Services, Tifton Physical Soil Testing Laboratory, and Turf Diagnostics and Design (see "Sources and Resources" for contact information). These labs specialize in physical soil analysis for turf environments; Brookside is also equipped to perform chemical analysis as well. Most of these labs are associated with other analytical companies so if they can't offer a specific analysis, they can have it done elsewhere. Some offer biological analysis as well.

Different labs use different procedures to extract calcium, magnesium, and potassium, and they may report them differently too. For example, potassium may be reported as potash (K_2O), or all three cation elements may be reported in pounds per acre instead of parts per million. Although this one is rare, some labs do not indicate the unit of measure. It is important not to assume the relationship of these values. An erroneous assumption could easily create a disaster. It's a good idea to call the lab and find out for sure. The different extraction chemicals used by labs can paint a bleaker or rosier picture than what plant roots experience. Labs attempt to mimic the natural soil chemicals that release plant available nutrients but can't possibly know the conditions in every soil. Most extraction chemicals are designed to imitate average soil conditions, which are relatively rare on most sports fields. The manager may need to communicate with the lab technician to ensure the tech's full awareness of the field's conditions. Often, a physical analysis (discussed later in this chapter) is a good prerequisite to chemical analysis.

LAB INFORMATION

Soil test interpretations are sometimes as different as the methodologies used to determine the results. If the turf manager uses the same lab each time analysis is done, interpretation should be relatively easy to learn. Unfortunately, some labs give recommendations along with insufficient data to make one's own accurate interpretation. Those labs generally cater to customers who want only the information necessary to balance and fertilize; they are not really interested in learning what the information means. Understanding how soil chemicals are measured and how they react with one another enables the manager to consider variables—unique to his fields—that lab technicians couldn't possibly know.

Lab recommendations are usually offered automatically but sometimes as an option (at extra cost). These recommendations can be useful only if the samples accurately represent the average conditions of the area in question. Recommendations are generally based on the nutrient needs of specific plants under average conditions, but many labs do take the soil's ability to store and exchange nutrients into consideration. Some labs ask for information such as type of grass, topography, acreage, and previous treatments before providing recommendations. Too often, however, the lab technician who tested the sample doesn't know squat about the field compared with the person who manages it every day. That manager should be able to interpret the analysis too. The tremendous number of analytical labs and methodologies makes it difficult to outline an interpretation method; however, there are basic tenets that can be used to interpret the data from most labs.

Managers who wish to implement ecological or organic practices are more or less forced to interpret the analysis reports themselves. Labs that offer nonchemical recommendations are few and far between. The main obstacle for most labs is that chemical analysis cannot fully reveal biological conditions. Nutrient deficiencies and imbalances often affect plant growth but can influence other soil organisms as well. An optimum balance of nutrients, however, doesn't guarantee adequate plant absorption. Leaf analysis may reveal deficiencies in the plant even when adequate nutrients are present in the soil. This can occur when soil chemical reactions bind certain nutrients into unavailable forms and biological activity is insufficient to free them. There are also circumstances under which soil organisms immobilize plant nutrients. Biological analysis is not yet considered in vogue, but more and more managers are recognizing its value in evaluating soil conditions.

This is not to say that traditional soil chemical analysis is not important. The condition of each soil component (physical, chemical, biological, etc.) affects all others. To better organize this chapter, information about chemical analysis is addressed before we move on to physical, biological, water, and leaf tissue analysis (see Figure 4-2).

Standard information on a soil analysis report can vary from lab to lab, but most reports provide values for pH (water and buffer), cation exchange capacity (CEC); reserve and available phosphorus (or phosphate); levels of exchangeable potassium, magnesium, and calcium; and base saturation. Many labs also measure the amount of organic matter. Most labs offer nitrogen or micronutrient analysis as an option.

PH

pH is probably one of the most important tests that can be performed for turf. pH can affect the availability of most nutrients (and toxins), the soil's structure, and the balance of soil organisms. Some believe that the initials *pH* stand for potential hydrogen or

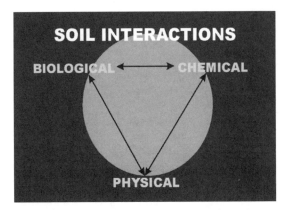

FIGURE 4-2   Biological, chemical, and physical reactions in the soil are inextricably linked.

power of hydrogen. The *H* in pH does, in fact, stand for hydrogen, but *p* is actually a mathematical expression that, when multiplied by the concentration of hydrogen in the soil, gives a value between 1 and 14 that expresses the acidity or alkalinity of the soil. Soil pH values are rarely found to be less than 4.0 or over 10.0. Values below 7.0 are acidic and those above 7.0 are alkaline. A value of 7.0 is neutral. As values get farther away from neutral, they indicate a stronger acid or base. A soil pH between 6.0 and 7.0 is ideal for most plants. Most species of turf plants grow best at a pH between 6.5 and 6.9.

Almost all labs offer a pH measurement in their soil analyses. Most conduct a water pH analysis, which determines the acidity or alkalinity of distilled water when mixed with an equal volume of soil. A few labs perform a salt pH analysis that takes into consideration the seasonal variation of soil soluble salts that can cause changes in pH. Salt pH values are normally 0.5 to 0.6 below water pH test results. The goal of these tests is an indication of whether or not the soil should be limed or acidified. Acidification recommendations can be made from the results of a water or salt pH analysis, but usually lime recommendations are not. Another test is generally needed to determine lime applications because the amount of reactive hydrogen held in the soil can vary significantly. Two soils with the same water pH can have completely different lime recommendations. A sandy soil, for example, with a pH of 5.5 may require only a half-ton of lime or less per acre to raise the pH to 6.5, whereas a clay soil with the same pH may need over 4 tons of lime per acre to achieve the same result. There are several acceptable methods of determining lime requirements, including a buffer pH test, reactive aluminum test, titration of soil acidity, or buffer estimations based on soil organic matter, soil texture, or both.

The buffer pH test is done with a special solution that determines the soil's capacity to hold exchangeable hydrogen (H^+) or hydronium ions (H_3O^+). The buffer test is normally used only if the water pH indicates a need for lime. If only one pH value is shown in an analysis report and there is no indication of how the test was performed, it was probably a water pH. The lab's recommendation for lime, however, is usually based on testing in addition to the water pH test, and it is a good idea to contact them and ask. Chances are good that the recommendation is based on the amount of organic matter in or the texture of the sample. Some labs test for exchangeable aluminum and, through a complex logarithmic formula, offer liming recommendations. This method was originally developed for semitropical and tropical regions where toxic aluminum can be the most limiting factor to crop production. The titration method measures the actual amount of calcium carbonate equivalent (CCE) needed to neutralize the sample. Carbonate is the component of lime (calcium carbonate or calcium magnesium carbonate) that neutralizes acidity in the soil.

The most commonly used methodology of the four mentioned above is the buffer test. There are several kinds of buffer tests; the two most commonly used are the Shoemaker-McLean-Pratt (SMP) and the Adams-Evans buffer. The SMP test is used mainly in the Northeast, where the soils commonly have a significant reserve of exchangeable aluminum. The Adams-Evans buffer is more appropriate for sandy soil that has a low CEC and a low level of organic matter. Fields that contain a lot of sand might be better served with lime recommendations based of the Adams-Evans buffer, but some analysts believe *all* buffer tests are too insensitive when it comes to sandy soil. Fields that contain calcareous sand, however, usually do not need lime at all; this would be apparent from a water pH test.

Depending on soil pH and the level of exchangeable cation bases (i.e., calcium, magnesium, and potassium) in the soil solution, the hydrogen that is adsorbed to the soil colloid may be pushed off. Once the H^+ ion enters the soil solution, a number of reactions can occur. The ion can chemically combine with other ions to form water, gases, or acids. Acids can work to liberate more base cations from the mineral components in the soil. H^+ can also liberate and transform phosphate ions into a form of phosphorus that plant roots can absorb.

Soil carbonates react with H^+ ions to form carbon dioxide and water, which reduces hydrogen ions in the soil and raises the pH. This is how lime (calcium carbonate) neutralizes soil acidity. Oxides, abundant components of many minerals, can also neutralize H^+ to form water. Hydrogen can also contribute to the formation of organic acids when reacting with residues of plants, animals, and microorganisms. These acids can often weather unavailable minerals attached to parent particles into available nutrients. This function is especially important in the rhizosphere, the zone immediately surrounding roots. Within the rhizosphere, biological activity can be high and the pH relatively low. The activity of H^+ ions in this zone can release mineral ions from soil particles that can then become available nutrients for the plant.

HOW MUCH LIME?

A buffer pH test usually gives a value of H in milliequivalents (meq.) per 100 grams of soil, and it takes ~½ ton (1,000 pounds) of pure calcium carbonate ($CaCO_3$) per acre to neutralize each meq. of H. (For a detailed explanation of milliequivalents, see the section on Cation Exchange Capacity later in the chapter.) Legally, lime has to be labeled with a calcium carbonate equivalent (a.k.a., total neutralizing value). This percentage indicates the degree of purity compared with $CaCO_3$. If, for example, a liming product is labeled 95 percent calcium carbonate equivalent (CCE), then it will take 1,053 pounds to neutralize one meq. of H per acre. The formula used to find this equivalent is:

$$\text{WEIGHT} \div \text{CCE} = \text{Equivalent}$$
(Note: percent = value ÷ 100; e.g., 95% = 0.95)

The lab's target pH may be higher than the manager's. Knowing how to determine the degree of neutralization enables the manager to tweak the lab's recommendations if necessary.

Some labs perform a reactive aluminum test to determine lime requirements; however, this may be an inappropriate test for sports fields, especially for turf established in very sandy soil. Lime recommendations based on reactive aluminum are often higher than those derived from a buffer pH test. It might be advisable to retest the water pH before too many applications of lime are made.

The recommendations from labs that perform titration tests are difficult to check, but such tests may be a more precise method of calculating lime recommendations, especially on sand fields. Sandy soil holds few cations (see below under "Cation Exchange Capacity"), including hydrogen, so buffer solutions are often not sensitive enough to give accurate readings. Titration is done with a water-soluble base such as sodium hydroxide. The base is slowly added to the sample until the desired pH is achieved. Then the calcium carbonate equivalent to the soluble base can be calculated.

Buffer estimations based on soil organic matter, soil texture, or both are often as accurate as any other. The experienced turf manager knows a sand-based field requires a lot less lime than a clay loam field to achieve the same change in pH. Lime applications of 10 pounds per 1,000 square feet or less may be adequate to achieve the desired pH. Lightly applying lime while monitoring pH changes is a good way to familiarize oneself with the response characteristics of sandy soils. Time, however, should not be the criterion for liming. There is no reasonable way to predict the effect of time on soil pH. Too many factors are involved in pH changes, and the only reliable method of determining the need for lime is a pH test.

It is also important to use the appropriate type of lime. Calcite or calcium lime is mostly $CaCO_3$ but may contain some magnesium carbonate. Dolomite contains ~22 percent calcium and ~11 percent magnesium. The decision to use one or the other should depend on the existing Ca:Mg ratio. To calculate this ratio, divide the calcium value by the magnesium value shown on the analysis report.

$$Ca \div Mg = x{:}1$$

If the analysis give values in parts per million (ppm) or pounds per acre (ppa), no conversion is necessary as long as all values are the same unit of measurement. If the result is less than 7, then using calcium lime is advisable. If the result is more than 10, dolomite is probably a better choice. If the result is between 7 and 10, see if the lab offers ranking values such as very low (VL), low (L), etc., or if a bar chart is available that ranks the results. If magnesium is ranked very low and calcium is ranked medium or higher, then dolomite should probably be used. In other scenarios, calcium lime is preferable. Much of the calcium lime on the market (especially in the Northeast) may contain up to 5 percent magnesium, so some magnesium is still being applied.

It is relatively rare that an established sports field needs a heavy dose of lime (especially if it was constructed from sand), but if conditions occur that warrant an application of more than 1 ton per acre (~50 pounds per 1,000 square feet), it is not advisable to apply all of it at once. Spring and fall applications of not more than 50 pounds per 1,000 square feet can be made until the necessary amount is applied. Also, it is not advisable to apply liming materials during hot, stressful times of the season.

TOO ALKALINE?

Some soils may require acidification, but beyond that flat fact it is important to understand *why* the soil's pH is elevated beyond optimum. If overzealous use of lime is the cause, it may be reasonable to slowly reduce the alkalinity with sulfur or some other acidifying material. If, however, the pH is elevated because of naturally calcareous soil or extremely alkaline irrigation water, pH reduction may be futile and attempts may cause more harm than good. Conditions such as these can be ameliorated, to a certain extent, by increasing the buffering ability of the soil with organic matter and the coincidence of biological activity. Turf can grow within a wide pH range, but some essential nutrients are often made unavailable when alkalinity (or acidity) reaches extremes. A more prudent approach to naturally alkaline soil may be to determine deficiencies (if any) through leaf tissue analysis and apply foliar applications of the missing nutrient(s).

Table 4-1 suggests application rates of elemental sulfur to lower the soil's pH. Rates should be reduced by one-third for sandy soil and increased by one-half for clay soils. Unless the application of sulfur is being thoroughly incorporated into the soil, it is not recommended that more than 20 pounds per 1,000 square feet are applied at one time. Sulfur bacteria use sulfur as energy and create sulfate ions (SO_4). Sulfate combines with soil hydrogen to create sulfuric acid, which reacts with carbonates in the soil to form carbon dioxide and water (and calcium sulfate). Removing carbonates in the soil lowers its pH. The soil temperature must be above 60°F (15.5°C), however, for these reactions to occur because sulfur bacteria are relatively inactive below that temperature.

TABLE 4-1
Application Rates Of Elemental Sulfur For Ph Reduction
(Expressed In Pounds Per 1,000 Ft²)

PRESENT pH	DESIRED pH				
	6.50	6.00	5.50	5.00	4.50
8.00	27	36	50	63	72
7.50	18	32	41	54	63
7.00	9	18	32	45	54
6.50		9	23	36	41
6.00			9	23	32

AN EYE ON IONS

One of the reasons different soils with the same pH have different lime requirements is that their capacity to hold cations such as H^+, K^+, Ca^{++}, Mg^{++}, and $NH4^+$ varies. To better understand cations (positively charged ions) and anions (negatively charged ions), a short review of elementary chemistry may be helpful.

All materials that are in, on, or above the planet, whether liquid, solid, or gaseous, are constituted of atoms from different elements that are often bonded to each other. The force that holds these atoms together is electromagnetic. It is similar to the force that holds dust to a computer screen. In order for this magnetic force to work, however, both positively and negatively charged ions must be present. Like charges do not attract.

There are 90 naturally occurring elements on earth. Elements are made up of atoms, and atoms are a combination of neutrons, protons, and electrons. The electrons move around the neutrons and protons (bunched in the center of the atom, called the *nucleus*) in orbit paths that differ in distance from the nucleus. Each path holds a set number of electrons. If the outermost electron path is filled to its capacity, then the atom has no charge and rarely bonds with anything. Elements with uncharged atoms are described as *inert*. In contrast, if there *are* vacancies in the outermost electron path, then the atom can share electrons with other atoms, creating a compound. These vacancies give atoms either a positive or negative charge, depending on whether they can take on or give up electrons. Most elements are made of atoms that have either a positive or negative charge. When the atom of one element bonds with the atom of another, the result is a molecule of a compound. The magnetic bonds between elements in many compounds satisfy the attraction each atom has for the other. These compounds are left with neither a positive nor a negative charge. If, however, the electrons in the outer ring of one atom do not completely fill the outer ring of another, a net negative or net positive charge is still available for yet another combination. These compounds are called *ions*.

Ions can be atoms of elements or molecules of compounds; both carry either a negative or positive electromagnetic charge. The ions of elements such as hydrogen, calcium, magnesium, and potassium have positive charges and are known as *cations*. Ions of phosphorus, nitrogen, and sulfur have negative charges and are called *anions*. Some elements such as carbon and silicon can act as anions or cations and bond to either charge. Ionic molecules such as nitrate, sulfate, and phosphate have negative charges and can bond with cations such as hydrogen, calcium, and potassium.

UNDERSTANDING COLLOIDS

There are very small particles in the soil, called *micelles* (short for microcells), that carry a negative electromagnetic charge. These particles are either mineral (clay) or organic (humus), and are referred to as *soil colloids*. Cations are attracted to these colloids like dust is to a TV screen.

Clay particles, viewed through a powerful microscope, appear as flat platelets adhering to each other like wet panes of glass. These particles are predominately made up of silicon, aluminum, and oxygen; depending on the type of clay, they can also contain a plethora of elements such as potassium, magnesium, iron, copper, and zinc. Clay's magnetism comes from the natural substitution of ions in its structure with other ions that don't completely satisfy the available magnetic charges. As more of these substitutions occur, the overall negative charge of the clay particle increases, and there is a relative increase in the amount of cations attracted to it (see Figure 1-5). Different types of clays have different capacities or potence for ionic substitutions, and their magnetic force differs accordingly. Clay particles with greater substitution potential create more magnetic force and attract and hold more cations. Some clay particles are not colloidal at all. Clay may be found in many sports fields, especially those constructed from native soil. There is evidence that a small amount of clay can significantly improve soil conditions. The indiscriminate use of clay as a soil amendment to improve CEC, however, is not suggested.

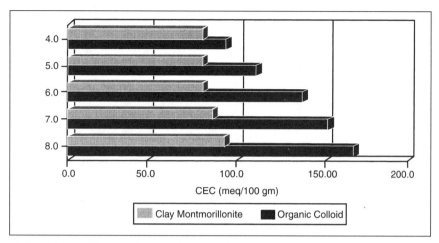

FIGURE 4-3   Influence of pH on the CEC of organic matter and clay. Adapted from Waksman, 1936.

Humus particles are also colloidal. Their cation exchange capacity per equal unit of weight is even greater than that of clay, but it is influenced by soil pH (see Figure 4-3). Humus becomes negatively charged from the surface compounds that contain hydrogen. In soils with a near neutral pH, hydrogen is displaced from humus to participate in a number of soil chemical reactions. When this occurs, the site that previously held the hydrogen ion is left vacant and available for another positively charged ion. If base cations such as potassium, magnesium, or calcium are present in the soil solution, they can be attracted to the humic particle (see Figure 4-4).

Humus and clay can form colloidal complexes together, which not only increases the overall cation holding capacity of a soil but also changes the structure of clay soil

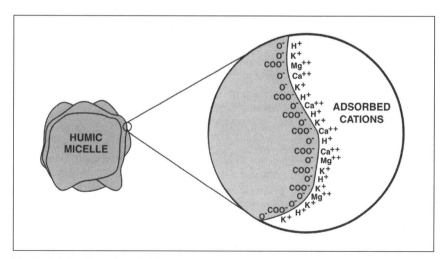

FIGURE 4-4   Organic colloid.

into a better habitat for turf roots and aerobic soil organisms. Humus, through complicated chemical bonds, can surround clay particles and break up their cohesive nature, which often prevents percolation of air and water through the soil. These bonds can also help extend the length of time humus particles exist in the soil.

Both clay and humus, with their unique structures and negative charge, *ad*sorb (as opposed to *ab*sorb) cation elements in such a way that the ions can be detached and absorbed by plant roots. Adsorption is simply an adhesion of ions to a particle surface, whereas absorption is more like consumption or assimilation. Hydrogen ions that are released by roots are traded back to the colloids. This process of cation exchange is nature's way of providing a sustainable source of cation nutrients for plants (see Figure 4-5). Essential nutrients such as calcium, magnesium, and potassium would be rare and unavailable in topsoil if it were not for the colloidal nature of clay and humus. When root hairs grow into proximity with exchange sites, cation nutrients from the colloid can displace hydrogen ions located on the root's surface and be absorbed by the plant. Cation exchange is essential not only for the mineral needs of the plant but also for the translocation of hydrogen throughout the soil.

Water also has a relationship with colloidal particles. Functions that are dependent on soil moisture are also limited in soils with low CEC. Organisms such as plants and microbes that depend on each other's biological functions for survival are inhibited by lack of water. A heavy clay soil with a low level of organic matter might have an opposite effect (a lack of air), causing problems associated with anaerobiosis. The CEC in

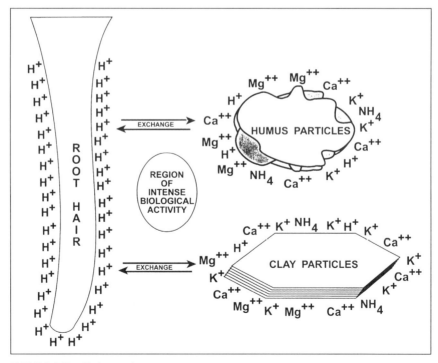

FIGURE 4-5   Cation exchange.

such a soil might be very high, but the lack of atmosphere in the soil can limit the amount and type of organisms it contains, causing dramatic changes to that immediate environment. A compacted soil likely has similar problems. Oxidized nutrients such as nitrates and sulfates may be reduced (i.e., oxygen is removed) by bacteria that need the oxygen to live, and the nitrogen and sulfur could be lost as available plant nutrients.

CATION EXCHANGE CAPACITY

The cation exchange capacity (CEC) is determined by the amount of clay and humus in the soil. However, not all clay or humus is colloidal. Certain types of clay have a higher CEC than others. Some clay is not colloidal at all. Labile humus has a relatively low CEC compared with stable humus. The right kinds of clay and stable humus establish the soil's cation warehouse or reservoir. Sandy soils with little organic matter usually have a low CEC. Clay soils, especially those that also contain substantial levels of organic matter, have a greater capacity to hold cations.

The CEC of a soil is a value given on a soil analysis report to indicate capacity to hold cation nutrients. CEC is not something that is easily adjusted; the value indicates a condition or possibly a restriction that must be considered when working with that particular soil. Unfortunately, CEC is not a packaged product. The two main types of colloidal particles in the soil are certain types of clay and stable humus, and neither is practical to apply in large quantities. Compost, which is an excellent soil amendment, is not stable humus, but over time compost can contribute to the bank of stable soil humus. This contribution, however, may amount to only a small percentage of the initial application.

Table 4-2 shows how much compost is needed at different thickness levels on a 1,000-square-foot area. Each percent of organic matter found in a soil analysis is equivalent to over 450 pounds per 1,000 square feet (~6 inches deep) of area (20,000 pounds per acre). Compost normally contains about 40 to 50 percent organic matter on a dry basis and weighs approximately 1,000 to 1,500 pounds per cubic yard (depending on how much moisture it contains). If the moisture level were 50 percent, it would take 2 cubic yards of compost per 1,000 square feet to raise the soil organic

TABLE 4-2
Compost Spread Rates

Thickness	To Cover 1000 ft^2
$\frac{1}{8}$ in.	0.4 yds^3
$\frac{1}{4}$ in.	0.8 yds^3
$\frac{3}{8}$ in.	1.2 yds^3
$\frac{1}{2}$ in.	1.5 yds^3
$\frac{5}{8}$ in.	1.9 yds^3
$\frac{3}{4}$ in.	2.3 yds^3

matter level 1 percent, and this change would be ephemeral. Large applications of compost to the surface of the soil, however, can do more harm than good. Abrupt changes in soil layers can inhibit the movement of water and restrict the soil's capacity to hold moisture and exchange gases. Building soil organic matter is not something that can or should be done overnight.

A soil with a very low CEC should be adjusted, but not solely because of the CEC. A soil with a very low CEC usually contains little clay or humus. Its texture is probably closer to sand or gravel than soil. It cannot hold much water or dissolved nutrients, and without relatively frequent irrigation and fertilization, plants may not grow well in it. The adjustment is not so much to increase the CEC but to condition the soil and make it a more appropriate environment for plants. A direct result of this adjustment will eventually be a higher CEC.

The disadvantages of a low CEC include limited availability of mineral nutrients to plants and the soil's inefficient ability to hold applied nutrients. Plants can exhaust a significant amount of energy—that might otherwise be used for growth, adapting to environmental stress, and developing adequate defenses—scrounging the soil for mineral nutrients. Soluble mineral salts (e.g., potassium chloride) applied in relatively large doses to soil with a low CEC cannot be held efficiently because the cation reservoir is too small. Plants are faced with a use-it-or-lose-it situation, and they don't have the ability to store mineral nutrients.

During the process of soil building, the turf manager must be aware of the soil's limitations. Soil with a low CEC cannot hold many nutrients, so smaller doses of fertilizer need to be applied more frequently. Turf growing on such a soil may have nutritional habits like most infants. It can't eat a lot, so it must be fed often. As the CEC of the soil improves, more fertilizer can be applied less frequently.

CEC is measured in milliequivalents (meq.) per 100 grams of soil (the metric equivalent is centimol or cmol per kilogram). An equivalent is actually a chemical comparison. It is a measurement of how many grams of a cationic element or compound it takes to displace 1 gram of hydrogen. A meq. is simply one-thousandth of an equivalent.

This sounds complex, so let's look at it in simpler terms. Picture a seat on a train. The capacity of that seat is one person. If Peter, who weighs 240 pounds, is polite enough to give up the seat to Jessica, who weighs 120 pounds, the capacity of the seat doesn't change, just the weight of the passenger occupying it. When considering milliequivalents, think of each ion as a passenger on the soil colloid. Unlike commuters, ions are far too small to count, so their numbers must be calculated using known factors such as atomic weight and electromagnetic charge (valence). The hydrogen ion has an atomic weight of 1 and has a valence of $+1$ (hydrogen is a monovalent ion). The potassium ion has an atomic weight of 39 and is also monovalent. Hydrogen$^+$ and potassium$^+$ are both cations and would not normally combine, so the equivalence here is in terms of displacement or competition. It takes 39 units (weight) of potassium$^+$ to replace one unit of hydrogen$^+$. Calcium^{++} and magnesium^{++} are divalent ions (i.e., they have a valence of $+2$), so each would occupy two seats on the colloidal express instead of one, and their atomic weight is divided evenly between the number of seats. Therefore, it takes half their atomic weight to displace one unit of hydrogen$^+$. Calcium^{++}, which has an atomic weight of 40, needs 20 units to displace one unit of hydrogen$^+$, and magnesium^{++}, which has an atomic weight of 24, needs 12 units.

So what has all this to do with the rate of meq. per 100 grams of soil? A CEC with a value of 1 meq. per 100 grams means that each 100 grams of soil can magnetically hold either 1 milligram (mg) of hydrogen$^+$, 39mg of potassium$^+$, 20mg of calcium^{++}, or 12mg of magnesium^{++} (more likely some combination of all four). Table 4-3 shows equivalent values of common soil cations.

TABLE 4-3
Equivalence Relation

Cation	Atomic Wt.	Valence	Equiv.	Meq. Factor
Hydrogen	1	1	1	10
Potassium	39	1	39	390
Magnesium	24	2	12	120
Calcium	40	2	20	200
Ammonium	18	1	18	180

The CEC is calculated from the amount of exchangeable base cations (i.e., calcium^{++}, magnesium^{++}, and potassium$^+$) and meq. of hydrogen$^+$ found during soil analysis. In a test where exchangeable cations are measured in parts per million, the equivalent value of the cation is multiplied by 10 and then divided into the parts-per-million value found in the analysis.

$$V_{exchangable} \div (V_{equivalence} \times 10) = V_{meq.} \text{ (where } V = \text{value)}$$

Multiplying the equivalent by 10 comes from the ratio between parts per million and milliequivalents per 100 grams, which is 10:1. If, for example, 125 parts per million of exchangeable potassium were found in a soil analysis, its equivalence in meq. per 100 grams would be:

$$125 \div (39 \times 10) \approx 0.3$$

The amount of exchangeable K found in the analysis is 125 parts per million, and the equivalent value of potassium is 39, which is multiplied by 10 to become the meq. factor.

Once calcium, magnesium, and potassium are calculated into meq. per 100 grams, they are added together. This total constitutes the portion of the soil's CEC currently occupied by the base cations (calcium, magnesium, and potassium). The meq. of hydrogen is calculated from a buffer pH test and then added to the bases to obtain the soil's overall CEC (see Figure 4-6).

An inherent weakness in this method is that some extraction methods may dissolve nonexchangeable cations. Strong acidic reactants may extract significantly more calcium from calcareous soil, for example, than what would normally be dissolved in the soil solution or adsorbed to soil colloids. The resulting CEC calculation would be misleading because much of the calcium found in this analysis may not be exchangeable.

BASE	PPM FOUND	MEQ/100 gr
Potassium	74	0.2
Magnesium	115	1.0
Calcium	850	4.3
	Total Bases	5.5
	Hydrogen	1.0
	CEC	**6.5**

FIGURE 4-6   CEC Calculation.

Consequently, base saturation values and the Ca:Mg ratio would also be distorted. In a case like this, where calculating potassium or magnesium using the base saturation method (see below, under "Cation Corrections") would be misleading, cation nutrients would have to be applied in accordance with plant needs and physical soil structure (i.e., application rates are lower and more frequent as the soil texture becomes coarser).

Labs that offer a CEC value calculate it from their findings. If a lab does not run a buffer pH test, however, it cannot include hydrogen in its CEC calculations. Some labs offer what is called *effective CEC* (ECEC), which is calculated from only the meq. of exchangeable base cations (potassium, magnesium, and calcium). If a buffer pH test is not done, the lab has no hydrogen$^+$ value to plug into this formula. (Some labs may perform a buffer pH test and still choose to report the ECEC.) If calculating the overall CEC is necessary, the lab's lime recommendation can act as a de facto hydrogen$^+$ value. If the lab recommends 3 tons (6,000 pounds) of lime per acre, for example, each 1,000 pounds of calcium carbonate or equivalent will neutralize approximately 1 meq. of hydrogen. (Some analytical chemists believe the factor should be 1,200 to 1,400 pounds.) Therefore, 3 tons of lime will neutralize ~6 meq. of hydrogen.

The inherent problem with calculating the meq. of H from a lime recommendation is that the recommendation may be a generalization and relatively inaccurate. According to one lab that reports ECEC, the CEC of a soil is pH dependent and fluctuates with variances in pH. This lab feels that the ECEC is a more accurate measure of cation exchange capacity. Others disagree.

Cation exchange capacity is somewhat dependent on pH, especially in soils where humus provides most of the colloidal exchange sites. This may be important when calculating potash, magnesium, or calcium requirements. If, for example, a lab reports ECEC instead of CEC and the soil is moderately acidic, it may be difficult to determine the actual amount of potash the soil can efficiently adsorb because as the pH rises, so does the soil's capacity to hold it. As the pH rises, the difference between CEC and ECEC narrows because the saturation of hydrogen eventually decreases to a point where it is no longer a significant cation. Once the soil's pH has been raised and the level of hydrogen$^+$ ions in the soil is nominal, potash requirements can be more easily calculated based on CEC (or ECEC) and the desired saturation using the method described below, under "Cation Corrections." The same method can be used to determine if both calcium and magnesium are in balance. If there is little organic matter—typical on sand-based fields—pH changes may not affect the CEC as much.

PULLING RANK

Many labs use ranking insignia such as VL for very low, L for low, M for medium (or O for optimum), H for high, and VH for very high. When ranking cation nutrients, most labs assign these values based on the soil's capacity to hold them. For example, if 70 parts per million of potassium were found in a soil sample that has a CEC of 3.0 meq. per 100 grams, the ranking insignia might be H or VH even though the actual amount may be too small to feed a healthy stand of turf. That same value (70 ppm), however, would be considered L or VL if the CEC of the soil were 12.0 meq. per 100 grams or higher.

This may seem confusing, so let's look at capacity in a different way. Envision a full can of soda next to an empty 5-gallon pail. The capacity of the soda can is 12 fluid ounces, and the pail holds 640 fluid ounces, or ~53 times the capacity of the can. The level of material in the can is VH—it's full—but if one were to pour the contents of the can into the pail, the level in the pail would be VL. The ranking values for potassium, magnesium, and calcium are relative to the soil's capacity to hold cation nutrients. A sandy soil with a low CEC might show H or VH rankings for cations on the analysis report, but these levels may still be inadequate.

BASE SATURATION

The balance of calcium, magnesium, and potassium in the soil can easily be calculated by comparing the meq. of each element to the CEC. The meq. of the cation element divided by the CEC and multiplied by 100 equals the percent of the CEC the cation occupies.

$$V_{meq.} \div CEC \times 100 = \text{percent base saturation}$$

For example, if the CEC of a soil is 10 and the meq. of potassium is 0.3, then:

$$0.3 \div 10 = 0.03 \times 100 = 3 \text{ percent}$$

The ratio of the percent potassium, magnesium, and calcium (K:Mg:Ca) represents the *base saturation*. Base saturation is the balance of base cations in the soil. Labs that offer base saturation values calculate these percentages automatically and usually offer ranges within which those values should fall. Typically, those ranges are 2 to 7 percent for potassium, 10 to 15 percent for magnesium, and 65 to 75 percent for calcium. Concentrations of different cations in the soil affect the base saturation, but so does the strength of attraction each cation has. Calcium has the strongest magnetic grip of the cation nutrients, followed by magnesium. Potassium and ammonium ions have the same attraction strength.

Some managers assign more importance to base saturation than others do. There is strong evidence that excessive saturation of calcium and magnesium can force potassium into the soil solution, where it is susceptible to leaching. There is also anecdotal evidence that a Ca:Mg ratio below 7:1 or above 10:1 can lead to an eclectic list of problems. The Ca:Mg ratio, however, is not calculated from base saturation percentages. To determine the Ca:Mg ratio, divide the value for exchangeable calcium by the value for exchangeable magnesium. For example, if analysis shows 1450 ppm calcium and 183 ppm magnesium, then:

$$1{,}450 \div 183 = 7.9 \text{ (to 1)}$$

Base saturation values significantly above the suggested range may not be cause for concern unless they are creating an imbalance in the form of deficiencies. Only deficiencies should be addressed and, when this is done, excessive saturation of other cation elements are often reduced. The CEC and base saturation tell two important details about the soil: (1) how much potash, magnesium, and calcium the soil can hold, and (2) the balance of those nutrients.

CATION CORRECTIONS

Correcting cation deficiencies, in most cases, should be done in accordance with the CEC. In other words, one should not apply more cation nutrients than the soil can hold. Determining how much to apply can be easily calculated by multiplying the CEC by the desired saturation percentage and then multiplying that product by the cation's meq. factor (see Table 4-3). For example, if an analysis reports the CEC of the soil is 6.3 meq. per 100 grams, exchangeable potassium is 24 ppm, and the base saturation of potassium is 1 percent, how much potash should be applied? If 4 percent potassium saturation is our goal, then:

$$6.3 \times 0.04 \times 390 \approx 98 \text{ ppm potassium}$$

In this equation, 6.3 is the CEC, 0.04 is equivalent to 4 percent, and 390 is the meq. factor for potassium. Since 24 ppm already exists, then an application of $(98 - 24 =)$ 74 ppm potassium is appropriate. Conversion is also needed from ppm potassium to pounds per acre potash as fertilizers guarantee soluble potash, not elemental potassium. The conversion factor is 2.4:

$$74 \text{ ppm} \times 2.4 \approx 177$$

177 pounds per acre or ~4 pounds per 1,000 square feet of actual potash must be applied. The formulae for calculating calcium and magnesium applications are:

$$\text{ppm calcium} = \text{CEC} \times \%\text{BS}_{calcium} \times 200$$
$$(\%\text{BS}_{calcium} = \text{the desired base saturation of calcium})$$

$$\text{ppm magnesium} = \text{CEC} \times \%\text{BS}_{magnesium} \times 120$$
$$(\%\text{BS}_{magnesium} = \text{the desired base saturation of magnesium})$$

To convert parts per million calcium or magnesium into pounds per acre, multiply by 2. Keep in mind, if the lab overestimates the CEC because of inappropriate extraction procedures, these formulae may not provide the most efficient results.

The level of cation nutrients (potassium, magnesium, and calcium) found in a soil analysis may indicate a need for correction, but the CEC indicates how much correction can take place at a time. Appropriate applications can be determined using the formulae mentioned above. Once the amount of potash, magnesium, or calcium has been determined in pounds per acre (or per 1,000 square feet), the application rate can be determined based on the percentage of nutrients contained in the fertilizing material. For example, say one determines that 4 pounds of potash are needed per 1,000 square feet, and sulfate of potash (potassium sulfate) is being used. Sulfate of potash contains 51 percent potash (0-0-51):

$$4 \div 0.51 \approx 7.8 \text{ pounds of material per } 1,000 \text{ square feet}$$

This calculation also can be used to determine calcium or magnesium applications. Table 4-4 shows the analysis of some materials containing potassium, magnesium, or calcium. The formulae (mentioned above) used to determine cation nutrient needs based on desired base saturation indicate the amount of material that should be applied in accordance with the CEC. This, however, may not be enough for the needs of the plant, especially for turf growing in soil that has a very low CEC. Increasing application rates beyond the soil's CEC may result in nutrient loss from leaching. Smaller, more frequent applications may be necessary. The advantages to a soil with a higher CEC are obvious, but such a soil requires greater application rates to correct a cation deficiency. Imagine yourself filling the 12-ounce soda can and the 5-gallon pail mentioned earlier with water—using a hand pump. The pail has ~53 times greater capacity than the can. Not only does the pail hold a much greater volume, but it takes more energy and resources to fill it. If both containers are filled to capacity, however,

TABLE 4-4

Materials Containing Calicum, Magnesium, And Potassium

Material	Percent Analysis		
	Potash	Magnesium	Calcium
Sulfate of potash (potassium xulfate)	52		
Potassium, magnesium sulfate	22	11	
Muriate of potash (potassium chloride)	60		
Gypsum (calcium sulfate)			23
Epsom salts (magnesium sulfate)		10	2
Calcitic lime		3	33
Dolomitic lime		11	22
Basic slag		4	29
Kieserite		18	
Bone meal		0.4	23

and the contents of both are used at the same rate, the advantages of the larger container are obvious.

IMPORTANT ANIONS

Cations are balanced by anions, which are ions that carry a negative electromagnetic charge. Cations, anions, and the exchange system in soil are crucial components in the cycles and chains of life on earth. Their importance is comparable to a vital organ—which, by itself, does not sustain life, but without which life could not exist. Because anions have the same polarity as soil colloids, they cannot be held or exchanged by clay or humus micelles. Important anionic compounds related to plant nutrition include nitrate, phosphate, and sulfate. Phosphate ions bond easily with several soil elements or compounds and rarely migrate far before developing a serious relationship with another soil chemical—or they can be assimilated by soil organisms or plants. Plants use phosphorus as a phosphate combined with hydrogen. Applications of highly available phosphate can, however, be eroded with normal surface runoff. This runoff can cause nutrient loss and possible eutrophication of ponds or lakes.

Phosphorus tests are inherently inaccurate because of the many variables in the soil that affect the availability of phosphate. If deficiencies of phosphorus are found, however, an application of some type of phosphatic material is usually warranted. The problem occurs when acceptable levels are found but soil conditions are such that the phosphorus cannot become available to plants. The chemicals used to measure phosphorus in a soil sample attempt to mimic the natural chemicals produced in a typical soil. The variations inherent in soils from one square foot to the next, let alone regional or continental variations, make it difficult to pinpoint typical conditions. Acids and other solubilizing substances created by soil organisms, plant roots, humic material, and soil chemical reactions are instrumental in freeing up phosphate by mineralizing organic phosphate from the residues of plants and other organisms and by biochemical reactions with soil compounds that contain phosphate. Ample soil organic matter is the key to a healthy and diverse population of organisms and adequate reserves of available phosphate.

Many labs report both available and reserve phosphorus and usually use symbols such as VL (very low), L (low), M (medium), H (high), and VH (very high) to compare the results of the analysis with what they consider acceptable levels. These symbols are used to indicate reserves of other nutrients as well.

Unlike potassium, magnesium, and calcium, phosphorus is not ranked in accordance with the soil's capacity to hold it. Phosphorus is assayed by many methods, and the results are not always comparable. The acceptable range for one methodology may be completely different than for another. Most labs use the Bray method to measure both available and reserves of phosphorus in the soil. The weak Bray (P_1) extracts readily available phosphorus. The optimal range for most plants using the weak Bray test is 25 to 40 parts per million. The strong Bray test (P_2) extracts water-soluble phosphates, weak acid-soluble phosphates, and a small amount of insoluble phosphates. Adequate levels using this test are generally between 40 and 60 parts per million.

The Olsen Sodium Bicarbonate Extraction method is usually used on calcareous soil samples but is also appropriate for neutral to slightly acid soils that contain less than 3 percent organic matter. The acceptable range using this test varies depending on the pH of the sample. A range of 12 to 15 parts per million may be adequate at a neutral pH, but 55 to 65 ppm would be needed at a pH of ~6.2. The Mehlich No. 1 (a.k.a. Double Acid Extraction) and the Morgan extraction methods are used primarily for low-capacity sandy soils with little organic matter and a pH of ~6.5. Optimum levels of phosphorus range from 20 to 50 parts per million extracted with these tests. There are still other acceptable methodologies, each with its own optimum range, so it is important to know which method the lab is using and what the analytical technicians consider adequate. Keep in mind that these ranges are more important during the establishment phase for turf. Once established, turf is normally efficient at removing phosphorus from the soil, and levels of phosphorus below the optimum ranges may still be adequate.

Phosphorus is usually measured in parts per million and, like other nutrients, must be converted to pounds per acre in order to calculate application rates. Fertilizers, however, are always labeled for their phosphate content, so conversion from phosphorus to phosphate is also necessary. To convert ppm phosphorus to ppa phosphate, multiply by 4.6. This factor includes the conversion of parts per million to pounds per acre (i.e., 2) and phosphorus to phosphate (i.e., 2.2951).

$$2 \times 2.2951 \approx 4.6$$

If, for example, it is determined that 10 ppm phosphorus per acre is required to correct a deficiency, then:

$$10 \times 4.6 = 46 \text{ pounds of phosphate should be applied per acre}$$
$$(\sim 2 \text{ pounds per 1,000 square feet})$$

If the phosphatic fertilizer contains 46 percent phosphate, then:

$$46 \div 0.46 = 100 \text{ pounds per acre } (\sim 2.3 \text{ pounds per 1,000 square feet})$$

Phosphorus is relatively insusceptible to leaching but can percolate beneath the root zone in sandy conditions, especially if there is little soil organic matter. Generally speaking, if the soil contains ample organic matter, not only is phosphorus unlikely to leach but also an adequate reserve of phosphorus is usually complexed into the soil.

Nitrates and sulfates *are* susceptible to leaching. Aside from the issue of groundwater pollution, the loss of these nutrients, when applied as inorganic compounds, can be significant, especially in well-drained, sandy soils. Soils with a greater capacity to retain soil solution can hold dissolved nitrates and sulfates more efficiently. This is not to say that a heavy soil is preferable. In heavy or compacted soils where the oxygen supply is limited, reduction (the biological or chemical removal of oxygen from compounds) can occur. Soil organisms (mostly bacteria) can reduce nitrate or sulfate to satisfy their own oxygen needs, which can transform these nutrients into gases that can escape into the atmosphere. A sandy soil with enough humus to hold an ample reservoir of soil solution without compromising drainage is ideal.

Tests for nitrates or sulfates are often optional—that is, not included with a lab's standard soil analysis. Nitrate analysis is a snapshot test because levels constantly fluctuate. Factors that influence nitrate content in the soil include soil temperature, carbon-to-nitrogen ratio, soil moisture, organic matter content, precipitation, biological activity, and the manager's fertility program. Samples from the same spot taken days apart can reveal significantly different levels of nitrate. If a nitrate deficiency (or superfluity) is suspected, soil samples can be drawn, dried, and sent to the lab via overnight delivery to get the most accurate results. Some managers refrigerate or freeze the sample and then ship it in an insulated pouch. The more time between sample extraction and analysis, the more likely that changes in nitrate level will occur.

Nitrate testing is most appropriate in arid and semiarid regions where the soil's source of water is primarily from irrigation and therefore can be controlled. In regions where the weather can change rapidly, the results of a nitrate test may be meaningless. Tests for nitrate in sandy soils, especially where precipitation is unpredictable, are generally unreliable because of nitrate's propensity to leach. Acceptable ranges of nitrate vary in different types of soils; whoever performs the analysis should know the relevant range for each sample.

Leaf tissue analysis may be a better indicator, and if soil nitrate analysis is important, on-site analysis may be a better method. On-site equipment can be purchased that measures the amount of nitrogen in plant tissue sap. These meters are relatively accurate and can assist in determining the nitrogen needs of the turf. Care must be taken to calibrate these tools regularly and avoid contamination of the reagents. Near-infrared equipment (NIR) is also available that can measure the nitrogen content in dry grass clippings. The equipment is not inexpensive, but it does give a quick and accurate nitrogen analysis. Kits that perform on-site analysis often contain nitrate tests. These are often more accurate than a lab analysis because of changes in the sample that can occur while it is in transit to a lab and because of changes that may occur in the soil while the manager is waiting for results (see below, "On-Site Analysis").

Testing for nitrate as part of an nitrogen management program may be profitable on large areas where significant applications of fertilizer are proposed. The appropriate timing of the test, however, may create a practical problem. Samples for nitrate testing should be drawn after the soil has warmed up and the biological component of the soil has become active again. This may not occur until mid- to late spring in some areas. It may be inappropriate or inconvenient to postpone nitrogen fertilization this long. If nitrogen fertilization cannot wait, then applications can adulterate the samples drawn later for nitrate analysis.

Some labs offer a calculated nitrogen analysis called *Estimated Nitrogen Release* (ENR) based on the percentage of organic matter found in the sample. ENR, which is expressed in pounds per acre, is usually calculated using one of several conditional equations. (*Note:* In these formulae, use percentage values as whole numbers; e.g., 2 percent = 2, not 0.02.)

- Soils with a cation exchange capacity (CEC) of >7 meq. per 100 grams and percent organic matter (%OM) <0.4%, then ENR = 20 × %OM + 24. If the CEC is >7 meq. per 100 grams and %OM > 0.4%, then ENR = 20 × %OM + 26.
- If the CEC >4 meq. per 100 grams but ≤7 and %OM <0.4%, then ENR = 20 × %OM +39. If the CEC >4 meq. per 100 grams but ≤7 meq. per 100 grams and %OM >0.4%, then ENR = 20 × %OM +41.
- If the CEC <4 and %OM <0.4%, then ENR = 20 × %OM +49. If the CEC <4 and %OM >0.4%, then ENR = 20 × %OM +51.
- To convert pounds per acre to pounds per 1,000 square feet, multiply by 0.023.

Reduce the ENR by 20 percent in northern soils because the cooler average temperatures inhibit the biological activity needed to release nitrogen from organic matter. The ENR never exceeds 140 ppa (~3.2 pounds per 1,000 square feet). Table 4-5 calculates several conditions using the above formulae and converts the values from pounds per acre to pounds per 1,000 square feet.

It is difficult to predict how much nitrogen will actually become available from organic matter, however, because of the large number of variables that affect its release. These variables include soil temperature, soil moisture, soil atmosphere, and the form and stability of the organic matter found in the sample. Peat, for example, has very little nitrogen to offer plants or soil organisms. On the other hand, nitrogen applications should not be based solely on plant needs either. The nitrogen that turf receives from organic matter, especially when clippings are recycled, is significant. Clippings can supply up to one-third of the nitrogen that turf needs, and the utilization is so efficient that less than 5 percent of the clippings' nitrogen is lost even in the worst of conditions. Organic matter is often a warehouse of nitrogen. Residing in every 1 percent of organic matter in 1,000 square feet of soil ~6 inches deep is an average of ~23 pounds of nitrogen. A soil with 4 percent organic matter might contain over 90 pounds of nitrogen per 1,000 square feet. This may sound excessive but normally, very little organic nitrogen is available at any given time. ENR estimates may sometimes seem higher than a steward might want to rely on, but they should not be ignored by any means. If only one- to two-thirds of the ENR value is considered reliable and factored into a fertility program, the reduction of applied nitrogen is significant.

Sulfate is not as transitory as nitrate, and few turf managers worry about sulfate deficiencies. Since the dawn of the industrial revolution, pollution from coal- and oil-burning facilities has deposited ample sulfur to the soil. As cleaner fuels have been introduced and more air pollution controls developed, less sulfur is being generated that might eventually enrich the soil. Given the drainage in some sports fields, the lack of organic sulfate reserves, and the propensity for sulfate to leach, occasional sulfate analysis may be in the best interest of the turf steward. The optimal range for sulfate is ~7 to 13 parts per million. If the lab reports results as ppm sulfur, multiply by 3 to convert sulfur to sulfate.

TABLE 4-5
Estimated Nitrogen Release (ENR) (Expressed In Pounds Per 1,000 Ft^2)

CEC	%OM																			
	0.1	0.2	0.3	0.4	0.5	1.0	1.5	2.0	2.5	3.0	3.5	4.0	4.5	5.0	5.5	6.0	7.0	8.0	9.0	10.0
1.0	1.2	1.2	1.3	1.3	1.4	1.6	1.9	2.1	2.3	2.6	2.8	3.0	3.2	3.2	3.2	3.2	3.2	3.2	3.2	3.2
1.5	1.2	1.2	1.3	1.3	1.4	1.6	1.9	2.1	2.3	2.6	2.8	3.0	3.2	3.2	3.2	3.2	3.2	3.2	3.2	3.2
2.0	1.2	1.2	1.3	1.3	1.4	1.6	1.9	2.1	2.3	2.6	2.8	3.0	3.2	3.2	3.2	3.2	3.2	3.2	3.2	3.2
2.5	1.2	1.2	1.3	1.3	1.4	1.6	1.9	2.1	2.3	2.6	2.8	3.0	3.2	3.2	3.2	3.2	3.2	3.2	3.2	3.2
3.0	1.2	1.2	1.3	1.3	1.4	1.6	1.9	2.1	2.3	2.6	2.8	3.0	3.2	3.2	3.2	3.2	3.2	3.2	3.2	3.2
3.5	1.2	1.2	1.3	1.3	1.4	1.6	1.9	2.1	2.3	2.6	2.8	3.0	3.2	3.2	3.2	3.2	3.2	3.2	3.2	3.2
4.0	1.2	1.2	1.3	1.3	1.4	1.6	1.9	2.1	2.3	2.6	2.8	3.0	3.2	3.2	3.2	3.2	3.2	3.2	3.2	3.2
4.5	0.9	1.0	1.0	1.1	1.2	1.4	1.6	1.9	2.1	2.3	2.6	2.8	3.0	3.2	3.2	3.2	3.2	3.2	3.2	3.2
5.0	0.9	1.0	1.0	1.1	1.2	1.4	1.6	1.9	2.1	2.3	2.6	2.8	3.0	3.2	3.2	3.2	3.2	3.2	3.2	3.2
5.5	0.9	1.0	1.0	1.1	1.2	1.4	1.6	1.9	2.1	2.3	2.6	2.8	3.0	3.2	3.2	3.2	3.2	3.2	3.2	3.2
6.0	0.9	1.0	1.0	1.1	1.2	1.4	1.6	1.9	2.1	2.3	2.6	2.8	3.0	3.2	3.2	3.2	3.2	3.2	3.2	3.2
6.5	0.9	1.0	1.0	1.1	1.2	1.4	1.6	1.9	2.1	2.3	2.6	2.8	3.0	3.2	3.2	3.2	3.2	3.2	3.2	3.2
7.0	0.9	1.0	1.0	1.1	1.2	1.4	1.6	1.9	2.1	2.3	2.6	2.8	3.0	3.2	3.2	3.2	3.2	3.2	3.2	3.2
7.5	0.6	0.6	0.7	0.7	0.8	1.1	1.3	1.5	1.7	2.0	2.2	2.4	2.7	2.9	3.1	3.2	3.2	3.2	3.2	3.2
8.0	0.6	0.6	0.7	0.7	0.8	1.1	1.3	1.5	1.7	2.0	2.2	2.4	2.7	2.9	3.1	3.2	3.2	3.2	3.2	3.2
8.5	0.6	0.6	0.7	0.7	0.8	1.1	1.3	1.5	1.7	2.0	2.2	2.4	2.7	2.9	3.1	3.2	3.2	3.2	3.2	3.2
9.0	0.6	0.6	0.7	0.7	0.8	1.1	1.3	1.5	1.7	2.0	2.2	2.4	2.7	2.9	3.1	3.2	3.2	3.2	3.2	3.2
9.5	0.6	0.6	0.7	0.7	0.8	1.1	1.3	1.5	1.7	2.0	2.2	2.4	2.7	2.9	3.1	3.2	3.2	3.2	3.2	3.2
10.0	0.6	0.6	0.7	0.7	0.8	1.1	1.3	1.5	1.7	2.0	2.2	2.4	2.7	2.9	3.1	3.2	3.2	3.2	3.2	3.2

MICRONUTRIENTS

Most turfgrasses do not have an especially high need for micronutrients, but all plants need some. A deficiency of any nutrient, no matter how little is required, can limit plant development and functionality. Testing for micronutrients is not usually warranted. However, if problems exist that are not explained by a standard test, such testing may be necessary. Most labs keep soil samples for ~30 days after the initial analysis, so if micronutrient analysis becomes necessary within that time, drawing new samples may not be necessary.

Most micronutrients are cations, but labs do not normally report results in relation to CEC (i.e., what the soil can hold). The levels of micronutrients needed in the soil are so small that almost any CEC can hold enough of them. Great care should be taken when correcting micronutrient deficiencies. The line between too little and too much is often very fine. The lab that does the testing usually makes recommendations, but these are only as good as the sample taken. Rusty or corroded tools used to draw samples can easily adulterate a micronutrient analysis. Because of their high zinc content, galvanized tools or containers should be avoided regardless of their condition.

Iron is one micronutrient turf needs that is rarely deficient in most soils, but if the pH of a soil is too high or biological activity is too low, it can become unavailable to plants. Excessive levels of phosphates, zinc, manganese, or even thatch can also lock out iron. Many managers apply commercial preparations of iron to compensate for these conditions. Turf color usually improves when small amounts of soluble iron (ferrous iron) are applied to the soil, but if soil conditions are such that the iron is immediately tied up, then much of the iron applied will quickly become unavailable to plants. If these soil conditions exist and it is impractical to correct them, foliar (leaf) preparations of iron or other susceptible micronutrients may be more efficient.

Some managers use iron as the weather turns colder to counter chlorosis caused by unavailable nitrogen. As the soil temperature drops, so does the biological activity that regulates the availability of nitrogen. Iron is also used to treat chlorosis when applications of nitrogen can exacerbate other problems, including certain turf diseases. The introduction of iron does not have an immediately apparent effect on the balance of nutrients in the soil and does not seem to alter the nutrient balance in the plant, but observations are often limited to aboveground appearance and don't take functionality into consideration (see Chapter 2, under "Trace Elements"). Some scientists believe the iron merely coats the leaves, as a paint would, and causes a surface reaction that manifests itself in a dark green color. Iron, like many other nutrients, is abundant in soil (not sand), but most of it is tightly bound in mineral compounds and unavailable to plant roots. Biological activity on and around the root system can dissolve some of these bonds and make insoluble micronutrients available. In general, the more resources that are available to soil organisms, the more soil-bound nutrients can become available to plants.

ORGANIC MATTER

Most soils are mineral soils because they were formed from rocks weathered into smaller and smaller particles by forces such as rain, frost, wind, and erosion (see Chapter 1, under "Soil Creation"). Eventually, the surface area of these mineral particles increased to a point where certain organisms could access its mineral nutrients. These pioneers of soil formation were likely photosynthesizing organisms whose needs consisted mostly of gaseous elements such as oxygen, nitrogen, hydrogen, and carbon dioxide derived from the atmosphere. Some of what they needed, however, was attached to the weathered rock particles that surrounded them. As generations of these photosynthesizing organisms cycled through life and death, decay and predacious organisms began to evolve. As time passed, the accumulation of organic residues from the biomass served to support a greater diversity and even larger populations of organisms and, eventually, higher plants. Contributions of residues from plants accelerated the growth and diversity of the biomass and the creation of humus. Organic matter has its own life cycle, however, and through oxidation, nitrification, and other natural processes on average amounts to approximately 5 percent in the top 6 inches of a mineral soil in the temperate zone of the planet. This figure varies as climatic and other conditions change from location to location.

Organic matter is often a barometer of soil health, and measuring it is a useful practice. The population of organisms supported by soil organic matter is of immeasurable benefit to plants. More organic matter usually means:

- more decomposers and faster recycling of nutrients (including carbon dioxide) from plant and animal residues;
- more nitrogen-fixing, phosphorus-solubilizing, and hormone-producing soil organisms;
- more beneficial organisms that help dissolve mineral, transport water from soil depths, and antagonize plant pathogens;
- more soil-dwelling predators that release plant nutrients;
- more earthworms that accelerate rainwater permeation; and
- more humus to increase the water- and nutrient-holding capacity of the soil.

Humus expands and contracts in the soil as its moisture level changes. This phenomenon increases porosity, which improves the movement of water and the exchange of gases with the atmosphere and alleviates compaction. Lighter soil absorbs water faster and can hold more of it.

It is important when drawing samples for organic matter analysis that undecomposed residues such as crowns, roots, and thatch be carefully removed from the sample. These residues do not represent the mature soil organic matter fraction and will distort the results of the analysis.

Burning is a standard method of testing for organic matter. The sample is dried before it is burned to minimize water weight, which will inevitably be calculated as part of the organic carbon driven off by combustion. Analytical chemists admit that even after thorough drying, some water molecules, steadfastly attached to hydrated compounds, may still remain, but the level of error from these persistent units of water is well within an acceptable range. The mineral portion of the sample doesn't burn and will remain after combustion. The percent of organic matter is determined simply by subtracting the weight of the ash from the total weight of the dry sample before it was burned.

Many labs use a colorimeter method for determining percent organic matter in the soil. The soil is mixed with a chemical that changes color when it reacts with organic matter, and the intensity of color is measured. This method is a valid and accurate way of determining the percent organic matter. Most labs use either method if a specific request is made. Many labs routinely perform organic matter analysis, not so much because they recognize the value of humus but because the biological activity inherent in a rich soil can interfere with the effectiveness of many herbicides.

USGA specifications recommend between 0.5 and 2 percent organic matter for field construction and recognize that there will be a natural increase in that percentage over time. Generally, when USGA analysts refers to organic matter as excessive, they include undecomposed thatch, roots, and other residues in their measurements and are not in favor of high levels of organic matter. If most of the organic matter in a soil is undecomposed residues, it is not helping the turf, the game, or the soil organisms. The situation is different, however, if the bulk of soil organic matter is stable or labile humus. Many managers and turf scientists would argue that an abundance of sand and lack of organic matter is necessary for a firm, well-drained playing surface. It's difficult to argue with that logic, but it begs the question of whether or not we must sacrifice so many of the benefits of a biologically rich soil for excessive drainage and inordinately rigid surfaces. Depending on the angularity of sand particles, the surface may be far less stable than if the soil is rich with organic matter (see Chapter 6, under "Sand and Drainage").

It may be difficult for most managers to maintain a level of soil organic matter (disregarding thatch and other undecomposed residues) above 5 percent no matter how hard they try. A biologically active soil consumes most organic residues and generates carbon dioxide for plants. Additionally, the longer and warmer the growing season, the lower the natural levels of soil organic matter are. A reading close to 4 percent in temperate regions is a good level, but even this may be difficult to attain and maintain. An analysis of soil extracted from an ecologically maintained golf green reveals organic matter levels at between 3 and 4 percent (Sachs and Luff, 2002). This is a surprisingly low figure after almost four decades of topdressing with compost twice annually; however, it represents an extremely functional soil ecosystem that consumes the energy in the compost to perform essential biological activities. Fields, where soil organic matter is below 2 percent, may not be able to maintain functional levels of many biological activities. In some cases, an analysis may reveal high organic matter without a correspondingly high level of biological activity. Bioanalysis and respiration tests are discussed below, under "Biological Analysis. Some labs calculate an estimated nitrogen release (ENR) from the amount of organic matter found in the sample (see "Important Anions," above). This value is usually given in pounds per acre. (To convert this value to pounds per 1,000 square feet, multiply by 0.023.)

BIOLOGICAL ANALYSIS

The importance of organic matter and the biological activity it supports is the thesis of this book. Unfortunately, the inherent problem with organic matter analysis is that it doesn't tell us about its stage of decay or anything about the biomass. A substantial amount of undecomposed residues in the sample may result in a high measurement of organic matter that doesn't necessarily indicate a high level of biological activity.

Organic matter analysis can indicate the potential for biological activity and improved cation exchange capacity (CEC), but the many variations in organic matter influence both the biomass and the CEC. Undecomposed residues, for example, do not contribute to the CEC of a soil but can provide food for many organisms, thus increasing their activity and the subsequent availability of plant nutrients. Some residues, such as thatch, may not contribute much to either the CEC or biological activity. This material is more resistant to decay than residues such as clippings, and because its contact with the soil is limited, organisms have less access to it. Labile humus, such as compost, contributes a tremendous amount of resources for soil organisms but offers few exchange sites for soil cations. Stable humus, on the other hand, has much less to offer organisms but can adsorb a substantial quantity cations.

The CEC contributions of organic matter can be measured to a certain extent. We know that the two soil particles that adsorb most cations are clay and humus. If the soil contains little to no clay, then humus must be responsible for most of its capacity to hold cations. The cornucopia of other benefits of organic matter can overshadow the importance of CEC derived from it. The energy stored in organic matter fuels the biological mechanisms in the soil ecosystem. One of the main objectives of this book is to convince the reader that the health and welfare of soil organisms is inextricably linked to the health of turf plants. With that in mind, the measurement of soil organic matter often indicates much more than its capacity to hold cations.

An experienced manager can employ analytical observation to determine some facts about the soil organic matter. The color, feel, and smell of a soil sample can give a relatively accurate indication of its characteristics. A dark, crumbly sample with the smell of freshly turned soil is a good indication of well-developed organic matter and an active biomass; however, it is impossible to judge the diversity and vitality of soil organisms. Respiration is a better indicator.

Most soil organisms generate carbon dioxide, and the volume produced is a good way to measure their activity. Woods End Research (see "Sources and Resources" for contact information) markets an on-site soil respiration test called Solvita® that measures biological activity (see Figure 4-7). A soil sample is placed in a jar (provided) along with a gel-coated paddle, and the jar is sealed with a screw-on cap. The gel changes color in response to the amount of carbon dioxide produced by soil biota. After 24 hours, the color of the gel is compared with a color key that identifies the level of biological activity. This test does not work properly if the sample is too dry, too wet, too hot, or too cold. The sample should ball up when squeezed, but no water should be expelled. The test should be conducted at room temperature (68°–77°F) and out of direct sunlight. If the soil must be moistened or dried, samples should not be drawn

FIGURE 4-7   Solvita is an on-site soil respiration test that measures biological activity by detecting carbon dioxide. Photo courtesy Woods End Research.

for a couple of days after treatment. The sample should not contain thatch, crowns, or any other undecomposed residues.

Solvita measures the active biomass rather than the resources upon which it is living. If the percentage of organic matter found from chemical analysis is high but the production of carbon dioxide measured by Solvita is low, then, for some reason, the organic matter is not providing resources to the biomass. Limiting factors can include moisture, temperature, or both but can also include pesticides, salt fertilizers, irrigation water, or the physical condition of the soil.

Soil Food Web and BBC Labs (see "Sources and Resources" for contact information) perform biological soil analysis. The tests each lab offers differ, but all are designed to measure the quantity and diversity of soil organisms in a sample. The larger and more diverse the soil's food web, the better the regulation of plant nutrients and the more protection from pathogens. Tests that determine total and active bacteria, total and active fungi, protozoa numbers, nematode numbers and diversity, and mycorrhizal fungi indicate the balance and interactivity of soil organisms. Some labs can also perform the same assay for leaf surfaces to determine if disease-suppressive organisms are colonizing the phyllosphere. These tests tell both the level of biological activity and the balance of organisms involved.

Biological analysis is relatively new, and we still have a lot to learn about the relationships of the multitudes of soil organisms. Indeed, the functionality of many soil-dwelling species has not yet been determined. Most biologists agree, however, that diversity and complexity are necessary for a stable soil ecosystem. Their main criterion for a healthy soil is that it contain a significant diversity of life.

LEAF TISSUE ANALYSIS

Sometimes macro- or micronutrient deficiencies (or superfluities) occur in plants, but a soil analysis does not reveal the problem. Some edaphic anomaly may be causing a nutrient deficiency even though the soil does not exhibit a shortage of that nutrient. Lackluster turfgrass performance in soil with ample nutrients may indicate a root pathogen, some type of stress, or a problem with the absorption of essential nutrients even if they are available.

Leaf tissue analysis can be performed to determine if turf is lacking some important factor. Most of the plant's physiological activity takes place in the leaves, and changes in the plant's nutrient absorption correspond with the balance of minerals in leaf tissue. Keep in mind, however, that neither leaf tissue nor soil analysis will reveal whether or not carbon is deficient.

To submit samples for leaf tissue analysis, gather 30 to 40 blades from fresh clippings and spread them out to air-dry overnight. Avoid contamination from soil or other debris that can adulterate the test results. Package the samples in a paper bag or cardboard box with ventilation holes punched through the walls; place the package inside an appropriate shipping container. Labs generally request information they need to provide a useful analysis. Most labs provide forms to be filled out and forwarded with the samples. Ideally, leaf tissue analysis is done in conjunction with a soil analysis so the condition of the plant and the soil during the same period can be compared. Conditions in the soil—especially in sandy soil—and in the plant can change relatively quickly. Tissue analysis performed months before or after soil tests may not accurately reveal the problem or problems.

Leaf tissue and concurrent soil analysis can provide information needed to both solve and prevent problems. If, for example, a tissue analysis indicates superfluous nitrogen in the plant, this condition may eventually lead to other problems such as thatch, disease, or insect encroachment. For another example, analysis may reveal that the level of phosphorus in the plant is below the acceptable range even though the soil contains an ample amount. This scenario is relatively common in cold soils or where biological activity is low. The analysis can also point out deficiencies of seemingly obscure micronutrients such as manganese, copper, and zinc. Leaf tissue analysis is a useful tool that can be instrumental in solving some mystifying problems.

PHYSICAL ANALYSIS

Physical analysis is performed most often during the construction stage of a sports field, especially if it is being constructed according to USGA specifications. The ideal texture, consistency, and particle size can, at least in the short term, mitigate potential problems. The consistency of a designed soil, however, inevitably changes over time. Natural phenomena that, from the perspective of the plant, may improve growing conditions eventually reduce porosity so that more soil solution is retained. These changes are rarely welcomed by managers who are trying to preserve superfluous drainage.

Physical analysis not only measures the percentage of sand, silt, and clay but also determines the diameter, sphericity, and angularity of sand particles. The USGA usu-

TABLE 4-6
Sand Particle Ranges

Screen Size	Percent Retained
2.0 mm (No. 10)	≤3 percent gravel ≤10 combined
1.0 mm (No. 18)	
0.5 mm (No. 35)	≥60 percent
0.25 mm (No. 60)	
0.15 mm (No. 100)	≤20 percent
0.10 mm (No. 140)	≤5 percent
0.05 mm (No. 270)	

ally divides sand particle diameters into seven size categories ranging from 0.05 mm to 2.0 mm. USGA recommendations are that soil contain ≤5 percent silt, ≤3 percent clay, and the rest sand. Table 4-6 shows the USGA's suggested ranges for sand particles. Physical analysis also measures particle density, bulk density, infiltration rate, total porosity, aeration porosity, capillary porosity, and organic matter. Suggested values from the USGA are shown in Table 4-7.

Some managers perform physical analysis on established fields to monitor changes, measure the effects of physical treatment, or justify renovation. Labs that do physical analysis want to see an undisturbed profile of the soil, usually about 12 inches deep. One lab, N.W. Hummel, suggests sharpening one end of a 2-inch-diameter PVC pipe and driving it ~12 inches into the soil. When the pipe is extracted, the sample is contained inside. The ends of the pipe are then packed with newspaper and sealed with tape and the entire assembly (pipe and all) is sent to the lab.

TEXTURE ANALYSIS

Texture analysis is slightly different than physical analysis. Texture analysis only determines the percentage of sand, silt, and clay in a given soil. Those findings are plugged into a texture analysis triangle (Figure 4-8) to determine soil classification. To use the

TABLE 4-7
USGA Physical Property Standards

Physical Property	USGA Values
Particle density	N/A
Bulk density	N/A
Infiltration rate	6–24 in./hr
Total porosity	35–55 percent
Aeration porosity	15–30 percent
Capillary porosity	15–25 percent
Organic matter	0.5–2.0 percent

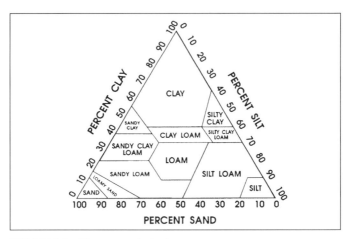

FIGURE 4-8   Texture analysis chart.

triangle, extend lines from the appropriate starting points, parallel to the sides of the triangle, which are counterclockwise to the sides where the lines began. Like tying shoes, the triangle is easy to use but difficult to explain. If, for example, a soil texture analysis discovered 40 percent sand, 40 percent silt, and 20 percent clay, the first line would begin on the 40 mark of the percent sand side of the triangle, drawn parallel to the percent silt side. The second line begins at the 40 mark on the percent silt side and is drawn parallel to the percent clay side. The intersection of those two lines indicates the texture classification of the soil. The third line may be drawn to complete the triangulation, but this is usually unnecessary unless the first two lines intersect directly between two classifications.

A simple, on-site texture analysis can be conducted by collecting a soil sample in a clear graduated cylinder, test tube, or other sealable graduated container and mixing it with an equal volume of water. Before adding the water, tap the container on a hard surface to compact the soil slightly and then measure the volume of the soil sample. After adding water, seal the container and shake it vigorously for ~30 seconds. Then place it upright in a location where it can remain undisturbed for ~24 hours. The sand particles will settle to the bottom and the silt on top of it. Clay will eventually settle on top, but the finer particles can take weeks to precipitate out of suspension. This is why we measure the dry sample before adding the water. If the volume of the original sample is known, it is easy to determine the percentage of sand and silt by measuring each layer and calculating what portion it is of the whole sample. To determine the percentage of sand or silt, divide the level of each by the total volume of soil and multiply by 100. If, for example, our soil sample measures 50 ml and we find that 20 ml of that is sand, then:

$$20 \div 50 \times 100 = 40 \text{ percent}$$

Once the percent sand and silt is determined, the texture analysis chart can be used to classify the sample. Physical and texture analyses are valuable tools. Familiarity with the soil one is working in allows for more informed decisions about irrigation, core aeration, liming, fertilization, and applications of pesticides.

IRRIGATION WATER ANALYSIS

Water analysis is an important test if the turf manager relies on irrigation. Insufficient water can quickly become the most limiting factor in turf performance, but contaminated water can slowly create enormous problems that do not show symptoms until it is too late. Labs that test the irrigation suitability of water commonly measure sodium, calcium, magnesium, chloride, conductivity, sulfate, nitrate, pH, carbonate, bicarbonate, phosphorus, potassium, boron, dissolved solids, and sodium absorption ratio. These analyses can pinpoint most problems with irrigation water. However, many other natural and manmade contaminants can affect turf performance, and discovering them can sometimes be difficult and expensive. Labs test for the presence of specific chemicals or conditions and can find unknown contaminants only by testing for different possibilities. If the list of those possibilities is long and if discovery occurs somewhere near the roster's end, considerable expense may be incurred (see Figure 4-9a).

FIGURE 4-9A   What's in this water? Natural or artificial contaminants may cause problems for turf.

Water analysis is usually done when a new water source is introduced to the grounds, but many managers also have their irrigation water tested periodically to monitor its quality. Depending on the source of water, prolonged drought conditions may increase the concentration of mineral or other compounds. As water evaporates from surface sources, such as ponds or reservoirs, the concentration of dissolved solids increases simply because they are diluted in less water. Water that is normally innocuous thus may become problematic under extremely dry conditions. Exceedingly wet conditions can also cause problems, depending on the path runoff water takes before arriving at the pond or reservoir where it collects. Heavy rains can move more surface contaminants and may create problems depending on what lies upstream. Periodic water analysis, especially after extremes in weather conditions, may be appropriate.

ON-SITE ANALYSIS

Many of the analyses discussed in this chapter can be performed on site. Test kits are available that provide everything from chemical reagents to test tubes and eyedroppers.

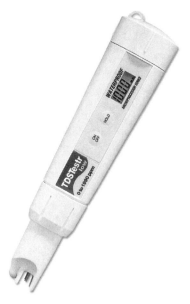

Additionally, many electronic instruments can measure conditions such as pH, conductivity, moisture, and the total dissolved solids in irrigation water, quickly and accurately (see Figure 4-9b). The results from these tests can be as dependable as those from professional labs, but it's important to remember that no analysis can reflect more than the conditions of the sample. The sample must represent the average conditions of the field, or the information derived from it is meaningless. Sticking a pH meter into one spot and assuming that the reading represents the pH of the entire field may lead to an over- or underapplication of lime or sulfur.

FIGURE 4-9B   LoMotte's handy TDS Tester measures total dissolved solids in irrigation water. Photo courtesy LaMotte Company.

Sampling procedures should be the same whether the analysis is perform on site or at a lab hundreds of miles away (see "Sampling," above). The advantages of on-site analysis are the immediacy of information, the selectivity of test data, and the reduction of changes that might occur while samples are in transit to distant labs. Often, a manager wants to measure only one parameter—pH, for example—to see if a lime application achieved an adequate adjustment. This information may be quick and easy to obtain with on-site testing equipment, and quicker and easier than if a lab is used. Nitrate tests are often

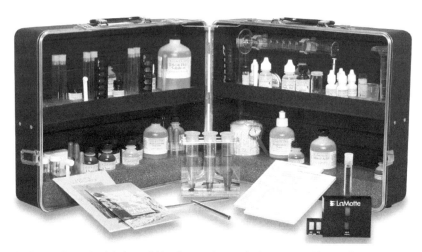

FIGURE 4-10A   Sophisticated kits for on-site analysis can provide results as accurate as professional labs but samples must represent the area in question. Photo courtesy LaMotte Company.

much more accurate with on-site analysis because of the changes that can occur while the sample is in transit to a lab and because of changes that may occur in the soil while the manager is waiting for results (see Figures 4-10a and 4-10b).

BE COOL

It is important to keep analysis reports in perspective. The results of most tests are an average of the area being evaluated. Soils do not respond like a high-performance engine, in which subtle adjustments can tweak out another 2 to 3 more horsepower. Fine-tuning the soil ecosystem is generally impractical. Not only are the results of most analyses relatively inexact but also factors that affect the physical, biological, and chemical conditions in the soil are constantly changing. If treatments are made with consideration for the entire soil ecosystem, then the whole solar-powered, biological turf-growing machine can benefit.

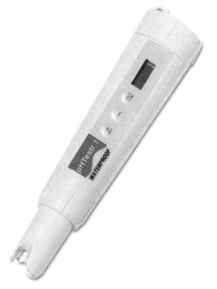

FIGURE 4-10B   pH meters are fast, accurate, and handy to use but sampling one spot does not necessarily represent the rest of the field. Photo courtesy LaMotte Company.

POINTS TO REMEMBER

- The soil ecosystem can be broken down into three categories: physical, chemical, and biological, each of which affects and is affected by the others.
- Soil samples should represent, as well as possible, the entire area. The more samples taken (and combined) from a field, the better the representation.
- Samples can easily be contaminated by rusty or corroded tools or tools that have leftover residues of foreign material(s), making soil test results useless.
- For laboratory analysis, choose labs that provide satisfactory service and consistent results. Do not compare the reports of different labs.
- The properties of cations and colloids enable the soil to hold and exchange certain nutrients with plants.
- Many managers use base saturation and CEC to determine application rates of cation nutrients. Calcareous soils may make this method inappropriate. Only the manager of the site in question can determine whether or not calculated application rates work for him or her.
- Nitrogen is not typically analyzed unless specifically requested because varying conditions in the soil are constantly changing its availability.

◆ Organic matter is often part of a lab's standard analysis, but test results may reveal ambiguous information. Generally speaking, if there are ample residues and high levels of biological activity (and the environmental conditions that favor that activity), then adequate levels of most plant nutrients will be made available.

◆ Other important analyses include leaf tissue analysis, physical analysis, texture analysis, and irrigation water analysis. Each of these tests can reveal important information individually and collectively enable the manager to make more effective management decisions.

◆ Physical, chemical, and biological conditions in soil are constantly changing, and there is no definitive way of predicting how those changes will affect our turf. But, if we can keep all three conditions in balance and in a good state, the ecosystem will likely function beneficially.

Chapter 5

PESTS

Technically, a pest is something that causes injury or damage to human concerns. On a playing field, those concerns can range from mosquitoes strafing players to teenagers leaving litter strewn under the bleachers. Pests that can cause severe damage to turf, however, are the greatest concern to turf managers. Severity is a subjective determination. It is the threshold of tolerance that the manager, school committee, or players are willing to accept. At one time, damage that didn't interfere with play may have been considered acceptable; however, over the years, aesthetic values have become an ever-increasing influence. On some fields, today's standards demand such intensive management that aside from photosynthesis, nature's contributions to the growing system are relinquished to management techniques. Artificial plant growth regulators do the job for natural hormone-producing organisms. Soluble salts of nitrogen and other immediately available nutrients do the work for free living nitrogen fixers and organisms that process organic residues into plant nutrients. The job performed by predators is (sometimes) accomplished with insecticides that too often harm the predators. Fungal pathogens need fear fungicides only because the natural populations of parasites, predators, and other disease-suppressive organisms have left for more lucrative jobs in other environments. And as these fungi evolve their tolerance to fungicides, they can be even more successful. Earthworms, microarthropods, and other beneficial saprophytic organisms move on to escape the grim realities of this chemical warfare.

In reality, most of these groups of organisms don't migrate to less hostile environments—they just don't survive. This micromanagement technique might not create so many problems if we fully understood the complexities of turf's ecosystem—but we don't. We *do* understand that the relationships plants have with the biological component of their environment are important for their survival. If materials are applied that suppress the functions of these organisms, problems that require other chemical remedies often appear.

Turf—or more accurately, the turf manager—can become dependent on chemicals as easily as people can become dependent on drugs. Also like drugs, the more often chemicals are used, the more often they seem to be needed. Although the playing field is largely a man-made system, it can be, nonetheless, a system that functions with balance and ecological grace. The occurrence of turf pests in large numbers might be a message to the manager that the ecosystem is somehow out of balance. Sometimes the message is simple: *You can't grow that here.* Other times the problems speak of infertility, excessive nutrient(s), compaction, poor drainage, excessive drainage, inadequate levels of organic matter, mechanical injury, or incorrect pH. Treatment of the symptom—that is to say, the weed, the insect, or the disease—does not necessarily recreate balance; it only eliminates the symptom, which nature often replaces with another. Additionally, applications of many pesticides often eliminate more than just their target. The subsequent depletion of beneficial organisms can create more unwanted symptoms.

This cycle is a relatively classic scenario in turf, and it can eventually result in a dramatic reduction of biological diversity and, consequently, grass quality in the immediate environment. Many of these changes may be unnecessary. The cause of the original problem might have been simple, but the situation is complicated by multiple treatments that alter the soil ecosystem.

Grasses are naturally resilient and competitive organisms designed to withstand the rigors of grazing animals. Grown under optimal conditions, grasses can compete with weeds and endure the occasional pathogen or small herd of grazing insects. Soil organisms react to optimal conditions in a similar manner. Huge populations of soil dwellers compete for resources in an ecological orchestration that maintains a functional balance throughout the soil system. Infestations of pests have difficulty becoming established in an environment where too much competition exists. Conditions that harbor pest problems are often optimal for the pest, not the health of the plant. Low levels of organic matter, inappropriate height of cut (HOC), shallow root systems, excessive thatch, soil compaction, poor fertility, overirrigation, and incorrect pH can all contribute to pest problems by not providing adequate conditions for grasses to be healthy and competitive.

Investigations from the USDA Agricultural Research Service present compelling evidence that plants can cultivate populations of specific soil-dwelling organisms in the rhizosphere. They accomplish this by releasing special pabulum through their roots that attracts and nurtures these select groups. These organisms colonize the roots and produce toxins that inhibit the growth of specific pathogens. They can also correct some nutrient deficiencies by making mineral ions, necessary for plant growth and health, available from the soil, and they can produce invaluable substances that regulate plant growth and help the plant develop resistance to environmental stress. These substances include amino acids, antibiotics, auxins, cytokinins, enzymes, giberillins, indoles, and vitamins. Some of these substances can be transported intact through the vascular system of the plant to help growth, resist stress, and defend against many pathogens and other foraging pests.

The side effects of many pesticides can include suppression, depletion, eradication, or an alteration in the balance and type of organisms in the rhizosphere. If symptoms of this biological malaise begin to appear, more pesticides are often applied—and the problem worsens. Some biologists believe that many pesticides can have subtle residual effects lasting for years and that some pesticide residues may combine to form new chemicals with unpredictable effects on soil organisms.

This isn't a claim that once a turf manager begins using pesticides, there is no turning back. Biological health and balance *can* be restored, but it is difficult to do this at the same time that the balance of soil organisms is being altered or destroyed with frequent applications of pesticides. Applications of concentrated, salt-based fertilizers can also affect developing populations of these select groups of root-dwelling organisms by changing the osmotic pressure of surrounding soil moisture and the soil's chemical balance. Certain kinds of organic matter added to or inherently in the soil can mitigate many of the harmful effects on soil organisms from both pesticides and salt-based fertilizers—providing these chemicals aren't being applied in overwhelming quantities (see Chapters 2 and 3).

Scientists know that healthy plants are not completely defenseless against pest organisms. Plant species that have no defenses, either their own or from symbiotic organisms, would have become extinct long ago. Most species of plants can synthesize chemical defense compounds that inhibit pest activity. The synthesis of these organic chemicals depends largely on the availability of the necessary elemental components (i.e., fertility) and the plants' overall health, strength, and vitality. In some cases, the introduction of a simple primary nutrient such as potassium can help the host plant create stronger defenses to certain pests. On the other hand, excessive applications of some nutrients, such as nitrogen, can significantly reduce the plant's ability to defend itself.

Plant resistance to insect pests and diseases is manifested in four basic forms:

1. The manufacture of toxins that affect the biology of the pest;
2. The ability to make itself unattractive via smell, taste, or nutritional value, forcing the pest to go elsewhere for sustenance;
3. The development of tolerances to pest damage—that is, the ability to thrive in spite of the adversity; and
4. A physical resistance created by thickening the outer layers of both stems and leaves.

Often, a plant may exhibit all four resistances.

All of these defensive reactions depend on optimum fertility and effective stress management. Fertility must include adequate supplies of carbon dioxide from biological activity in the soil. Plants cannot process nitrogen into proteins and enzymes (insoluble forms of nitrogen) without adequate carbon, and soluble forms of nitrogen in plant tissue are often what attract pathogens and insects.

It is also known that many plants can sense imminent pest problems and alert other plants to the threat. When nearby plants are attacked, natural plant hormones are often released, signaling adjacent plants to produce defense compounds in anticipation of attack. The production of these hormones and the implementation of defense mechanisms depend on a healthy plant growing in a sound soil ecosystem.

Soil organisms also have the ability to produce allelopathic chemicals. Researchers believe that there are as many natural toxins in the environment as there are kinds of organisms. These toxins are usually formed by plants, fungi, or bacteria, but some may be mineral in nature. Antibiotics, for example, are made by soil fungi and are toxic to many bacteria. In some soils, fungal organisms can maintain prominence by suppressing bacterial growth. Bacteria, on the other hand, also produce toxins that can inhibit populations of fungi. Bacteria-dominated soils can naturally inhibit the establishment of many pathogens.

Toxins are usually produced as metabolites of biological activity or as compounds formed from the decay of some organic materials. Some species of organisms produce compounds that are toxic to themselves, thus providing their own control for overpopulation. Substances that are toxic to one organism may be nutritious to another. The best balance of these natural toxins in the soil is both directly and indirectly related to resources that provide food and habitat for a large diversity of soil organisms. It is true that many of nature's toxins have been isolated, synthesized, and concentrated by scientists into biocidal substances called *pesticides*; however, introducing these substances into the environment in unnatural concentrations can cause an ecological chain reaction with unpredictable consequences.

Plants can display a variety of reactions to grazing pest organisms. The amount of organic nutrients released into the soil through plant roots generally increases, creating a relative increase of soil organisms in the root zone. Biological activity can, in turn, increase the amount of carbon dioxide and mineral nutrients available to the plant. Most plants respond to aboveground damage by increasing root growth and the amount of nutrients stored in the root system. Apparently, reducing the amount of nutrients located in the shoots and leaves makes the plant tops less nourishing and less attractive to grazing insects and pathogens. The stored nutrient in the root system increases the plant's ability to recover from pest damage. Plants can also significantly increase their production of alkaloids, substances that are often toxic or distasteful to insects. When fertilizers are applied, however—especially concentrated, highly soluble salts that trigger lush growth—the production of these toxins is dramatically reduced. The more energy the plant has to expend growing, the less is available to produce defense compounds (see Figure 5-1). A rich diet for turf can result in many problems including disease, drought intolerance, and insect invasion.

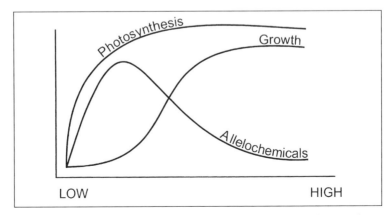

FIGURE 5-1   Growth versus defense. As more energy is used for growth, less is available for defense.

Sometimes a manager's best efforts to produce a healthy turf actually reduce turf quality by inflicting stress at inappropriate times. Mechanical injury caused by top-dressing, core cultivation, mowing, rolling, or grooming is more difficult to overcome if heat, drought, or other environmental conditions are already stressing plants. Implementing these activities while ignoring the stressed condition of the turf is analogous to jogging with the flu. The same is often true for irrigation and fertilization. The more stress introduced to turf, the more likely pest problems will develop.

Stress is not usually obvious until after damage from pathogens or insects occurs. What an advantage it would be if a manager could detect stressed plants before damaging insects or pathogens could! According to research, chlorophyll levels drop when a plant is stressed, and equipment is available that can measure this change (Spectrum). In fact, special eyeglasses designed by the National Aeronautics and Space Administration (NASA) can be purchased (Spectrum, Gempler's) that allow the wearer to identify stressed plants before they show symptoms to the naked eye (or the pest's naked eye). A manager equipped with a stress-detection device may be able to identify potential problems before symptoms appear but must also be able to identify the cause of the stress if he is to alleviate it. This can often be difficult (see Figures 5-2a and 5-2b).

FIGURE 5-2A Technology developed by NASA lets the viewer detect stressed plants from a distance. Photo courtesy Spectrum Technologies, Inc.

FIGURE 5-2B Chlorophyll meters measure relative chlorophyll content, a key indicator of plant health...or stress. Photo courtesy Spectrum Technologies, Inc.

DISEASE

The simultaneous occurrence of a plant pathogen and a suitable host does not necessarily result in infection. Other conditions musts be favorable for pathogens to succeed. These conditions include but are not limited to temperature, humidity, precipitation (rain or snow), base fertility balance, pH, nitrogen management, irrigation management, height of cut, soil biological activity, and plant stress.

Turfgrass diseases once considered inconsequential have become major problems on many playing fields due to excessive amounts of stress from traffic, low height of cut, sandy root zones, and other intensive management practices. After years of research, little doubt remains that stress is related both directly and indirectly to the vast majority of turf diseases. If the turf steward is attempting to manage disease with less or no fungicides, the mitigation of stress must be a high priority.

The Stress Relationship

Like the human body, a plant can protect itself from diseases. Plants produce many chemical compounds that are antagonistic to pathogens. The ability of the plant to successfully resist disease depends on many factors. When stressed, the plant's normal metabolism is disturbed and free oxygen radicals accumulate that cause the breakdown (oxidation) of lipids, proteins, chlorophyll, and nucleic acids. Plants normally produce antioxidants to defend against this loss, but production of antioxidants during stressful times is not always adequate to prevent damage. The plant responds by using lots of energy to create more lipids, proteins, and nucleic acids. However, photosynthesis occurring in the blades is often yielding less energy than the amount being consumed because of stress factors like traffic, heat, and drought. Height of cut is often a problem too. If turf is mowed too closely, less leaf surface area is exposed to synthesize energy from the sun. As stress increases and energy production decreases, the plant becomes more defenseless against pathogens.

A substantial amount of research establishes a correlation between inadequate production of antioxidants and the occurrence of disease in turf. If the turf plant can produce adequate amounts of antioxidants during periods of stress, photosynthesis and metabolism are often maintained at normal levels and the plant is stronger, less susceptible to, and better able to defend itself against pathogen infection.

Researchers discovered that certain natural plant hormones, such as auxins and cytokinins, significantly increase concentrations of antioxidants (such as alpha tocopherol, superoxide dismutase, and beta-carotene) in plants during periods of stress. These hormones are available in synthetic preparations but are also abundant in natural seaweed (*Ascophylum nodosum*) extracts. These extracts are commercially available in both liquid and dry-soluble preparations and can be used often and in varying concentrations without risk of overdose. Most seaweed formulations are compatible with fertilizers and pesticides and can mitigate the ecological impact caused by some of these materials. In fact, researchers found that seaweed extracts can counter the osmotic effects of some salt-based fertilizers. Seaweed can be applied as often as once per week, and some studies suggest that when applied with fungicides, insecticides, or herbicides, the seaweed improves the performance of the pesticide. Apparently, this phenomenon is due to the seaweed's ability to improve plant health despite the pesticide's ecological impact. Pesticides are not always as discriminating as manufacturers would like us to believe, and applying them often has an ecological side effect. Many researchers believe that seaweed minimizes the plant stress caused either directly or indirectly by pesticides (see Figures 5-3a and 5-3b).

Humic acids and humates have also been investigated and found to increase the plant's production of antioxidants. Research using combinations of seaweed and humic materials shows promising results.

The use of seaweed, humic derivatives, or both is more effective as a prophylactic than a control. Strengthening a plant (or any other organism) after it becomes sick is generally more difficult than maintaining its strength while it is healthy. A better tactic than waiting for symptoms to appear is to regularly apply seaweed through the irrigation system or mixed in the spray tank with other materials. This approach can prevent disease or make unavoidable disease symptoms less severe.

Natural Defense Systems

Plants have strong defenses against disease, but for these systems to function properly, the plant must be healthy. The defense systems of over- or underfed plants and plants experiencing severe stress are often unable to operate adequately. A strong plant allows only selective movement of materials through its tissue. The cellular structure of the plant is normally impermeable to everything plants want excluded. Under certain conditions, however, movement through and between cells changes from selective to passive. Cell walls are weaker, and their tightly knit arrangement is loosened. This is often a result of too much nitrogen, not enough potassium, or both. It can also be caused by a long list of other conditions. Nitrogen can exist in plant tissue in soluble forms such as nitrate, ammonium, and amino acids. These forms are attractive to pathogens, and the loose-knit cellular structure makes it easier for penetration and infection.

FIGURE 5-3A   Ascophyllum nodosum is the most widely researched seaweed used for agricultural and horticultural purposes. Photo courtesy Acadian Seaplants Limited.

FIGURE 5-3B   In Nova Scotia and New Brunswick, harvesters gather seaweed from government-licensed areas using specially designed cutting tools. Photo courtesy Acadian Seaplants Limited.

Once the plant transforms soluble nitrogen into protein, it is more difficult for pathogens to become established—and they are less inclined to try, as the plant is less attractive to them. It is harder for pathogens to assimilate and digest protein than more soluble forms of nitrogen. Plants need carbon, hydrogen, and oxygen to make protein from nitrogen. Their only source of carbon is carbon dioxide in the atmosphere. In a rich soil, carbon dioxide is constantly being generated by soil organisms, and turf plants have their best opportunity to absorb it as it seeps from the soil's surface. If inadequate amounts of carbon dioxide are evolved in the soil and too much nitrogen is applied, weaker and nutritionally more attractive plants (that is, attractive to pathogens) are often the result.

Carbon is also needed for the production of many defense compounds. Plants can produce enzymes like chitinase, which breaks down the penetrating component of pathogens. Carbon is also a component of lignin and callous, materials that plants can produce to inhibit pathogen penetration.

Healthy plants can also produce bursts of hydrogen peroxide—a particularly lethal substance to most pathogens. Research has found that seaweed extracts, humic acids, or both can help plants increase production of many defense compounds (Senn 1978).

Choosing disease-resistant cultivars is wise, especially in regions where certain turf diseases are common. Most land-grant universities have data on the disease resistance of seed varieties, and new information is always emerging. Plant diversity can also be an important strategy for disease control. Most pathogens are specific about which plants they infect. If several varieties coexist, the infection of one species may be less noticeable, and it may be more difficult for the disease to spread. Research has shown that mixing grass cultivars, especially when resistant varieties are included, can improve natural disease control (Beard 2002, Brede 2000, Leslie 1994, Sachs and Luff 2001).

Indigenous varieties, if available, are sometimes the most disease-resistant. Many areas in the country, and probably the world, spawn native grasses, paspalum, or other species that are particularly suited for the region in which they grow. These nameless varieties look good, spread well, and spring back more quickly after pest or environmental damage. Some managers who have the time and space cultivate native grasses in nurseries and use them to repair damaged areas in the field.

Soil Allies

Other protection from disease pathogens comes from the soil—or, more accurately, from soil organisms. As cliché as it may sound, there is truth to the axiom that a healthy soil promotes healthy plants. In the soil are thousands of different species of organisms that exist for two common purposes—to survive and to reproduce. Their most limiting factors are resources such as food, water, and proper atmosphere. If these organisms were given an unlimited supply of resources, their populations would increase beyond the earth's spatial capacity in a matter of weeks.

Organisms must compete with each other for the limited resources in soil. Most soil organisms can be categorized into one of four groups—parasite, symbiont, saprophyte, or predator. The parasite is an organism that derives its energy from another life form, whereas a saprophyte derives its energy from the dead tissue or residues of other organisms. Many soil organisms—in fact, most turfgrass pathogens—can be both parasitic and saprophytic. A symbiont also derives energy from another living organism but in a mutually beneficial relationship. As resources dwindle in a given environment, certain segments of the biomass may become dormant or die off, thus giving some surviving organisms a distinct competitive advantage. In an environment depleted of organic residues (energy for saprophytes), parasitic organisms tend to dominate. In fact, some saprophytic organisms may become parasites. Several important turfgrass pathogens exist as saprophytes until conditions prevail that allow this change to occur. If the dominant organisms happen to be plant pathogens, then a microbial imbalance may be manifested as plant diseases. Poor soil and other adverse conditions can cause an organism to change from being saprophytic to pathogenic. Fusarium, for example, is most often a saprophytic fungus that decays organic residues, but it can become a pathogen when it encounters poorly nourished roots. Unfortunately, its reputation is only that of a pest, and it is usually treated with a fungicide, which can deplete or destroy beneficial organisms. Saprophytic organisms are valuable for their production of carbon dioxide, a vital component of a plant's diet.

A rich soil, as its name implies, contains a wealth of resources. Many of us imagine a rich soil to be one that contains an abundance of plant nutrients capable of producing excellent crop yields. The term, however, has a deeper meaning. Resources are in many forms and benefit many aspects of the soil system. Most of them are linked, either directly or indirectly, to one another and to an important soil component—organic matter. Although the percentage of organic matter in a mineral soil is relatively small, the function of this component is responsible for a lion's share of the system's benefits. The proteins, carbohydrates, humic substances, and other compounds that constitute the soil's organic fraction are resources for billions of soil organisms, many of which are disease-suppressive.

Many managers have discovered that the incidence of disease diminishes significantly when the area is biologically enriched with well-aged compost (see Chapter 3). Apparently, the amount and type of organisms living in mature composts are antagonistic to most pathogens. Some biologists believe that many pathogens may revert to a saprophytic existence when an area is enriched with compost, but the reasons may have more to do with plant health than the availability of organic residues. Researchers from Ohio State University, in fact, discovered what they term *compost-induced systemic acquired resistance* (Zhang, W., et al. 1996), which describes a phenomenon that occurs in plants growing in a compost-based potting mix. Their experiment was conducted in containers where half of the plant's roots were separated from the other half by an impermeable wall through the center of a container. The peat-based potting mix on one side of the container was infected with *Pythium ultimum, P. aphanidermatum,* and *Colletotrichum orbiculare*. The other side of the container was filled with either a soil mix, a peat mix, or a compost mix. Apparently, not only did the plant roots growing in the compost show resistance to infection, but so did the rest of the plant. In the other containers, disease symptoms were evident on the roots in both sides of the container and on the aboveground portion of the plants.

Many turf managers have found that soil management practices that encourage the development of organic matter, soil organisms, or both have a similar effect. Researchers believe that plant defensive mechanisms are triggered by organisms in the rhizosphere, and either signals or chemicals are routed through special pathways in the plant. They also believe that systemic acquired resistance can be triggered by pathogens attacking the plant but that the defense mechanism of stressed plants may not initiate an adequate response.

The incidence of organisms is often related to the soil's organic matter content. Organic matter levels are controlled primarily by plant growth and climate. Cultivation practices such as tillage, aeration, irrigation, and liming, however, can accelerate the decomposition process (see Chapter 6). Plants are the main source of raw materials for the formation of organic matter and the main influence on the development of microbial biomass. The roots of plants release into the soil up to 50 percent of the organic compounds produced by photosynthesis, creating an area of intense biological activity around the roots. This activity serves many functions that affect the soil, plant, and atmosphere. Antagonism and competition directed at pest organisms are only two of them.

The Compost Connection

Scientists at Cornell University have done a significant amount of research on the suppression of turf diseases with applications of aged compost (Nelson 1997). They attempted to isolate the bacterium causing the disease suppression but found that many species of microorganisms are responsible. In fact, they discovered that between 65 and 100 percent of microbes found in compost may have disease-suppressive characteristics. This discovery suggests that healthy soils, growing in soil with ample organic matter, are also inherently rich with disease-suppressive organisms.

Cornell's studies were conducted primarily on golf course greens, where the researchers applied as little as 10 pounds of topdressing mix containing as little as 20 percent compost per 1,000 square feet 5 to 7 times per year. They warn, though, that not all composts are created equal, and they suggest that the more effective composts for disease suppression are those aged for two years or more. They also found that yard waste compost is relatively inferior for disease suppression. This is probably because the abundance of cellulose and lignin in yard waste does not support the types of organisms needed for disease suppression. Ten to 15 years of disease suppression studies using compost show, without a doubt, the potential of well-aged compost, made from the proper ingredients, to significantly reduce the severity of many turf diseases that affect both the roots and shoots. The studies also show that the incorporation of high-quality compost into the soil during construction or renovation can provide disease suppression for many years.

Research also shows disease suppression from the use of compost teas, but Cornell's data are incomplete (personal communication). Dr. Eric Nelson and other Cornell researchers formulated compost tea by mixing 1 part mature compost with 5 parts water and allowing it to soak for 3 to 7 days. They then filtered the liquid and sprayed it on plants infected with pythium root rot. The results in the lab were far more encouraging than those in the field, and funding was exhausted before further study could be accomplished. Dr. Nelson felt that better results could have been observed if the team were able to continue with the research, but that using high-quality compost solids instead of the tea would always net better disease control.

Dr. Elaine Ingham of Oregon State University had better results with compost tea, but hers was a much more complex production system that constantly incorporates air into the water so valuable aerobic organisms can proliferate. Her research (and others') demonstrated that compost tea, made correctly from well-aged compost (also made correctly), can be an important tool for turf managers confronting plant diseases (Ingham). Brewers made specifically for the production of aerobic compost tea are available (Earth Tea Brewer, EarthWorks, Ground UP, Growing Solutions, Northwest Irrigation). Testimonials from managers and golf superintendents who have used compost tea from an aerobic brewer have been positive. These turf stewards report the reduction—and, often, the elimination—of fungicide use.

Inoculation

Inoculation with disease-suppressive organisms is a popular practice of many turf managers, but applications must be repeated—frequently—because average soil conditions do not support large enough populations of these microbes to sustain disease suppression for a prolonged period. Additionally, many of the suppressive organisms used are ultraviolet (UV) sensitive and must be applied in the late evening or at night. In fact, a recent study found that natural radiation from sunlight can significantly reduce populations of some organisms colonizing leaf surfaces (Yuen et al. 2002). A wide variety of organisms has been found to be disease suppressive and, although many have been tested—with positive results—few are both EPA registered and commercially available. Inoculants can be applied in dry material, via sprays, mixed with topdressing materials, and through irrigation systems. In fact, brewers that ferment large populations of disease-suppressive strains are commercially available—for example, the BioJect® (EcoSoil Systems). The brewers are connected directly to the field's irrigation system and usually deliver the microbes in the late evening to avoid exposure to UV light (see Figure 5-4).

One of the problems associated with using microbe inoculants is making sure an adequate population is not only delivered to but also sustained in the turf. Commercially available organisms, such as *Trichoderma harzianum*, applied at labeled rates, should provide an adequate population, as will many of the brewers, but distributing them evenly and sustaining adequate populations—a million or more microbes per gram of soil—is significantly more difficult. Soil environments with higher levels of humus and organic residues can sustain greater populations of soil organisms for a longer period, but the conditions necessary to sustain the specific microbes in inoculants are unknown. The fierce competition for resources in the soil favors indigenous organisms, but the diversity of those native groups also changes as environmental conditions vary.

Factors that influence groups of disease-suppressive soil and leaf surface organisms include moisture, temperature, soil conductivity, pH, soil atmosphere, turfgrass variety,

FIGURE 5-4   Brewers like the BioJect® ferment large populations of disease suppressive organisms and deliver them throught the irrigation system. Photo courtesy EcoSoil Systems, Inc.

and organic matter. Introduced inputs such as fertilizers, pesticides, and topdressing material also influence the soil's biota. Research at Oregon State University has shown that different biological environments in the soil are highly influential (Ingham et al. 1989). A fungi-dominated soil, for example, favors a forest environment, and a soil with a population of bacteria slightly larger than that of fungi favors grasses. It is not unreasonable to assume that conditions favoring a balance of bacteria and fungi can also favor disease suppression.

Inoculants found successful at reducing the severity of turfgrass diseases usually contain only one or two species of bacteria or fungi. The list of those organisms tested includes *Acremonium sp., Azospirillum brasiliense, Bacillus subtilis, Enterobacter cloacae, Flavobacterium balustinum, Fusarium heterosporum, Gacumannomyces spp., Gliocladium virens, Lactisaria spp., Phialophora radicicola, Pseudomonas aureofaciens, P. fluorescens, P. lindbergii, P. putida, Rhizoctonia spp., Serratia marcescens, Streptomyces spp., Trichoderma hamatum, T. harzianum, T. polysporum, Typhula phacorrhiza,* and *Xanthamonas maltophilia.* Of those listed, only a few are commercially available as EPA-registered products, but the list grows. Many others are commercially available (with new ones appearing on the market regularly). Although most are effective, some have not been tested thoroughly; it is advisable to contact the nearest land-grant university that conducts turfgrass research for advice. (The EPA web site http://www.epa.gov/pesticides/biopesticides lists all of the registered biopesticides.)

Exciting new research has emerged from the University of Massachusetts about a new antifungal bacterium (accidentally discovered) labeled APM-1. (Torello et al. 1999) This organism produces powerful antifungal toxins that seem to affect most fungal pathogens and can be applied at much greater intervals than the brewed organisms mentioned above. The bacteria can exist in spore form and be delivered on a dry carrier to the turf canopy. The soil rarely has enough nutrients to sustain the growth of this organism, but trials using an organic fertilizer as a carrier are showing positive results. Since spores can remain dormant for prolonged periods, a bagged product can have a shelf life of several years. Preliminary findings show sustained disease control for longer periods after a single application and that plant growth is significantly enhanced. This additional benefit is puzzling to researchers, but they think the bacterium lives endophytically (within the tissue of the plant) and is somehow able to both protect and promote from the inside. The University, along with the New England Turfgrass Foundation, have applied for a patent on this new bacterium; availability may soon be forthcoming.

Biological control of diseases with inoculation is a viable alternative to fungicides. Handling and applying microbes often requires more attention and vigilance than fungicides do, but the microbes don't have the ecological impact of most fungicides. Further, because so many native organisms are able to suppress turf disease to varying degrees, it is logical that developing a resource-rich habitat for them in the soil would serve the turf manager well.

Cultural Practices

Some of our cultural practices may be responsible for altering the system's capacity to defend against diseases. Mowing, for example, is a stressful experience for grass, but mowing with a dull blade significantly increases stress. Turf mowed with a dull blade is often torn rather than cut, and the jagged wound left behind is an ideal place for pathogens to become established. Additionally, the extra stress inflicted on the plant can lower its natural defenses against infection. Rotary mower blades can dull after only 6 to 8 hours of use. On reel mowers, the front face of the bed knife should be sharpened and the reels backlapped every 1 to 2 weeks or more often if topdressing material or fertilizer causes dullness. If a bed knife or reel is nicked, it should be repaired immediately (see Figures 5-5 through 5-7).

Cleaning the reels or the underside of the mower decks is also an important practice. Removing potential inoculum from the mower can check the spread of pathogens and even some insect problems. Problematic areas should always be mowed last. Other stress-producing practices such as improper mowing, excessive traffic of maintenance vehicles, excessive use of pesticides, clipping removal, excessive applications of lime, poor drainage, and improper fertilization (especially with nitrogen) can significantly decrease the turf plant's resistance to many diseases.

FIGURE 5-5A   Damage to grass from dull rotary blades is unsightly and can lead to disease or other problems that may spread elsewhere on the field. Mower blades can loose their edge after only six hours of mowing.

FIGURE 5-5B   Keep spare blades sharp and change them frequently.
Changing blades should only take minutes.

Mowing too short reduces photosynthesis, which takes place in the plant blades.
The synthesis of organic compounds is essential for plant systems to function. Up to
50 percent of these compounds is exuded through the roots into the soil, nourishing
large and diverse populations of organisms. These organisms are capable of, among
many other tasks, disease suppression and the generation of carbon dioxide, a vitally

FIGURE 5-6A   Extensive damage to grass blades from dull rotary blades can stress
turf beyond a tolerable threshold and can lead to disease and other problems.

important nutrient for plants. Mowing at a greater height is always beneficial for grass health, but pressure from coaches can keep the grass short—too short. Generally speaking, the lower the HOC, the higher the risk for disease. Many managers would consider fields mowed at 2 inches as shag, but such fields are much less susceptible to disease. The leaf surface area of most grasses increases by 30 percent for every $\frac{1}{8}$ inch the mower is raised.

Compaction and Aeration

Excessive foot or vehicle traffic can cause soil compaction, which inhibits the movement of water and the exchange of gases between the atmosphere and the soil. This condition reduces the amount of oxygen available to

FIGURE 5-6B   Shredded turf from dull rotary blades is unsightly and unhealthy. Disease pathogens have better opportunities here.

roots and the amount of carbon dioxide available to blades, both of which causes stress to turf plants, decreasing their natural resistance to pathogens. Pythium root rot, summer patch, anthracnose, and other shoot and root pathogens gain an opportunistic advantage with compaction and poor drainage. Once disease organisms become established, traffic serves to spread the problem to other areas. Areas subjected to excessive traffic must be conditioned. The compaction must be relieved, and a program for

FIGURE 5-7   A sharp blade cuts cleanly, uses less fuel, and presents fewer opportunities for pathogen infection.

building soil organic matter should be considered. Topdressing with well-aged, good-quality compost after core aeration is an excellent practice whenever and wherever possible (see Chapter 6, under "Compost," "Compaction," and "Aeration").

Research from Cornell University suggests that core aeration, by itself, offers only temporary relief of compaction problems (Rossi 2000c). Aid from earthworms and soil-aggregating organisms is still needed, and resources such as compost are necessary for their populations to grow. Some fields see more activity than the turf can withstand. Added to tightly scheduled practices and games are often marching band practices, concerts, pep rallies, and other activities that don't allow the turf any recovery time. Practice fields or other open areas may be needed to dilute the wear and tear.

Aeration is an extremely important practice. It reduces compaction caused by foot and vehicle traffic and immediately resuscitates the exchange of gases between the below- and aboveground atmospheres. Oxygen from above can reach the roots, and the turf canopy can absorb carbon dioxide from below. On severely compacted fields, aeration may be analogous to finally getting a breath of air after swimming the entire length of a large pool—underwater. Proper aeration is a necessary cultural practice to control many turfgrass diseases, but timing and frequency are critical. Aeration should always be done when the grass is thriving because, as helpful as it is, aeration still stresses turf. If the turf is already stressed by heat or drought and signs of disease are beginning to appear, aeration can aggravate the problem. Once compaction becomes the cause of severe stress, the logical remedy—aeration—may be too late.

Another counterproductive side effect of aeration, especially core aeration, is the inadvertent depletion of soil organic matter (humus). Oxygen introduced into the soil increases root growth but also increases the oxidation of organic matter. Removal of cores may be a direct evisceration of the some of the best soil on the field. Cores that are collected can be saved and added to a compost pile. Core holes can be filled with a compost/sand topdressing mixture to replenish the loss of organic matter and inoculate the field with disease-suppressive organisms (see Chapter 3).

Stress from Pesticides

The excessive use of pesticides is another factor that can contribute to the severity of turf diseases. The purpose of pesticides is to kill biological entities that are injuring the health or appearance of cultivated plants. Unfortunately, many pesticides do not discriminate sufficiently between pest and beneficial organisms. They can alter the biological system enough to stress the preferred species of plants. Whether the product is a fungicide, herbicide, insecticide, nematicide, or rodenticide, there is evidence that other, nonpest organisms contributing to the well-being of the soil and cultivated plants are affected. The degree to which these biocides are used can impact some of the beneficial functions in the soil or plants, causing stress and presenting opportunities for disease organisms to become established. Researchers at Clemson University and Cornell found that a variety of products designed to control weeds and insects increased the severity of brown patch (Nelson 1995; see Figure 5-8). It is not unreasonable to assume that the pesticide is decreasing the plant's ability to resist infection. It is also likely that stress inflicted by many pesticides might give an advantage to other

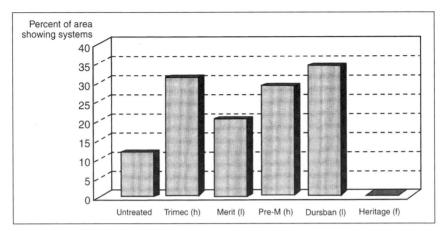

FIGURE 5-8   Pesticide effect on disease severity. Adapted from Nelson, 1995.

pathogens. In fact, some field studies show that diseased plots treated with fungicides had more severe symptoms at the end of the spray interval than did untreated plots.

The vast majority of fungal organisms in the soil function beneficially. They perform such tasks as the decomposition of organic residues and the generation of carbon dioxide—a vital nutrient for photosynthesis. Some, such as mycorrhizae, have symbiotic relationships with plants that offer access to water and nutrients otherwise out of reach from the plants' roots. Others are parasitic or antagonistic to many plant pathogens. Mycorrhiza is a family of beneficial fungi that colonizes plant roots and not only provides nutrients and water for plants but also protects them from root pathogens like pythium. Most fungicides, however, do not discriminate among these organisms and can destroy more beneficial fungi than pathogens. Fungicide is not a logical strategy. Additionally, applications of fungicides rarely kill 100 percent of a disease outbreak. The pathogens that survive may develop resistance to the fungicide, and their offspring will also be resistant.

Nematicides, used to control phytopathogenic nematodes, also kill beneficial nematodes, many of which are vital to plant health or antagonistic or parasitic to fungal pests. The *Labronema* nematode, for example, lives on many fungal organisms, some of which may be pathogens.

A secondary but significant price paid for using certain fungicides is earthworm mortality. The suppression or decimation of earthworm populations from fungicides can eventually cause problems such as thatch buildup, soil compaction, reduced water infiltration, and the reduction of plant vigor. Earthworms are sometimes considered a nuisance by managers because of the casting piles left on the surface of the field. The benefits they provide, however, far outweigh the inconvenience of these castings, which can be easily dispatched (see Chapter 6, under "Earthworms").

Clippings Management

Plant pathologists recommend removing the clippings from diseased areas pathogens are not spread into other areas, but research suggests that leaving heal.

clippings behind can suppress many disease organisms (Dest 1992, 1995). Apparently, some of the organisms that decompose clippings are antagonistic to many plant pathogens. Additionally, the recycling of nutrients and organic matter back to the soil promotes the growth of healthier plants that are better equipped to defend themselves against diseases. Pathogens can be spread by foot and vehicle traffic, mowers, wind, irrigation, and even by birds and insects. The key defense is a soil rich in microbial life and stalwart plants capable of suppressing pathogen infection. If fields are mowed early in the morning when the grass is normally wet from dew, clippings may have to be collected, or they can form clumps. If late afternoon mowing can be arranged, the dry clippings can often be left behind without causing problems for players.

Researchers at the University of Kentucky found that early morning mowing was the single most effective cultural control of dollar spot. The removal of dew and the guttation fluid attached to clippings as early as possible reduced dollar spot infection and severity significantly more than the control or other cultural practices (Williams and Powell 1995). However, a golf course superintendent in New Hampshire reported a discernable decrease in the incidence and severity of disease when his greens were mowed in the late afternoon and the clippings were left behind (personal communication). *Note:* Mowing severely heat-stressed plants is never a good idea. If the clippings must be collected, their final destination should be the compost pile so that, eventually, the compost can be returned to the field for its disease-suppressive characteristics (see Chapter 3).

pH

Proper pH and nutrient balance can also play a major role in the management of diseases. Stress associated with nutrient deficiencies or incorrect pH can make the difference between a turf that resists infection and one that does not. Annually testing the soil, leaf tissue, or both is an excellent way to monitor the balance of nutrients in the soil and plant (see Chapter 4). Proper fertility is essential for a healthy, disease-resistant stand of turf. Disease resistance depends on an adequate supply of all essential nutrients. Excessive applications of nutrients or lime, however, can be as detrimental to plants as deficiencies are. Time should never be the criterion for applying lime—only a pH test. Different soils have different capabilities to hold nutrients, and the optimal capacity of one soil may be twice that of another. These holding capacities are usually measured and considered by soil testing laboratories making fertility recommendations. Exceeding those recommendations can cause as many problems as (or more problems than) not applying enough. Attention to the calcium:magnesium ratio in the soil analysis may also increase disease resistance. Many manager and agronomists believe that ratios lower than 7:1 can make soils more prone to compaction and, subsequently, to disease as well. If a soil analysis indicates a low calcium:magnesium ratio but lime is recommended, dolomitic lime should be avoided (see Chapter 4, under "pH").

Some turf diseases are sensitive to a high or a low soil pH, and some scientists suggest raising or lowering the pH on fields that are prone to infection by these acid- or alkaline-intolerant pathogens. Unfortunately, other organisms—including turf plants—may also be sensitive to changes in pH, and many of those organisms may be beneficial, perhaps even disease suppressive. A lower pH generally inhibits bacteria but has little effect on fungal organisms. Bacteria typically antagonize pathogens more than any other group of soil organisms. Optimum pH for turf and soil organisms is logically the best for disease suppression. Healthy plants and a balanced biomass yield the strongest defenses against disease. In a naturally alkaline soil, it may not be practical to lower the pH. The amount of sulfur or other acidifying material needed to reduce the pH to an optimum level can cause more problems than it solves. Fields where calcareous sand has been applied year after year may have pH anomalies that cannot be completely corrected (see Chapter 4, under "Too Alkaline?").

Diseases that are more successful where fertility or pH is either inadequate or excessive include Rhizoctonia diseases (brown patch), Pythium diseases, Bermuda grass decline, Leptospaeria spring dead spot, Curvularia, dollar spot, zoysia rust, Bipolaris leaf blotch, yellow patch (winter patch), Fusarium, take-all patch, summer patch, necrotic ring spot, snow molds, snow scald, red thread, pink patch, anthracnose, brown blight, melting out, powdery mildew, rust diseases, stripe smut, downy mildew, gray leaf spot, fairy ring, and virus diseases.

Nutrient Management

Proper nitrogen management is especially important. Too much or too little nitrogen encourages the vast majority of the diseases mentioned in the preceding section. The plant's use of nitrogen varies because of many factors including soil texture, organic matter (quantity and quality), precipitation (or irrigation), soil and air temperature, turf variety, root mass, clipping management, cultural practices (HOC, verticutting, aeration, topdressing), solar exposure, and the type of nitrogen applied. Even if best-guess nitrogen recommendations were correct, they don't take into account these conditions. Considering the multiple factors that influence turf's assimilation of nitrogen is important if the turf manager wants to control diseases with less or no fungicides. Controlling diseases this is also extremely difficult. Biological management of nitrogen can be a much more efficient method of regulating its availability to turf plants (see Chapter 2, under "Nitrogen").

Dr. Gail Schumann of the University of Massachusetts produced a chart (see Table 5-1) outlining cultural controls of specific turf diseases. Seventy five percent of the recommendations involve either increasing or decreasing soil fertility. The chart suggests that too much or too little soil fertility can encourage plant pathogens. Common sense dictates that optimum soil fertility cannot be improved upon, but achieving this ideal is nearly impossible. Too many variables affect the availability of and the plant's need for nutrients. On ecologically maintained sports fields, most nutrients are applied in a form that is unavailable to plant roots. The release of these nutrients is facilitated by biological activity in the soil, regulated by many environmental conditions such as climate and soil moisture. Coincidentally, the conditions that encourage this activity also encourage the growth of plants. This natural coincidence synchronizes the availability of nutrients from natural organic and natural inorganic sources with plant need and very often regulates the release of those nutrients for optimum plant utilization. In addition, the biological activity stimulated by organic resources can compete with, antagonize, or parasitize many turf pathogens. Where Schumann suggests lowering pH, it's important to note that in some instances this is not only impractica, but nearly impossible (see Chapter 2, under "Sulfer," and Chapter 4, under "Too Alkaline?").

TABLE 5-1
Cultural Controls For Certain Turfgrass Diseases

Anthracnose	Fertilize; aerate; raise HOC; reduce water on leaf blades.
Brown patch (rhizoctonia blight)	Avoid excess nitrogen and water; minimize leaf wetness time.
Dollar spot	Fertilize; aerate; minimize leaf wetness time; use resistant cultivars.
Fairy ring	Core and water; mask symptoms with N or iron; in severe cases, remove soil.
Fusarium leaf blight, crown and root rot	Avoid drought; minimize leaf wetness time; reduce thatch.
Leaf spot melting out	Avoid excess nitrogen and water; minimize leaf wetness time; raise HOC; use resistant cultivars.
Necrotic ring spot	Avoid water and fertility stress; aerate; reduce thatch; use resistant cultivars.
Powdery mildew	Improve air flow; reduce shade; avoid excess nitrogen.
Pythium blight	Avoid excess nitrogen; improve drainage; don't irrigate at night or mow in wet weather.
Pythium root rot	Improve drainage; aerate; raise HOC.
Red thread/pink patch	Fertilize; avoid low pH; minimize leaf wetness time; use resistant cultivars.
Rust	Fertilize; aerate; avoid water stress; minimize leaf wetness time; use resistant cultivars.
Slime molds	Minimize leaf wetness time; hose or rake away mold.
Snow molds	
Typhula blight (gray snow mold) Fusarium patch	Let turf go dormant; mow until growth stops; minimize snow cover time.
Stripe smut	Purchase smut-free seed; avoid excess nitrogen in spring; avoid water stress in summer; use resistant cultivars.
Summer patch	Raise HOC; lower pH if possible (see also Necrotic ring spot).
Take-all patch	Improve drainage; lower pH if possible; raise HOC; avoid phosphorus and potassium deficiency; avoid using lime.
Yellow patch	Minimize leaf wetness time; avoid excess nitrogen; reduce thatch.
Yellow tuft	Avoid excess nitrogen; minimize leaf wetness time; improve drainage; mask symptoms with iron.

Adapted from Schumann, May 1994

Research suggests that trace elements may play a role in a plant's susceptibility to infection. If plants cannot absorb all the nutrients they need, regardless of how obscure each may be, it is logical that they cannot achieve optimum health, strength, and resistance to infection. A soil test may show the availability of trace elements, but it is difficult without a leaf tissue analysis to determine if adequate levels are reaching the plant (see Chapter 4, under "Micronutrients" and "Leaf Tissue Analysis"). The assimilation of nutrients into the plant often depends on the balance of those nutrients in the soil, the pH, and the level of biological activity. Natural acids and enzymes created by soil organisms free trace element ions from parent material or other insoluble sources; the ions can then be absorbed by plants. The optimum pH for trace element availability is ~6.5. In some cases, a pathogen may cause a trace element deficiency resulting in a better opportunity for infection. The organism that causes take-all patch, for example, metabolizes manganese from the soil, which reduces the amount available to the plant. This deficiency can weaken the plant's resistance to the disease. Supplemental applications of manganese during take-all attack can reduce its severity.

As mentioned earlier, research has shown that optimum fertility, especially with regard to nitrogen, can aid in the natural suppression of turf diseases. Natural organic nitrogen may be better suited than conventional nitrogen fertilizer for this task because of its slow release properties and because it encourages the growth of microbe populations that can ultimately compete with, parasitize, or antagonize plant pathogens. Populations of saprophytic organisms that generate carbon dioxide for plants and of hormone-producing organisms that help plants resist stress are also encouraged. Clippings contain more than half of the nitrogen applied to turf, and probably in the ideal form. If it is impractical to leave clippings behind, then they can be saved, composted, and eventually returned to the turf during topdressing procedures.

Heat and Drought Stress

Stress seems to be the common denominator when diseases (and other pests) are being discussed. Simple practices that can reduce stress—even a little—can often accomplish significant gains in damage control. A researcher at Michigan State University found that light watering of approximately $1/10$ inch (an average of ~10 minutes of irrigation) each very hot afternoon suppressed most turfgrass diseases (Vargas 1994). The research suggests that stress is involved in the establishment of an infection and that mitigating stress by lowering the soil and plant temperatures can ameliorate conditions to the point where natural plant resistance is able to prevent or mitigate infection. The research also found that insect, weed, and thatch problems were suppressed in the treated plots. Fields with irrigation may be able to control many turfgrass pests with about $1/10$ inch of water in the mid- to late afternoon throughout the heat and drought season. This stress relief does not necessarily replace normal irrigation programs; its main purpose is to cool the plant and the soil surface.

Heat and drought take their toll on turfgrass. Both inflict a tremendous amount of stress and often result in weaker plants that are less able to defend themselves against disease. Many of the most damaging turf pathogens gain significantly better opportunities for infection when the temperature rises. Surprisingly, high air temperature is not as much of a problem as high soil temperature. Turf roots growing in warm soil (60°–70°F) can mediate the leaf response to 100°F (38°C) air temperature. However, if the soil is 100°F, turf roots are often damaged, and no matter how cool the air is, grass quality will decline. This may be part of the reason why light, frequent irrigation during the hottest part of the day can relieve stress and mitigate infection. Not only does it cool down the plant but also the combination of the water temperature and the cooling effect of evaporation reduces soil surface temperature.

In hot soils, root growth is inhibited and transpiration is reduced. This in turn affects the water balance between the roots and tops of turf plants. High air temperature also increases the demand for water uptake by the plant's roots at the same time that high soil temperature reduces the roots' ability to do so. Consequently, the plant becomes stressed. In hot soil, carbohydrate production also is decreased. The plant uses carbohydrates to produce materials that bind water, protect important proteins, and increase overall stress tolerance.

High temperatures reduce photosynthesis (energy production) but increase respiration (energy consumption), resulting in a negative energy balance. The longer the plant consumes more energy than it creates, the weaker and more susceptible it is to pathogen infection.

Fortunately, the turf manager has several ways of mitigating high soil temperature:

1. Raise the height of cut. Turf mowed higher has deeper roots and more root mass, and it consumes less energy. Additionally, cutting higher creates a denser canopy, shading the soil. This not only reduces soil temperature but also decreases the amount of moisture evaporated from its surface.

2. Precondition turf in anticipation of drought. Studies indicate that turf can be conditioned to be more tolerant of drought. Exposing plants to mild drought conditions at low ambient (soil and air) temperatures triggers deeper root growth and more diffusive branching, resulting in better access to water when high heat conditions occur. Infrequent irrigation during cooler periods (i.e., spring and fall) encourages deeper roots and prepares turf for the hot, dry season.

3. Reduce nitrogen use. Many studies have shown that the more nitrogen (beyond optimum) applied to turf, the less root mass is produced. In fact, some studies have found that the roots of unfertilized turf plots were significantly deeper than the roots in fertilized plots (Hull 1996). Plants growing in soils with slight nitrogen deficiencies grow deep roots in search of nitrogen. More root hairs are created, and the efficiency at which nitrogen is used increases dramatically. This is not to say that nitrogen should not be used on turf, only that it should not be applied in excess. High concentrations of nitrogen in the soil slow and sometimes arrest turf root development, especially when applied in early spring. Excess nitrogen also reduces the amount of carbohydrate reserve in the root system and changes the balance of natural hormones that regulate photosynthesis, respiration, and the

production of antioxidants. High levels of nitrogen significantly reduce the plant's heat and drought tolerance.

At the same time all of this is going on under the soil's surface, shoot growth is increased, placing an even greater demand on roots for water. Plant tops become more succulent and have thinner cell walls that can be penetrated more easily by pathogens. Some studies show that varying levels of nitrogen have different effects on different cultivars of grass (Vargas 1994). High levels of nitrogen, for example, caused brown patch suppression in ryegrass, but the opposite was true with tall fescue. Other studies show that some diseases such as Bipolaris and Drechslera leaf spot, Pythium diseases, stripe smut, summer patch, and pink and gray snow molds are favored by higher applications rates of nitrogen and that others, such as stem and crown rusts, anthracnose, red thread, and dollar spot, are suppressed (Tani 1997). Prescribing a set amount of nitrogen for every cultivar growing in every situation is not advisable; it is, however, much easier to apply more nitrogen where needed than removing some where too much is applied. There are two schools of thought regarding the dormant feeding of nitrogen. Some experts believe the best time to apply nitrogen is late fall, after the turf has reached dormancy. They believe dormant feeding favors root growth, which, in turn, increases photosynthesis and the storage of carbohydrates for the following spring. Others feel that applying nitrogen late in the fall increases the likelihood of winter diseases such as pink and gray snow mold and pythium snow blight. Where snow mold is a perpetual problem, dormant feeding may not be appropriate.

4. Irrigate lightly and frequently during hot, dry periods. About $1/10$ inch of irrigation significantly reduces the temperature of both the plant and the soil's surface. Subsequent evaporation provides further cooling to leaf and soil surfaces. Some managers monitor soil temperatures and syringe only when the temperature is elevated beyond a certain point (see Figure 5-9).

5. Apply seaweed extracts. The natural hormones in seaweed help plants produce more antioxidants, which reduce stress and sustain a balance between photosynthesis and respiration.

6. Leave clippings behind when mowing. These organic residues are food for earthworms, and their ability to aerate soil is powers of 10 better than any mechanical system. An acre of rich soil can be home to as many as 500,000 earthworms creating as much as 250 miles of tunnels per week. These tunnels are glued together with earthworm excretions, which are rich in hormones that help plants resist heat and drought stress. There is a linear

FIGURE 5-9   A pocket soil thermometer can monitor the potential of stress from high soil temperatures. Photo courtesy Spectrum Technologies, Inc.

relationship between the number of earthworms living in the soil and the amount and speed of water absorption into the soil.

7. Increase mowing frequency, but cut no more than one-third of the plant's height. Frequent mowing encourages deeper and more diffusive roots that have better access to soil moisture.

8. Avoid using herbicides, which can inhibit the vigor of turf roots.

9. Encourage biological activity. Humus produced by soil organisms holds more water and stimulates plants to produce finer root hairs. The increased surface area on these roots has greater access to soil moisture.

Drainage and Air Movement

Drainage is an important consideration for disease management, one that is usually addressed when the field is constructed. Consequently, copious amounts of sand are often used to provide what some designers believe to be a healthy soil environment. Unfortunately, this soil environment cannot support a large and diverse population of soil organisms that others believe is an essential component of a healthy soil. The point is moot. Using a rototiller on fields just to incorporate organic matter is not being suggested. On the other hand, switching from sand (or mostly sand) as a top-dressing material to something a little more enriching might prove worthwhile. Using mixes of sand with 10 to 40 percent topsoil is a common procedure, but questions like where the topsoil came from; what the soil analysis showed; how much organic matter it contained; and how biologically active it was it cannot be easily answered. And what about sand? What is being accomplished with layer upon layer of sand? Thatch reduction? Maybe. A truer, harder surface? Perhaps, but at what cost? The surface created by sand topdressing is admittedly smoother—but not so much smoother that it is worth sacrificing the natural, biological protection offered by well-aged compost. Many managers believe that drainage must be preserved at all costs or disease will prevail—but maybe not. Drainage is good to have, but not at the expense of everything else that functions in a healthy soil. Substituting well-made, well-aged compost for some of the sand and most of the topsoil is a compromise that will feed a broad diversity of disease-suppressive organisms without jeopardizing drainage. A golf course superintendent in New Hampshire has been using a 50 percent sand, 50 percent compost topdressing mix since 1965, and drainage has never been a problem (Sachs and Luff, 2002).

Dyed-in-the-wool sand users may want to consider another handicap. A new disease called *Ophiospharella agrostis* is spreading across the country . This extremely pernicious pathogen attacks both warm- and cool-season grasses but only appears on turf growing in soil with a high sand content. *O. agrostis* develops in warm weather and is most commonly found in open, sunny areas. The disease initially looks like a golf ball mark but as its size increases, it takes on a copper color and has some characteristics of pink snow mold or Fusarium patch. Dead spots have different shapes, which makes diagnosis more difficult. The disease leaves crater spots in the field that take a long time to recover because the pathogen kills the stolons before they can fill in. Fruiting bodies can shoot spores 5 to 6 inches into the air; these can then be carried by wind or water. Spores can germinate in one hour in the presence of light and leaf tissue. Damage can begin in less than two hours, and the pathogen can infect both leaves and roots. No resistant cultivars have been found, but some recover faster than others do. Turf growing in soil—not sand— seems to be unaffected by this pathogen.

The importance of good drainage underscores the danger of having a wet environment for a prolonged period. The longer turf leaves and the soil surface remains wet, especially in hot, humid weather, the greater the opportunity for pathogen infection. Good air movement is as important as good drainage. Air moving over the grass leaves evaporates moisture and cools their surfaces. Some managers resort to using mechanical devices such as fans or blowers to improve air movement over problem areas. Research has shown that ten or more consecutive hours of leaf wetness can be conducive to disease development such as brown patch and dollar spot (Williams and Powell 1995, Tani and Beard 1997, Vargas 1994, Dernoeden 2000).

Air movement is most often dictated by Mother Nature, but the manager can take steps to improve the hand she deals us. First, note the prevailing winds. From what direction do they normally originate? Are there any natural windbreaks such as trees or hedges between the field(s) and the direction from which the wind blows? If yes, thinning may be in order. If a building or some other solid structure is blocking air movement to an area prone to diseases encouraged by prolonged moisture, mechanical air movement might be a viable option during hot, humid periods.

If overseeding is a regular practice, it might be a good idea to take a look at the turf's density. It's common knowledge that a thick, healthy stand of turf is the first line of defense against weeds—but, taken to its logical extreme, this desirable condition can create problems too. A stand dense enough to it inhibit air movement may increase the likelihood of disease infection. Fields grown on soil enriched with compost or high-quality organic fertilizers may, on rare occasions, grow too thick. Thinning may be advisable before the hot, humid days arrive.

Another side effect of deliberate overseeding is the increased likelihood of Pythium disease. Pythium spores sense the chemicals released by germinating seeds. These chemicals act like an alarm clock that wakes up dormant Pythium spores and tells them it's time to go to work. The more seeds are germinating at once, the louder the alarm. In a biologically active soil system, competition for these chemicals is fierce, which reduces the amount available for Pythium spores, but planting seed too heavily can make it difficult for natural biological controls to prevail. Turf seeds inoculated with appropriate varieties of mycorrhizae are often protected from pythium infection. The mycorrhizal organisms coat the plant's roots and leave little opportunity for the pathogen to become established.

Detection

Early detection of turfgrass diseases is as valuable to turf health as early detection of cancer or heart disease is to human health, but it is difficult for a manager to scrutinize large areas daily. Ground crewmembers, however, can be trained to recognize the signs of disease outbreak. It's not important that they be able to identify the pathogen or its stage of growth—only that they be on the lookout for mycelium, discoloration (especially in circular patches), and any other abnormalities. If every member of the crew were required to carry a small notepad and pen, they could record where and when they observed the symptom and report it to the supervisor promptly. Incentives could be offered to heighten their vigilance. Treatment at early stages of development is usually more effective than at later stages, and the disease can often be controlled with less fungicide. Treatments with well-aged compost or compost tea are also more effective at earlier stages of disease development.

Even under the best management practices, some turfgrass loss can occur during prolonged periods of stress. Treatments to the entire field in hopes of preventing a relatively minuscule loss are economically and ecologically impractical. Small losses, especially in problem areas, present opportunities to incorporate disease-suppressive compost during renovation. Sometimes it is prudent to give nature an opportunity to resolve the problem on her own before intervening. Often, a combination of natural factors, such as weather changes, will enable turf to quickly repair itself. If overseeding becomes necessary, an application of seaweed extract can hasten the establishment of new seed or sod and also reduce the plants' susceptibility to infection. This relatively brief inconvenience to players, coaches, and fans can provide long-term benefits to the turf and turf manager.

WEEDS

Weeds are often the biggest problem on sports fields because athletic activities often wear or tear turf away from the soil, leaving opportunities for weeds to become established. Sports like football and rugby probably cause the most damage because the players often struggle directly against each other. The turf underneath their cleated shoes endures as much force as the opponent against whom they are pushing. The center of the field is typically the most worn from football games. When games are played during wet conditions, most of the field can easily be destroyed. Soccer fields see most damage in front of the goals, where struggles for position are most intense. Soccer players do not push against each other as often or aggressively as football players do; the damage to turf comes more from quick changes in direction, stops, and starts. Each time the soil is exposed from athletic wear or tear, the opportunity for weeds is presented (see Figure 5-10).

Weeds are plants—often plants with value—that are in the wrong place. In a natural, uncultivated setting there are no weeds. Ralph Waldo Emerson wrote that a weed is "a plant whose virtues have not yet been discovered." The natural tendency of plants is to use every available space on the soil's surface. If sun, water, and nutrients are available in a space where little or no competition for those resources exists, then there will soon be a thriving plant. Nature provides this opportunity to protect the soil from erosion and to provide the cooling and moisture preserving effects of shade. Many so-called weeds are cultivated and sold as valuable plants for different locations. An expensive installation of ground cover becomes a weed at the garden's border. Perennials that propagate underground and spread into turf become weeds no matter how rare or beautiful they are.

FIGURE 5-10   Soccer fields often see significant damage in front of the goals where struggles for position intensify the most.

What makes a plant a weed is the intolerance of the coach, the turf manager, the school board, or fans. Most weeds cannot survive constant and low mowing, so relatively few invade turf and significantly fewer that can actually interfere with the game. The problems created by weeds are more aesthetic than they are disruptive to the game. An old tree with limbs hanging over the fence in the corner of right field can influence the course of a well hit baseball significantly more than a dandelion, but few people would consider the politically incorrect action of using herbicide on the tree (or cutting it down) because the tree has aesthetic value—whereas the dandelion does not. Depending on the tolerance level of the turf manager, coaches, school board, or just someone who can make a lot of noise, weeds may be much more difficult to control without pesticides than diseases or insects. Zero tolerance on weeds is a tough stance even with an arsenal of herbicides. Part of developing an ecological maintenance program may be learning to live with a few weeds.

Most weeds play an important role in the broad scheme of things. Dandelions, for example, are beneficial plants. Their deep roots return leached nutrients to the surface and are large producers of organic matter. Earthworm populations thrive in their vicinity, and the plant does not compete with turf for consequential amounts of nutrients, water, or light. Clover is another beneficial plant that has gained undeserved notoriety. Clover is a legume that can fix free nitrogen from the atmosphere and share it with turfgrass. Clover roots are extensive and contribute a significant amount of resources to soil organisms. These plants are also extremely drought resistant and can stay green long after turfgrass has gone dormant. Unfortunately, an abundant canopy of clover can be slippery when it is wet; depending on the sport, that may pose a safety problem.

Poa annua (annual bluegrass) is a problem weed for many managers. It doesn't wear well, but stands of *Poa*, especially where its coverage is expanding, may be a sign of poor drainage, overirrigation, too low a height of cut, or excess nitrogen. Nitrogen applied at inappropriate times of the season can also cause weed problems. If nitrogen is applied soon after annual weed seeds germinate, those plants will be able to compete more aggressively with turf. On the other hand, nitrogen applied before annual weed seed germination can help develop a dense canopy that blocks the sunlight crucial to the survival of weed seedlings.

There are two subspecies of *Poa*, the annual variety (*Poa annua ssp. annua*) and a perennial variety (*Poa annua ssp. reptans*). Differences between the two include root system, growth patterns, seed production, and life cycle. The annual variety has a shallow root system, grows erect, produces seed heads in May and June, and has only one life cycle per season. The perennial variety has a strong, fibrous root system, grows prostrate, produces seed several times per season, has a life cycle that can last several seasons, and is more difficult to control. Some managers have successfully controlled *Poa annua ssp. annua* by allowing the affected field to go dormant for a short period during the hot summer months. Cool-season grasses recover from a brief period of dormancy, but the annual variety of *Poa* almost always dies off. Unfortunately, if *Poa* occupies a conspicuous percentage of the field, the result of this strategy is more unsightly than the weed. *Poa annua ssp. reptans* cannot be controlled in the same way. Conditions that favor *Poa* over other grasses include compaction, excess nitrogen, low height of cut, uncollected clippings, and excessive irrigation. The lower the manager must mow the fields, the more likely he will have a problem with *Poa*.

Diversity

Evidence is strong that the incidence of insect predators, parasites, and antagonists increases where plant diversity is greater. Some weeds act as bait plants, drawing herbivorous pests away from turf. Plant diversity is an important ecological strategy. Depending on only one species of plant to survive and thrive in a given area is too high a risk for Mother Nature. The diversity of a natural setting not only provides better survivability but also creates a habitat for a more balanced ecosystem. Only one variety of plant in a given habitat can limit the diversity of other organisms, which may also limit the natural protections they offer.

In terms of weed control, a diverse mixture of grasses is often more competitive than a single cultivar and variety would be. If grasses are to dominate an area without the use of herbicides, they must adapt well to environmental conditions. Given the diversity of conditions that exists in most settings, a successful strategy may be to cultivate a diversity of grasses so at least one or two cultivars will thrive if others fail. A diverse combination of turf cultivars and varieties is often a reliable strategy for maintaining a dense sod in spite of nature's unpredictable conditions.

Whenever a cultivated plant does not adapt well to existing conditions, Mother Nature provides a substitute. Unfortunately, the plant she chooses is often not acceptable to the turf manager. Diversity on the football or soccer field is easier to tolerate than on bowling greens or croquet courts. However, researchers recently found that a mix of bent grass varieties has better resilience in the face of stressful conditions (Leslie 1994).

Insects, Pathogens, and Weeds: Contemplating the Unforeseen

Soil conditions have a profound effect on the strength and competitive abilities of turf. Many weeds that exist in turf are a result of poor soil conditions, such as compaction, infertility, improper pH, and excessive porosity, that do not favor the preferred turf cultivars. Intervention at the soil level can often provide a solution that is not only effective but long-lasting as well. Many agronomists have observed that the proper balance between calcium and magnesium can significantly reduce the need for herbicides. The relationship between this balance and the rollback of weeds is not well understood, but balanced fertility offers both plants and support organisms optimum conditions for competitive performance. Observations indicate that soils with a low calcium-to-magnesium ratio (below 7:1) are more prone to compaction, which favors weeds that can tolerate heavier soil density (see Chapter 4, under "Cation Corrections").

Herbicides may eradicate weeds, but they do not change the conditions that gave the weeds their competitive edge. Additionally, some herbicides can increase pest insect activity by suppressing predators, stressing plants, or both. Research from Cornell University shows that applications of certain herbicides can also increase the severity of some disease symptoms (Nelson 1995).

An increase in populations of herbivorous insects can stress turf to the point where weeds are more easily established. Researchers discovered that all living things give off radiation in specific wavelengths (Callahan 1975). When flawed conditions cause problems for plants, those wavelengths are altered and may act as signals to herbivorous insects. The insects can, in turn, create conditions that favor one species of plant over another. In a situation where turf is subclinically ill (i.e., plants that have a health problem but are not as yet showing symptoms), the plants' altered wavelengths may attract insects that then cause further stress to the turf. Insect activity can suppress the health and vigor of turf and favor the establishment of weeds. This phenomenon can be a double-edged sword. Weeds that are subclinically ill due to the unyielding competition from healthy turf may signal insects to act as a selective biological herbicide. The general message nature gives us is to strengthen the preferred species rather than weaken the unwanted. Mowing with a dull blade, for example, may exert just enough stress on a stand of turf to trigger a disease or insect problem that could eventually create the ideal setting for weed infestation.

The unforeseen circumstances that thin out an area of turf are sometimes unavoidable. Vigilant attention to injured areas, however, can mitigate problems without resorting to herbicides. If these areas are prepped for new seed as soon as possible, weeds may not have time to encroach. Plant and weed residues should be removed to avoid the possible production of allelopathic chemicals that could inhibit the germination of new seed. Some managers create a mixture of seed and aged compost, which they rake and tamp into injured areas. This method is successful; however, compost that is not well cured can have a high salt level, which may kill germinating seeds. If one employs this method, it is a good idea to have a maturity test performed on the compost before use (see Chapter 3, under "Analysis"). Generally, a conductivity value above 4 millimhos per centimeter (0.4 siemens per meter) is too salty for seed.

If all else fails and herbicide use becomes necessary, it is wise to investigate the tolerance of different species of grasses to the product you intend to use. If the herbicide will weaken the turf you are trying to protect, then the overarching goal of the product is defeated. In addition to weakening the turf, every herbicide ever tested has effects on nontarget organisms. Qualifying or quantifying these effects is difficult in light of the other factors that influence the diversity and quantity of soil and leaf surface organisms. Tests indicate, however, that natural disease and insect suppression is often inhibited after one or more applications of certain herbicides. Healthy populations of soil organisms are responsible for numerous other benefits that indirectly affect weed growth. These benefits generally favor the turf, which can then be more competitive and successful. Soluble seaweed extract, humic extracts, or a combination of both can be applied with most herbicides to mitigate the impact the chemical might have on turf and soil organisms. These materials complement the application of just about any pesticide—but a physical compatibility test is always recommended first.

Weeds Versus Height of Cut

Often, effective weed control in turf is as simple as raising the height of cut. This action makes the turf more competitive because it can use the sun's energy for itself and block it from fueling unwanted species of plants. For every $1/8$ inch a mower is raised there is a 30 percent increase in leaf surface area. That increase causes a relative increase in photosynthesis, which feeds a larger and healthier root system and a larger, healthier population of organisms in the rhizosphere. The lateral roots (rhizomes) of some turf varieties often develop new plants that thicken the stand, providing even more competition.

Spring is an important time to mow higher, as the plant is in its reproductive stage and creating new tillers, stolons and rhizomes. Raising the height of cut in the spring can help control weeds all season long. Turf roots can produce allelopathic chemicals capable of suppressing weed seed germination. The more diffusive and massive the root system, the more allelochemicals can be produced. Additionally, the lush growth typically observed in spring is the plants' way of processing nutrients into proteins, carbohydrates, and other compounds via photosynthesis. Mowing at an extremely low height of cut inhibits this process and can lead to a host of problems.

Height-of-cut experiments have demonstrated that grass mowed higher can suppress many weeds, including crabgrass, annual bluegrass, goosegrass, and dandelions (Dernoeden et al. 1993). It is obviously impractical to mow at heights that impede games. On the other hand, mowing stressed turf at an unreasonably low height of cut is an open invitation for weeds, especially annual bluegrass.

Mowing lower can be a useful strategy for controlling some already established annual weeds, but timing is important. The height of cut must be lowered and the clippings collected when seed heads have formed but the seeds are still attached. If timed correctly, the amount of viable seed can be significantly reduced—but the height of cut should not be lowered too much. Stressing the turf by cutting too low can give other weeds a distinct advantage. Weeds effectively controlled with this strategy include annual bluegrass, crabgrass, goosegrass, foxtail, barnyardgrass, fall panicum, and dallisgrass. A single weed plant can produce from 1,000 to 500,000 seeds. Under the right conditions, many of those seeds can become more seed producers.

Weed Identity

Identifying weeds is as important as recognizing insect pests and plant pathogens, especially if the plan is to use herbicides. Conventional controls work best if they are treating the pest for which they were designed. Identity is also important because certain weeds thrive under certain conditions. For example, crabgrass seems to like sandy, well-drained soil that can send cultivated grasses into early dormancy. Dandelions can indicate soil compaction, low pH, or both. Paying attention to the stories weeds tell is a valuable approach to controlling them, but, in a situation where many weeds are telling many stories, cultural controls may be difficult to prescribe. If symptoms such as weeds are indicating problems with soil fertility, then a soil test may be an easier way to pinpoint those problems (see Chapter 4). Soil tests, however, do not expose physical problems such as compaction, drought, and excessive moisture. Some of these conditions could be recognized while drawing samples from the area. Most labs do not test for available nitrogen unless asked specifically, so a soil analysis may not indicate a condition of excessive nitrogen—but a leaf tissue analysis would. When a human patient exhibits classic symptoms of a certain condition, a doctor nevertheless performs a test to confirm the condition before prescribing medication. In turf, weeds may be indicating a specific condition such as infertility or incorrect pH, but a soil test, leaf tissue analysis, or both can confirm the diagnosis.

It is helpful to understand weeds and in what conditions they thrive (see Table 5-2), but it is more important to analyze the soil as a first step in developing a weed control plan (see Chapter 4). Biological respiration and bioassay tests are other tools that can help the grounds manager grow stronger, more competitive turf. The balance of soil organisms is as important to turf performance as the correct balance of soil nutrients. One lab worth mentioning that performs bioassay tests and makes recommendations to establish and maintain optimum balances of organisms on sports fields is Soil Food Web (SFI), which has laboratories in Oregon, New York, Australia, New Zealand, and Holland (see Sources and Resources).

Much has been published over the years that identifies various conditions in which certain weeds tend to thrive. This information may help us figure out what is causing a weed problem. It makes sense, however, to look first at the conditions in which the *desired* species of grasses thrive, because optimal conditions for turf will do more to limit weed invasion than will anything else. Balanced fertility, correct pH, good soil structure and porosity, ample amounts of organic matter, adequate level and balance of biological activity, and proper maintenance procedures are the factors that influence the aggressive nature of turf. If all of these conditions are addressed and there is

TABLE 5-2
Common Conditions That Promote Certain Weeds

Weed	Conditions
Algae	Excessive surface moisture
Annual bluegrass	Excessive surface moisture; compaction; mowed too low; high nitrogen
Barnyardgrass	Poor drainage
Birdsfoot trefoil	Drought conditions; low nitrogen
Black medic	Drought conditions; low nitrogen
Broadleaf plantain	High pH; compaction
Buttercups	Poor drainage
Chickweeds	Mowed too low
Cinquefoil species	Drought conditions; excessive surface moisture; low pH; general low fertility
Clover species	Low nitrogen
Coltsfoot	Poor drainage; low pH
Common chickweed	Too shady
Common mullein	Low pH; general low fertility
Corn chamomile	Poor drainage; high pH
Corn speedwell	Compaction
Crabgrass	Drought conditions
Creeping bentgrass	Poor drainage; excessive surface moisture; mowed too low
Creeping speedwell	Too shady
Creeping thyme	High pH
Curly dock	Drought conditions
Docks	Poor drainage; low pH
English daisy	Low pH
Foxtail species	General low fertility
Goosegrass	Drought conditions; compaction
Hawkweeds	Low pH; general low fertility
Henbit	General low fertility
Hop clover	High pH
Knawel	Low pH
Lady's thumb	Poor drainage; low pH
Leafy spurge	Drought conditions
Mallow	General low fertility
Moss	Excessive surface moisture; mowed too low; too shady
Mouse-ear chickweed	Too shady
Nutsedge	Poor drainage
Pigweed	Drought conditions
Pineapple weed	Compaction
Plantains	Poor drainage; mowed too low
Prostrate knotweed	Compaction
Prostrate spurge	Drought conditions; compaction

TABLE 5-2
(Continued)

Weed	Conditions
Rabbit-foot clover	Drought conditions; low pH; high pH
Sheep or red sorrel	Low pH
Speedwell	Drought conditions; mowed too low
Vetch species	Low nitrogen
Wild carrot	High pH; general low fertility
Wild parsnip	General low fertility
Wild radish	General low fertility
Wild strawberry	Low pH
Yarrow	Drought conditions
Yellow wood sorrel	Drought conditions

Adapted from Bosworth

still a weed problem, then the weed information may become valuable. However, most of the conditions that favor weeds do not favor turf, so if ideal conditions for turf are already in place, chances are that the conditions that favor weeds have already been addressed.

Preemergents

The broad use of preemergent herbicides is accepted by many turf managers who do not actually know that it is necessary. One reason may be paranoia—the fear of losing one's job should weeds rear their ugly little heads, especially just before a big game. The expense of using preemergent herbicides should be considered even if the ecological factors are ignored. Using preemergent herbicides is analogous to a person taking antibiotics to protect himself or herself against a bacterial infection. The outcome for this person, however, would be a weakened system that is more susceptible to infection. Preemergent herbicides are designed to suppress the germination of weed seeds while having no effect on nontarget organisms. Ecologically speaking, it is not logical to assume that dose after dose of these products has no impact on the natural system. Unfortunately, if any part of the natural system is stressed, the resulting chain reaction may eventually result in other problems. Tests from Cornell (see Figure 5-8) show increased severity of disease symptoms when herbicides and insecticides are used, which suggests that the pesticides are adversely affecting disease-suppressive organisms, plant defenses, or both (Nelson 1995).

Preemergent herbicides are sometimes used for a much longer period than they are needed, especially for controlling crabgrass. Preemergents, by nature, allow seeds to germinate but not grow. The resulting depletion in the seed bank lessens the need for preemergents unless some crabgrass plants succeed in growing and setting more seed. It is reasonable to assume that after a few years of annual preemergent applications, the seed bank is sufficiently depleted and there is no immediate need for preemergent applications. The manager, however, will never really know if he continues with the annual (or more frequent) tradition of applying preemergent herbicide. In the meantime, it is likely that repeated applications of herbicide are affecting soil organisms and turf plants. Although these effects are difficult to quantify or qualify, it is likely that the impact reduces the opportunity and the ability for turf to compete as a healthy member of the ecological community.

Preemergents also pose a problem if overseeding is employed. Worn areas on sports fields often require new seed, but it is difficult to predict when and how often. Applications of preemergents may make it impossible to overseed areas thinned by athletic activity. Preemergents may even affect dormant seeding because germination generally does not occur until spring. If preemergents are necessary, their use should be avoided in areas prone to wear so that new seed can be applied whenever it is needed. On a football field, the area most prone to wear is the oval in the center of the field between the 20-yard lines. On soccer, lacrosse, and field hockey fields, worn areas typically appear directly in front of each goal and about 20 yards out from the goals, where defenders are most active. Soccer fields also show wear in the corners, where corner kicks are made. Sidelines are also prone to wear from the congregation of spectators, coaches, and nonplaying team members (see Figure 5-11).

Open Opportunities

Weeds such as crabgrass are opportunistic, but they have a difficult time getting established if conditions are not right. First and foremost, crabgrass needs open space. Experiments at Cornell University confirmed that the larger the open area, the more likely it is that crabgrass or goosegrass will become established (Rossi 1999). Researchers also discovered that a small amount of thatch was a deterrent to crabgrass germination. This research suggests that paying close attention to scuffed areas on the

FIGURE 5-11   The corners of a soccer field take a lot of abuse. Attention to wear can reduce the opportunities for pests to succeed.

field can significantly reduce the opportunity for crabgrass or goosegrass establishment. Vigilant applications of a repair mix that quickly reestablishes turf can reduce the need for herbicide.

Repair mixes can vary considerably, but it is advisable that well-aged compost be a component. Compost retains moisture and contains organisms and compounds that can not only increase the germination time and percentage but also protect the seedling from pathogens such as Pythium. It is important that the compost be well aged and well made. Immature compost may contain salts that can suppress or kill germinating seeds. If seed is used in the repair mix, and the mix is used to fill deep ruts or divots, only those seeds within $\frac{1}{2}$ inch of the surface are likely to germinate and survive.

Some golf managers use equal proportions of clippings, sand, and compost as a repair mix with surprisingly good results. It looks green and adds nitrogen, organic matter, and moisture. If creeping grass varieties surround the damaged area, the mix fills in remarkably faster than nothing. Some managers apply seed in anticipation of openings in the turf canopy. Certain athletic activities typically cause openings in the field, and the savvy manager can often predict when and where this wear will occur. Building a seed bank in advance can give some control over what grows back in these open spaces.

Compaction gives many weeds an advantage, but core aeration should only be done during periods when turf is growing vigorously. Aeration, verticutting, brushing, and other activities that open the turf canopy should be avoided during times that are ideal for weed seed germination. Core aeration during dormant or slow-growth periods (e.g., summer) increases the potential for weed encroachment.

Sometimes nature delivers superfluous water and, aside from the field's crown or an underground drainage system, the turf manager can do little about it. Redirecting traffic and vehicles away from areas where the soil tends to stay saturated longer can prevent compaction, which often results in an outbreak of weeds that tolerate a heavier soil density.

Clipping Management

Another aid to controlling some weeds is grass clippings management. The question is whether or not to collect, and the answer may significantly reduce the need for herbicide. Depending on conditions, the decision to collect clippings may encourage or discourage weeds. Clippings from many species of turf plants are thought to contain allelopathic compounds that suppress the germination and/or growth of certain weeds. Furthermore, the distribution of clippings can act as temporary mulch, prior to decomposition, that not only suppresses weeds but also provides nutrients and preserves moisture for the established turf. Fifty-eight percent of the nitrogen from turf fertilizers resides in the clippings. Redistribution of that nitrogen and the other nutrients in clippings gives turf fuel to compete even more aggressively with weeds. The benefits of leaving the clippings behind include improved water infiltration, higher populations of earthworms, greater root production, and disease suppression.

All these benefits may have a direct or indirect influence on the suppression of weeds. In instances where excess nitrogen is favoring weeds like annual bluegrass, crabgrass, foxtail, barnyardgrass, and fall panicum, or weed seed heads are visible, clippings can be collected to reduce available nitrogen and limit seed dispersion. Collecting clippings can significantly reduce annual bluegrass seed dispersion. However, there is no need to discard the valuable essence of the clippings; they are an important ingredient for the compost pile (see Chapter 3).

Nutrient Management

Nitrogen applied insufficiently or to excess can favor some weeds directly and others indirectly. Crabgrass and annual bluegrass are both more competitive when levels of available nitrogen are above optimum, whereas clover and other legume weeds are favored by low levels of available nitrogen. Excess nitrogen that encourages disease outbreak indirectly favors many opportunistic weeds that become established in the bare spots that remain. The same is true where excess nitrogen in plant tissue makes turf shoots, roots, or both more appetizing to herbivorous insects or larvae. Inadequate nitrogen can also trigger insects problems because the plant is weaker and less able to produce defense compounds. Anything that thins turf also gives weeds an opportunity to move in. Knowing the nitrogen needs of each type of turf in the field is an important step toward preventing the encroachment of weeds, not to mention pathogen infections and insect invasions. Biological regulation of nitrogen can synchronize plant needs with availability (see Chapter 2), but resources that support soil organisms must be present.

Timing

Renovation in the fall instead of the spring is another practical way to control many weeds in cool-season turf. Competition from weeds is usually greater in the spring than in the fall, when most annual weeds are beginning to die off. There is evidence that when seeds germinate, they give themselves a competitive edge by releasing natural plant hormones that inhibit the germination of other seeds in their immediate surroundings. This might be as true for weed seeds as it is for grass seeds. This factor makes fall planting, when the germination of weed seed is at a low ebb, more sensible. In the many regions of the United States, the reliability of rain is greater in the fall than in the spring. High grass seed mortality in the spring is something most managers have experienced, and the replacement seed never seems to do as well, possibly because of the natural hormones released by other germinating seeds.

Renovation timing is often beyond a manger's control. When a field sustains irreparable midseason damage from excess play, inclement weather, or both, aggressive renovation is often immediately necessary. Unfortunately, fields located in northern climes may have to wait if it's too cold for seeds to germinate or sod to take root. Bentgrass's best chance for successful establishment is generally in the summer or early fall months, when soil temperatures are higher. If overseeding is necessary in the spring and summer months, choose a variety that germinates and establishes quickly. The opportunity of weeds is limited if a canopy is established as soon as possible.

Varieties

Another important method of weed control is the proper selection of seed varieties. Varieties struggling to survive under unsuitable conditions are less able to compete successfully with weeds. A reiteration of the virtues of diversity is appropriate here. Conditions such as sun and shade may be easily identified, but invisible conditions may limit the success of a select varieties of grass. Diversity in a mix can offer strength over a broader range of conditions and increase the odds of producing a dense sod capable of crowding out most weeds.

Weed Seeds

The soil inherently contains millions of weed seeds deposited by wind, water, and animals. These seeds can stay dormant for hundreds of years until, somehow, they reach the soil depth where proper warmth, moisture, and other factors trigger their germination mechanisms. Deep tillage during turf renovation can bring many of these seeds to the surface, where they can germinate. Shallow soil preparation may be a better alternative if the creation of a seedbed is all that is necessary. It's impossible to escape bringing *some* seeds to the surface, but if conditions are less than ideal for germination, the established turf has a distinct advantage.

Harvesting cores after aeration can reduce the amount of weed seed spread over the soil's surface. Seeding machines that plant without turning the soil also help reduce the number of dormant seeds that can germinate when the soil is disturbed. If it is necessary to burn down existing foliage before overseeding, choose from the effective contact herbicides with relatively benign active ingredients. Some are made with citric acid (St. Gabriel Labs) and some with natural fatty acids (Mycogen). This leads to the subject of regular overseeding.

Overseeding

The term *senescence* refers to the natural aging process of all living things. The shoots (and roots) of turf plants live an average of about six weeks and then die off. Fortunately, new growth is constantly being produced from the crown to replace the loss, and it is difficult to actually observe senescence in turf. Regular applications of seaweed extract can retard senescence, help maintain stand density, and suppress weeds. Theoretically, the perennial grass plant is supposed to generate new growth from its crown year after year ad infinitum. In many varieties, it will even generate new crowns. Unfortunately, other factors in nature tend to interrupt this tradition and cause permanent senescence in turf.

Overseeding fields can inhibit senescence and thwart the typical invasion of weeds in a declining turf. The infusion of new seed into existing turf is, in essence, an injection of youth into a natural aging process, especially in a field with clumping turf varieties that do not naturally spread. If a parcel of turf is in natural decline, bare spots are eventually filled in by nature's choice of seed. If overseeded, a preferable variety is selected to accomplish the same end. This philosophy is practiced successfully by many managers.

FIGURE 5-12 The infusion of new seed into existing turf is, in essence, an injection of youth into a natural aging process. Overseeding machines come in many shapes and sizes. Photo courtesy Land Pride.

Some managers choose to overseed each time they aerate and topdress. This opportunity typically increases soil-to-seed contact, increases germination, and decreases mortality, especially if mature compost is used in the topdress material. A limitation for new grass seedlings is the abatement of sunlight caused by established plants. Lowering the height of cut increases available sunlight but can cause another set of problems (see "Weeds Versus Height of Cut," above; see Figure 5-12).

Overseeding dense, low-growing varieties like bent on croquet courts, bowling greens, and tennis courts is a more challenging proposal. The most difficult part is making the transition from the existing surface invisible to players and coaches. This may be easy if the manager's goal is an area of annual bluegrass (*Poa annua*). Mowing without the basket dispenses the *Poa* seed quite effectively. Increasing the percentage of bent on a bowling green or croquet court, however, can be more difficult. Before interseeded new bentgrass can be successful, the conditions that favor its existence over *Poa* or other weeds must be established. Overseeding areas of *Poa* with bent is difficult to hide. If the transition must take place in a short period, *Poa* needs to be noticeably stressed before bentgrass can succeed. This procedure is most often used to repair large damaged areas that can't repair themselves in a reasonable amount of time. If, however, the manager can make the transition slowly, over a period of several years, it is possible. Conditions that favor *Poa* over bent include low height of cut, superfluous nitrogen, and compaction. Changing these conditions and overseeding can slowly increase the percentage of bentgrasses to acceptable levels.

As with everything else, overseeding can be overdone. If seed is applied to excess, the resulting turf can become prone to certain diseases, especially those that thrive in environments where moisture is retained for long periods and air entrainment is inhibited. Pythium root rot can also be a concern because of an increase in chemical signals that activate Pythium spores. These signals come from germinating seeds, and the more seeds are germinating, the stronger the signal. Overseeding an already dense turf is often a waste of time and money. As soon as the grass plant begins to grow from a seed, it requires sunlight to produce energy. If a dense canopy of established turf is blocking sunlight, the new seedlings are unlikely to succeed. Common sense should intervene when one is about to overseed an area that could not look any better than it already does.

When overseeding (or interseeding), it is often necessary to stress the establish turf in order for the new plants to be competitive and successful. Established turf may need to be mowed very short after overseeding to allow the new plants access to ample sunlight. Mowing height can be raised gradually as the new plants begin to be established.

Using the correct amount of seed is also important. Many experts believe that overseeding rates should be up to 25 percent greater than regularly prescribed rates, while others recommend 10 to 15 percent less. Generally, more is used if seeds are broadcast and less when they are planted with a slit seeder (also called a *slice seeder*). For the sake of argument, let's assume the prescribed rate for a new seeding is appropriate for overseeding in optimal conditions (i.e., balanced fertility, low soil density, adequate levels of organic matter, and suppressed competition from established turf). Some rates must still be calculated. The label on any bag of seed will claim the percent *purity* (*p*) and the percent *germination* (*g*). Purity is determined by subtracting the percentages of crop seed, weed seed, and inert matter from 100 (if the bag contains only one variety of seed). From those values, a *pure live seed* (*pls*) percentage can be calculated:

$$p \times g = pls$$

If several varieties of seed are blended, these calculations should be done for each variety. If, for example a bag of perennial ryegrass (all one variety) contains 1.07 percent crop seed, weed seed, and inert matter combined, then the purity of the seed is:

$$100\% - 1.07\% = 98.93\% \text{ (or } 0.9893)$$

If the germination percentage is 92 percent (0.92), then:

$$0.9893 \times 0.92 \approx 0.91 \text{ or } 91\% \text{ } pls$$

In other words, only 91 percent of the seeds have the potential to become plants under ideal conditions. Therefore, it is often advisable to amend the recommended application rate to compensate for the 9 percent loss. If the recommended seeding rate is 7 pounds per 1,000 square feet, then:

$$7 \div 0.91 \approx 7.7 \text{ pounds of seed}$$

Another important consideration is the test date on the seed label. Germination rates generally decline as time accumulates between the testing and the planting date. There is no set formula for calculating the reduction in germination, but if seed is stored for more than nine months after the test date, it's a good idea to retest the germination rate. Seeds can be easily tested on site by putting a fixed number between two wet paper or cloth towels. The towels must be kept damp and ambient temperatures maintained at ~70° to 80°F. After the appropriate germination time, the rate can be calculated by dividing the number of sprouts by the total number of seeds. If 100 seeds were tested and 85 germinated, then:

$$85 \div 100 = 0.85 \text{ or } 85\%$$

Then recalculate the *pls* value:

$$0.9893 \times 0.85 = 0.84 \text{ or } 84\% \text{ } pls$$

and the application rate:

$$7 \div 0.84 \approx 8.3 \text{ pounds of seed.}$$

Overseeding with the correct amount of seed can promote a thick turf that can compete effectively with weeds.

Natural Herbicides

Organic herbicides are commercially available. These weed control products are biologically or botanically derived, exhibit little or no environmental persistence, and do not inhibit soil biological activity. Some of them (e.g., corn gluten) actually stimulate and feed biological activity to the benefit of grass plants. Corn gluten is a byproduct of the corn syrup industry that releases allelopathic chemicals as it decomposes in the soil. These chemicals act as a preemergent herbicide by suppressing the growth of roots on germinating seeds. Because it is a food protein, the gluten also provides nitrogen to the existing turf. In some cases, the amount of corn gluten needed to control weeds may deliver too much nitrogen, so although the level of weed control may be adequate, the potential for disease to develop is increased. Experiments with corn gluten suggest that the more biologically active a soil is, the more effective it will be and the less of it is needed. Smaller application rates reduce nitrogen contributions and the possibility of disease outbreak. Corn gluten contains 10 percent nitrogen. Fertility programs that include nitrogen must be adjusted when corn gluten is used so excessive nitrogen is not applied. Corn gluten—labeled as an herbicide—is commercially available under a number of brands.

Scientists isolated five of the dipeptides identified as herbicidal compounds in corn gluten and found that one, alaninyl-alanine (endearingly referred to as *Ala-Ala*) had the greatest impact on root growth (Unruh et al. 1997). Small amounts of this dipeptide had numerous herbicidal effects on the roots of germinating ryegrass plants. This research may, at some point, produce a corn gluten derivative that can effectively control germinating weed seeds without adding excessive nitrogen.

As innocuous as some of these new tools seem, they still address only a symptom, not the problem. They do not correct the conditions that allow weeds rather than turf to be successful. Using these products is like putting heroin addicts in a methadone program. The addiction doesn't change, only the substance of abuse. Using more environmentally benign materials is always preferred, but it is not necessarily the solution to the problem. If a product like corn gluten is used as a tool to accomplish the objective of soil and turf improvement to a point where herbicide is no longer needed, it becomes extremely beneficial. However, if it is used only to eliminate symptoms on a regular basis, it can eventually begin to cause other problems.

Biological weed control is being researched with increasing vigilance. Pathogens that infect only the target plant (weed) are being isolated and tested, some with promising results. Most of these organisms, however, are facultative, which means that infection depends on a specific set of conditions. Those conditions may vary with each pathogen and might include temperature, moisture, compaction, fertility, pH, height of cut, and competition from other soil organisms. Since one of the main objectives in an ecological sports field program is to maintain a high level of biological activity and reduce conditions that stress turf, the effectiveness of biological weed control inoculants may be low. If the turf manager has created conditions that are hostile to plant pathogens, then introduced pathogens may have the same difficulty getting established. Researchers at the University of Guelph, instead of isolating and breeding a specific pathogen, discovered some of the foods that enable certain biological weed control agents to flourish. They found that adding durum semolina, guar gum, and gluten flour increased the effectiveness of indigenous pathogens that attacked dandelions (Neumann and Boland 1999).

Hand weeding may seem ludicrous on acres of open area, but there are cases where it is the only means of effective control. A golf course in San Francisco, for example, had a big problem with infestations of English daisy. Faced with a city ordinance that mandated the reduction or elimination of pesticides and the fact that no herbicide to date had been successful at eliminating English daisy, hand weeding became the only option. Although laborious (50 workers) and expensive (over $1,500 per acre), course managers experienced 99.9 percent control three years after the operation was done. The project took six days to complete (Ash 1998).

Most coaches and fans can overlook a few weeds. (Players usually have other issues on their minds.) If the grounds crew practices integrated pest management (IPM) and regularly scouts for problems, a few minutes per day spent hand-extracting weeds can often keep up appearances without resorting to herbicides. Some weeds are better off being left alone, though. Dandelions, for example, are annual weeds that almost always reproduce via wind-blown seed. It can, however, regenerate itself from a broken taproot, and it is next to impossible to extract the entire dandelion root without breaking it Vigilant removal of flower heads before they disperse their seed is a more effective method of managing this weed. A thick stand of turf that is cut 2.5 to 3.5 inches tall offers more competition than most dandelions can manage.

Analysis

No matter how a soil looks or feels, it may need to be tested and perhaps treated to obtain balanced fertility and active biology. Beginning with a well-balanced and fertile soil environment will do more to prevent weed problems than any arsenal of herbicides. Cornell University often prefaces weed control information with this statement: "The first line of defense against weeds is a dense sod." To obtain a dense sod, one must provide the necessary conditions.

There are many conditions, either physical, chemical, biological, or combinations of the three that favor the proliferation of weeds over turf. Table 5-2 shows some of the conditions that can give weeds a competitive edge, but the occurrence of just a small number of weeds or different varieties of weeds in the same place may indicate a problem other than those listed. Sometimes weeds grow well under conditions opposite to those indicated on the table just to prove there are exceptions to every rule. One rule, however, does seem to apply to every situation: Weeds tend to proliferate where turfgrass won't. Conditions that stress turf plants generally favor weeds. Any time the growth of a grass plant is inhibited by stress, infertility, or other suppressive conditions, another species of plant can gain a competitive edge. If fertility is the problem, testing the soil can often discover it and administering the proper inputs can usually correct the imbalance—but timing is also an issue.

Common sense suggests that the best time to feed turf (or any other living thing) is when it is hungry. Turf, like most other living things, has the greatest appetite when it is expending the most energy—that is, when it is growing. Fertilizing at times when turf growth is waning may supply nutrients to less desirable plant species. If a soil analysis indicates an adequate level and balance of nutrients in the soil, care must be taken to give plants only what they need. Phosphorus, for example, is a nutrient that is important to germinating seeds, but established turf rarely needs much more than what is already in the soil. Applications of phosphorus in excess of turf needs may only serve to increase the germination of weed seeds.

Low levels of organic matter are not as easy to correct, but the problem can be addressed by several methods, including mowing higher for greater root development and applying well-made, well-aged compost as part of a topdressing mixture. Organic matter plays a major role in establishing and maintaining a dense turf. It is home to billions of soil organisms that perform hundreds (if not thousands) of beneficial functions, including disease and insect suppression. Bare or thin spots created by insects or pathogens are susceptible to weed encroachment. Soil organisms are also responsible for making many mineral nutrients available to plants. Growing and maintaining a dense turf without adequate organic matter requires more intensive management (see Chapter 6).

Heat and Drought Stress

Stress caused by heat or drought is difficult to control. Mowing higher can help because not only do the longer leaves shade the soil, preserving moisture and lowering the soil surface temperature but also the higher HOC encourages deeper rooting and greater access to more soil moisture. Additionally, greater leaf surface area has more stomates (pores), enabling the plant to increase transpiration—its ability to cool itself. Irrigation can mitigate the effects of heat and drought, but irrigation techniques are extremely important (see Chapter 6, under "Irrigation"). The last thing turf needs when it is already stressed by heat and drought is to be drowned. Overirrigation forces oxygen out of the soil and can suffocate roots. It can also make the soil more prone to compaction. In many cases, light, frequent watering (~0.1 in./day) during the most stressful part of the day can help maintain turf density. Most of the water from this procedure evaporates, so deep, infrequent watering may also be necessary from time to time. Avoid saturating the soil.

In the spring, some of us get a false sense of financial stability—until we remember that Uncle Sam hasn't been paid yet. That same feeling of euphoria, followed by frustration, comes when summer heat and drought hammer the spring (cool-season) turf that the ground crews have maintained so beautifully. The stress from high temperatures and low levels of moisture can change a thick, healthy turf into one peppered with problems. The turf's ability to compete with weeds, resist disease, and recover from insect damage are all but gone in just a few short weeks. Aside from irrigation, it seems as though there is little to do except to stand by and watch its decline.

Fortunately, there *are* a few things we can do to combat the summer's impairment of turf. First and foremost is raising the height of cut. Taller grass can shade the soil, significantly reducing the amount of heat the soil absorbs from the sun and the amount of moisture evaporated from the soil surface. Taller plants grow deeper roots that have both better access to water and better storage capabilities. Water use is actually increased slightly from the increased leaf surface area of taller plants. The physical process of transpiration through the leaves, however, can cool the ambient temperature by 7° to 14°F. The longer the grass can stay green, the longer the cooling mechanism can remain working. The slightly higher water consumption is more than compensated for by increased access to soil moisture from a deeper and more diffusive root system.

Seaweed extracts and humic biostimulants are inexpensive materials that can also mitigate the effects of stress. Research has discovered that the natural growth regulators in seaweed products can give turf significantly greater drought resistance and stimulate greater root development (Schmidt and Zhang 1997, Senn 1987). The greater resistance turf has to stress, the better it can compete with weeds.

Vesicular arbuscular mycorrhizae (VAM) is a family of beneficial fungi that colonize the roots of perennial plants and, on the plant's behalf, reach into the soil's depths for moisture and mineral nutrients. All they ask in return is a small amount of the photosynthesized carbohydrate that is routinely released through the roots. This symbiotic relationship exists in over 80 percent of all grass species and can significantly increase the plants' heat and drought resistance. Commercial preparations of VAM and other mycorrhizal inoculants are available that can colonize the roots of turf plants, but they are best applied when seed is initially set. These inoculants must make contact with the plant roots in order to begin colonization, and they are not able to move through the soil. Core aeration presents an opportunity to inoculate roots, but if turf is grown in a healthy, biologically active soil, chances are good that natural inoculation will eventually take place.

Mycorrhizae, although they have been around for over 400 million years, are highly sensitive to soil disturbances. They are ubiquitous in forests and other areas where the soil is largely undisturbed, but adequate populations do not exist in urban and suburban environments, where the soil has been moved, removed, shifted, turned, relocated, piled, and compacted. Their numbers are also impoverished on agricultural lands that have been plowed, harrowed, tilled, and treated with chemical fertilizers and pesticides. These are the environments where sports fields are often located, so natural inoculation may be difficult, especially if an abundance of chemical pesticides and fertilizers are used. Mycorrhizal inoculants are most successful on turf roots if they are applied at planting, but they can also succeed if they are worked down into the thatch layer during topdressing operations. Commercially available inoculants come with specific instructions, but, as a general rule, 30,000 to 70,000 spores per 1,000 square feet are necessary for good inoculation. Unfortunately, if fungicides are used, that relationship may be compromised or eliminated.

Combating disease with well-made, well-aged compost, compost tea, or a program of building soil organic matter can not only provide long-term disease protection but also encourage the useful relationships VAM have with turf. Mycorrhizae fungi are aerobic organisms and need oxygen to live. As the soil becomes compacted and oxygen levels are reduced, so are the symbiotic abilities of VAM. Once this occurs, they form dormant spores on the roots and wait for conditions to improve before they become active again. Mycorrhizae can form a protective layer around the roots and prevent pathogen spores, such as Pythium, from becoming established. Pythium and other root diseases indirectly encourage weeds by creating openings in the turf canopy. VAM indirectly suppress weeds by improving drought resistance and resilience in the face of other environmental stresses that inhibit turf's ability to maintain a dense canopy.

Another nonaction we can take to alleviate heat and drought stress is to stop collecting clippings. Clippings returned to the turf can provide several benefits. Between the time that they fall and the time they decompose, they act as temporary mulch that can lower the soil surface temperature. As moisture evaporates from the fallen clippings, the surrounding air is cooled and stress from heat is mitigated.

As mentioned before, clippings can produce allelochemicals as they decompose. Some researchers believe that these allelopathic chemicals can suppress some crabgrass germination (Dest et al. 1992). The nitrogen and other nutrients inherent in clippings is a perfect slow-release fertilizer that can help grass stay vital during stressful periods. Additionally, as clippings decompose, valuable carbon dioxide is generated for grass plants. Clippings left behind have also shown disease-suppressive properties, which can offer some protection when plants are susceptible to infection.

Bare spots created by pathogens are open invitations for weeds to become established. Clippings should be collected if there is any sign of disease. Mowing fields with the baggers off may form clipping clumps if mowing intervals are too infrequent. These clumps are unsightly and can block sunlight from sections of turf. Generally, clumps do not form if less than a third of the top growth is mowed—but, if they do, mowers can easily break up and disperse them. Clippings encourage earthworm activity, which increases the soil's water holding capacity and reduces thatch. Pesticides that suppress earthworms inadvertently contribute to thatch, which does not help the drought resistance of the turf. Excessive thatch can decrease the turf's resistance to drought because it holds little moisture and encourages shallow roots. A small amount of thatch, however, can be beneficial to sports turf. It can mitigate stress from traffic, lessen the impact of heavy rain, reduce direct sunlight to the soil's surface, and help exchange gases with the atmosphere. A thin thatch layer can also suppress the germination of many annual weed seeds by preventing them from making adequate contact with the soil.

Irrigation, if available, can be the ultimate treatment for stress caused by heat and drought. The misuse of this tool, however, can do more harm than good. Experts disagree on the ideal frequency and duration of irrigation. Some believe that deep and infrequent watering is best (Jordan et al. 2003, Richie et al. 2002), while others feel that high-frequency, low-volume irrigation is optimal (Vargas 1994). Some research suggests that light watering ($\frac{1}{10}$ inch) on a daily basis is best for relieving heat and drought stress. Common sense dictates that no single irrigation program ideally fits every field under every condition. Deep sandy soils with little water holding capacity may be better served with low-volume, high-frequency irrigation, especially in windy areas where moisture is quickly evaporated from the surface. But this may be inappropriate for heavy soils that do not dry out as quickly.

Many managers irrigate based on evapotranspiration calculations—that is, the amount of water they apply matches, as closely as possible, the amount of water lost from both evaporation from the soil and transpiration from plant leaves (see Chapter

6, under "Irrigation"). Maintaining this balance seems to provide turf with the ideal amount of moisture, which, in turn, maintains its competitive characteristics throughout the hot and dry season. Replacing only the amount of moisture lost from plant transpiration and soil surface evaporation is often ideal and can eliminate the often costly errors of excessive or insufficient irrigation.

Using a moisture meter to monitor soil water is a good idea, but the optimum amount of moisture varies in different types of soil (see Figure 5-13). If moisture meters are used, it is necessary to analyze the texture of a soil to determine its field capacity (the volumetric percentage of moisture that fills half of the soil's pore space). If a manager works with many types of soils, it may be expensive and laborious to do a texture analysis of each. This information, however, is valuable if the overall goal is to maintain a dense turf canopy. (See Chapter 4, under "Texture Analysis," for an inexpensive on-site method.)

Algae and Moss

Algae, although they are not really weeds, can be a problem on some sports fields, where the turf is mowed very close and irrigation is at a maximum for maintaining health and color during the hot, dry months. Algae usually occur where there is excessive moisture, high fertility, and low competition from turfgrass. Algae are photosynthesizing organisms and like full sun, but they can also exist in shady areas. Controlling algae ecologically is similar to managing weeds. A well-maintained, thick turf is the best defense against algae.

Often, algae begin in areas of poor drainage. Chronically moist conditions can stress turf and lower its ability to compete for space and sunlight. Algae, on the other hand, thrive in excessively wet areas. Problem areas may require a drainage system as a permanent solution, but it is important to understand that if a soil is heavy or compacted and has low spots, drainage may not help. Reconstruction with a crown or slight incline

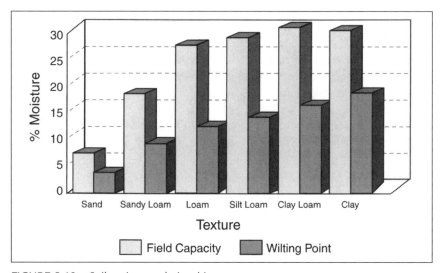

FIGURE 5-13   Soil moisture relationships.

may be the only way to shed excess water. Overirrigation may be another cause of alga encroachment. Too much water can stress grass and provide favorable conditions for algae. Fertilizers applied in excess (especially acidulating fertilizers such as ammonium sulfate) can also encourage algae. Additionally, fertilizers with high salt content can stress turf, whereas algae can tolerate higher levels of nutrients. Mowing higher can protect against algae, which tends to grow in thin layers close to the ground.

Eradication of established alga colonies requires either physical removal or some type of algicide. Household products such as Lysol Disinfectant and Clorox Bleach with a surfactant are effective at killing algae, but they can create problems. The first is that these products are phytotoxic—they can kill the grass if the dose is too large. This may not be a big problem if not much grass is growing in the first place. The second problem is a legal one. Household disinfectants and bleaches are not labeled as algicides and technically cannot be used as such. Copper sulfate is relatively successful at defeating algae, and some brands are labeled for turf. Greenhouse disinfectants made from quaternary ammonium compounds are effective, with the least amount of damage to grass plants. BioSafe Systems makes an algicide from hydrogen peroxide and acetic acid that is both effective and relatively innocuous in the environment.

However, eradicating existing algae is rarely a long-term solution. The conditions that allowed the algae to flourish are still there. The permanent solution to alga problems is cultural. Creating an environment that is favorable to turf and inhospitable to algae is usually less expensive and more effective in the long term. Aerating the soil, improving drainage, balancing fertility, and providing other conditions that allow turf to flourish are more permanent remedies for algae.

The occurrence of moss on turf usually indicates a wet and cool environment, probably a low soil fertility and pH, and improper mowing. Moss is a slow-growing plant that tolerates low pH, little to no fertility, and dense shade. Low mowing is a cultural activity that encourages the existence of moss. Fortunately, moss does not tolerate wear and tear, so removal can be accomplished easily with a verticutter or other tool that scarifies the surface. Preventing moss from reoccurring involves making changes to the soil so it will support a healthy stand of turf. Adjustments in soil fertility and pH should be done in accordance with a soil test (see Chapter 4). Core aeration may be necessary, as well as the introduction of quality composts to boost organic matter and biological activity. Areas subjected to dense shade may require renovation with a grass seed blend containing several types of fescues or other shade-tolerant cultivars. Trees causing excessive shade may have to be thinned. Some areas may be too shady for turf and might be better off with a shade-tolerant ground cover. Mowing turf at a reasonable height also helps prevent an invasion of moss.

INSECTS

It is unfortunate that most managers have little appreciation for insects and other arthropods. Most that inhabit the turf ecosystem are not only beneficial but actually crucial to its mechanics. Well over 90 percent of the world's arthropods are neutral or beneficial. The percentage is even higher in turf.

Creating a healthy and balanced ecosystem for turf would, in theory, control all important pests, but we are unable to accomplish this for a couple of reasons. First, we don't know how. Research has discovered a tremendous amount about the relationships among the soil, plants, biomass, and atmosphere. If, however, we could fit all that we know in a thimble, what we do not understand would be hard to contain in a large truck. Second, even if we did know how to create the quintessential ecosystem, nature would always be throwing variables at us that we could not control. Even a completely natural system, untouched by human management, does not respond favorably to excessive and unusual heat, drought, cold, or precipitation. Eco-complications such as these make the turf manager's job more challenging and create an atmosphere that can tempt even the most reluctant applicator to the chemicals shed. This is unfortunate, because a healthy, ecologically balanced system does provide checks and balances that constantly protect turf plants. This natural aegis is invisible to all but the highly trained eye, so its need for protection is often overlooked.

There is ample evidence of instances where a healthy soil ecosystem initiates a chain reaction of biological, physical, and chemical phenomena that effectively controls many damaging insects—or at least limits the amount of damage they can cause. We don't know all the relationships that organisms in the turf ecosystem have with plants and each other, but we do know that organisms need certain resources to live and function. We also know that some insects and other arthropods offer protection to plants and that these organisms are often affected by biocides applied to control target insects. It's questionable whether we will ever discover how to effectively exploit beneficial organisms to a point where insecticides are obsolete, but most biologists agree that pesticides can be counterproductive.

Factors that control the success of herbivorous arthropods and their predators include climate temperature, precipitation, soil structure, and biomass. But the plant itself is also a consideration. There is evidence that all living things emit radiation in specific wavelengths that can be recognized by other organisms. Many insects rely on these signals for both sustenance and reproduction. According to some researchers, the insect's antennae receive the infrared frequencies given off by plants, predators, and insects of the opposite sex. Regardless of wind direction, the insect is able to locate the source of the radiation. It is thought that plants growing in suboptimum conditions generate altered wavelengths that attract grazing insects. This theory has been difficult to substantiate, but evidence of radiated signals from plants and reception of similar signals from insects does exist (Callahan 1975). If insects begin to cause damage because of signals from subclinically ill plants and insecticides that further stress biological functions are applied, then the turf may be rendered even more vulnerable to further attack. Treatment of the insect, which is a symptom, without analysis of the conditions in which the plant is growing can be counterproductive and lead to further biocidal treatments in the near future.

Insects and other arthropodan pests that damage turf generally fall into one of four main categories: root feeders, stem burrowers, juice suckers, and leaf eaters. Root feeders include white grubs, ground pearls, nematodes, and mole crickets. Insects such as billbugs and annual bluegrass weevils burrow into stems and often damage the crowns. Chinch bugs, greenbugs, mites, mealybugs, and spittlebugs are important juice suckers, and the leaf eaters include armyworms, cutworms, sod webworms, and other turf-eating caterpillars. Almost all of these insects are most damaging to turf during the immature stages (larvae or nymph) of their life cycle.

Fertility

As mentioned earlier in this chapter, plants have strong defense systems, and stimulating these defenses is the least exploited approach to insect control. Mechanisms such as the production of defensive compounds, translocation of nutrients, and strengthening of cell walls depend on the condition of the plant, which is largely reliant on a biologically active ecosystem. Fertility alone does not necessarily result in a healthy plant. In fact, excessive fertility can actually suppress plant defense mechanisms. Additionally, herbivorous insects need nitrogen more than plants do. Plants overfertilized with nitrogen often contain high levels of free amino acids that are known to stimulate both feeding and egg laying. Underfertilized plants, on the other hand, have a diminished capacity to defend themselves and cannot recuperate as quickly from insect damage. A biologically active soil has the ability to regulate fertility so plants are neither under- nor overfed and healthy turf is the first and most important defense against all pests.

Nitrogen is not the only important nutrient for plant defense mechanisms. Phosphorus, potassium, calcium, magnesium, sulfur, and many trace elements are also considered essential. All these elements combined, however, constitute only 5 percent of the turf plant's diet. Carbon, hydrogen, and oxygen from carbon dioxide and water are needed in much larger quantities than the manager can apply. Deficiencies in any essential element can limit a plant's ability to defend itself against pestilence.

Excesses can also create problems. Carbon, hydrogen, and oxygen are elements we cannot apply (with the possible exception of hydrogen and oxygen in irrigation water), and it is commonly assumed that nature provides the ideal amount. Carbon, however, is not always available in ideal amounts. Carbon dioxide is diluted in the inner atmosphere, which is about 100 miles thick, but a turf plant has access to only 1 to 3 inches (or less in some cases) of that gaseous envelope. Carbon dioxide produced by soil organisms seeps to the surface, where the plant's leaves can capture it. When the wind blows, carbon dioxide from the soil is diluted with the rest of the atmosphere. Typically, winds are calm in the morning and early evening. The pores on the underside of plant leaves (called *stomates*) are, coincidentally, open during the same periods. If, however, little carbon dioxide is being generated from biological activity, small plants like closely mowed turf must exist on a relatively austere diet, which can limit its defense capabilities.

Sandy soils often cannot support large enough populations of soil organisms, and their respiration of carbon dioxide is therefore limited. Heavy clay soils can compact more easily and inhibit the exchange of soil gases with the atmosphere. Without adequate carbon dioxide, the plant's ability to process soluble forms of nitrogen into protein—a form of nitrogen that is more difficult for insects to assimilate—is retarded.

Nitrogen, phosphorus, and potassium are commonly applied during fertilization. Calcium and magnesium are delivered if lime is applied. Some managers use iron to enhance turf color without promoting growth. Most other trace elements, including manganese, boron, copper, cobalt, zinc, and molybdenum, are often ignored unless a leaf tissue analysis determines they are lacking. Many other elements are not considered essential to plants but are used by soil organisms. If the theory that a healthy ecosystem produces healthy, resilient plants is correct, then the needs of both plants and soil organisms should be considered (see Chapter 2, under "Trace Elements"). The severity of insect damage is often related to plant health and vigor. Stressed plants are rarely as resilient.

Predators

When insect problems become apparent, the usual reaction is to identify the pest and find the appropriate insecticide to eradicate it. Applications of pesticides, unfortunately, often eradicate more than just the pest. In many cases, the insecticide used also suppresses predators that are capable of controlling the target pests. This suppresses some of the plant's natural resistance to the pest if a resurgence of the same pest occurs. Other predators, unrelated to the target pest, may also be impacted, and their inactivity may create a new insect problem. The popular insecticides used to control chinch bugs (*Blissus leucopterus*), for example, often kill big-eyed bugs (*Geocoris bullatus*), a species of insect that is capable of controlling chinch bugs. If the chinch bugs return, there may not be any big-eyed bugs to control them.

Dr. Daniel Potter and Stephen Cockfield at the University of Kentucky discovered another example of predator suppression (Cockfield 1984). They found that predation of sod webworm eggs was significantly suppressed for weeks after a single application of chlorpyrifos (Dursban). These researchers put 500 sod webworm eggs out at one-, three-, and five-week intervals after one treatment with chlorpyrifos. The number of eggs that were either eaten or carried off by predators was measured in replicated tests, and the averages are shown in Figure 5-14. For more than three weeks, predator activity

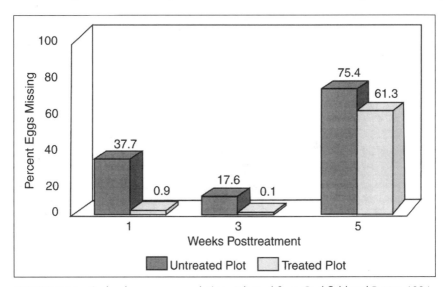

FIGURE 5-14   Sod webworm egg predation. Adapted from Cockfield and Potter, 1984.

was significantly suppressed by a single application of the insecticide. Known predators of sod webworm eggs are ants, rove beetles, predatory mites, and ground beetles. Insecticides known to affect one or more of these insect groups include chlorpyrifos (Dursban), isofenphos (Oftanol), trichlorfon (Proxol), and bendiocarb (Turcam). Beneficial organisms such as collembola, enchytraeid worms, and saprophytic mites, which play a valuable role in recycling organic matter and producing carbon dioxide—a vital nutrient for plants—are also affected by one or more of these materials.

Another test done by Cockfield and Potter shows suppression of spider and rove beetle populations (both of which are voracious predators) in areas treated with chlorpyrifos (see Figure 5-15). Both spiders and rove beetles are common turfgrass inhabitants.

The establishment of natural areas can add beauty; reduce maintenance, inputs, and water consumption; and attract important insect predators. Many research papers over the past five decades support the notion that plant diversity can suppress arthropodan pests. The two main theories supporting these pest control observations are the natural enemies hypothesis, which suggests that plant diversity promotes effective biological control, and the resource concentration hypothesis, which surmises that pests are less able to locate a food source in a more diverse environment (Quarles, 2002[b]).

Although most research is in agriculture, evidence is sufficient to suggest that a greater plant diversity surrounding turf can mitigate some insect problems. Unfortunately, there is no known way to attract predators specific to the pest problem at hand—at least not yet. Many experiments have been conducted using flowers, pheromone lures, and sugar or nectar solutions. More often than not, predators were successfully attracted, but predation was inconsistent. In one experiment using a sugar solution, large numbers of tiphia wasps (parasites of white grubs) were successfully lured into the desired area, but they preferred the lure to the prey, and less predation occurred than in an area where no attractants were used. Most researchers agree that the most effective attractant for predators is prey and that the reduction or elimination of insecticides that cause predator mortality is a sure way of increasing their activ-

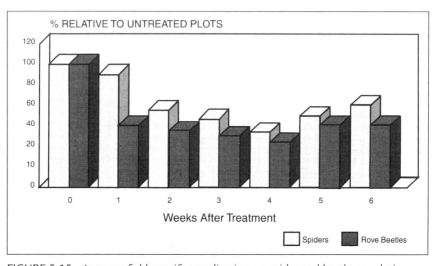

FIGURE 5-15   Impact of chlorpyrifos application on spider and beetle populations.

ity. Natural areas can be mowed once or twice per year to avoid the establishment of unwanted trees or shrubs. Managers may be reluctant to establish natural areas if they believe that trees and shrubs may eventually get established.

Many inhabitants of turf and surrounding areas are insect predators or parasites. The list includes ants, spiders, rove beetles, big-eyed bugs, ground beetles, tiger beetles, green lacewings, lady beetles, predatory mites, syrphid flies, soldier beetles, fireflies, blister beetles, stink bugs, assassin bugs, minute pirate bugs, damsel bugs, ambush bugs, robber flies, praying mantises, roaches, crickets, dragon flies, and dozens of parasitic insects such as Scoliid wasps, Typhiid wasps, and Trichogrammidae wasps. The population of these organisms depends on resources, climate, habitat, and other conditions that may be beyond the turf manager's control. Pesticides that suppress these predators, however, are always applied by choice. Ants can sometimes cause visible damage, especially on bowling greens and croquet courts, but eradication with an insecticide is often counterproductive. When the size or abundance of damaged areas reaches beyond the tolerable threshold, the unsightly bits can be easily repaired by plugging with a turf repair tool. Small piles of sand or soil excavated by ants can usually be smoothed with a drag cable or whipping pole (see Chapter 6, under "Earthworms"; see Figure 5-16).

Reasearch shows that some insecticides have a negative impact on some groups of soil organisms (Colinas et al. 1994). The vast majority of these organisms are beneficial to turf in one way or another, and when their activity is suppressed, fewer of these benefits are available. Slowing or stopping the flow of these biological gifts at a time when the plant is already stressed may make it even more susceptible to insect damage. As more research is conducted on the ecological side effects of pesticides, it is becoming clearer that a more holistic thought process is necessary to produce and maintain healthy turf.

Botanical and biological products are available that offer effective control; however, timing is important (as it is with conventional pesticides). Proper identification of the

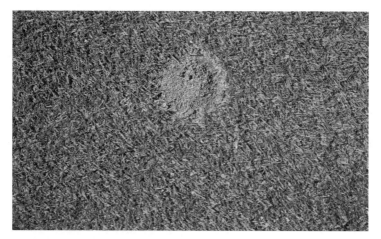

FIGURE 5-16   Ants are beneficial predators of many turf pests but their colony building activities can cause minor damage. Pesticides to control ant may be counter-productive.

pest and familiarity with its life cycle are key to effective control. Almost all of the arthropodan pests have natural enemies that constantly offer free help to the groundskeeper. Care should be taken to protect this resource. These beneficials include arthropods, nematodes, protozoa, fungi, and bacteria. Pesticides that affect these groups should be avoided unless absolutely necessary and, if they must be used, they should be used only where needed.

Cultural Controls

Cultural practices can result in a significant reduction of insect damage (see Chapter 7). Black cutworm moths, for example, lay their eggs on leaf tips. If the turf manager's timing is right, mowing the fields with the baggers on can reduce black cutworm population by 80 to 90 percent. The key is knowing just when the female moths oviposition. Pheromone traps are available that attract males and, generally, when males are being caught on a sustained basis, egg laying has begun. Black cutworms are capable of two to six generations per year, depending on the length of the season, so if black cutworms are a prevalent problem, vigilance is a priority.

The manager's familiarity with the habits of insect pests can reduce their opportunities to succeed. Failure to completely fill core holes after spring aeration, for example, can result in sod webworm problems. Adult female moths find partially filled core holes a convenient place to lay eggs. Damage from larvae usually begins along the edges of the core holes. In the fall, incompletely filled core holes do not usually present the same opportunities. Sod webworms can usually be eradicated without insecticides by flooding the affected area with water. Some managers mix in a little mild detergent. Within a few minutes, the webworms come to the surface, where they can be dispatched with a whipping pole and, if the sun is shining, left to desiccate. Birds often clean up the litter. If detergent is used, the turf should be rinsed to avoid scorching. Flooding can also be an effective control for chinch bug problems.

Stress

Often, turf can tolerate damaging herds of foraging insects by engaging a defense mechanism, outgrowing the damage, or both. Unfortunately, during the hot, dry part of the year, turf is often stressed and unable to defend against or outgrow even a small amount of insect damage. A researcher at Michigan State University found (entirely by accident) that the amount of damage caused by many foliar-feeding insects was reduced or eliminated by low-volume, high-frequency irrigation (Vargas 1994). The treatment consisted of daily applications of $1/10$ inch of water during the hottest part of the day. The result was a reduction of insect damage to below tolerable levels. If irrigation is available, using it to reduce stress makes more sense than applying pesticides, which may stress turf plants even more.

Stress also has a tendency to change the chemistry of a plant, producing a buildup of free amino acids, sugars, and other components of protein and carbohydrates that, in a free state, can stimulate insects to both feed and lay eggs. This phenomenon also occurs from nutrient imbalances, especially excess or deficient nitrogen. There is strong evidence that a biologically active soil mediates the amount of nitrogen and other nutrients available to plants, resulting in conditions that are better for turf than for insect pests. Stress management can include the use of seaweed or kelp extracts that contain natural plant hormones. These hormones help plants resist stress; in addition, several reports clearly correlate the application of seaweed extracts with a measurable increase in the production of defense compounds (Senn 1987, Schmidt 1997). Experiments have shown average feeding reductions of 60 percent on plants treated with seaweed extracts compared with control plants.

Thatch and Earthworms

Excessive thatch can provide habitat for many herbivorous insects, including chinch bugs, billbugs, and many species of damaging caterpillars, cutworms, and webworms. At the same time, thick thatch can weaken turf, making it less able to tolerate insect damage. Thatch is caused when the residues of stems, crowns, stolons, tillers, leaves, and other plant parts intermingled with living roots and shoots accumulate faster than they can be decomposed. Excessive thatch can inhibit water infiltration and promote the volatilization of nitrogen from fertilizers, especially when urea is used. Thatch is often a result of poor management practices (see Chapter 6, under "Earthworms and Thatch"). Excessive applications of nitrogen that promote fast growth and the use of pesticides that inhibit the activities of decomposing organisms (especially earthworms) are the leading causes of thatch accumulation.

Earthworms are probably the most valuable soil organisms for thatch control. They quickly decompose surface residues and enrich the soil with castings while providing aeration, improving water infiltration, and mitigating soil compaction. Grass clippings contain slow-release nitrogen that favors turf. Excessive soluble nitrogen can sometimes acidify soil, inhibiting the activities of earthworms and other thatch-decomposing organisms. Contrary to what many believe, collecting clippings can actually favor thatch accumulation. Grass clippings can be returned to fields inconspicuously if less than a third of the top growth is cut at a time. Double cutting can usually disperse clumps if too much grass is cut at once.

Pesticide use may play a role in the development of thatch; for example, pesticides that inhibit the activities of decay organisms inadvertently advance thatch. A single application of products containing bendiocarb, benomyl, carbaryl, fonofos, or ethoprop can kill 60 to 99 percent of an earthworm population. Other compounds such as chlorpyrifos, diazinon, isazophos, isofenphos, and trichlorfon also cause significant mortality of earthworms and other saprophytic organisms. Many of these compounds also reduce certain predator groups. Pesticides used to combat disease or insect problems may, in the long term, serve only to increase these problems if they harm beneficial organisms.

Thatch problems are relatively rare in low-input or organically maintained turf because most of the inputs are as beneficial to soil organisms as they are to turf. Composts and organic fertilizers stimulate the biological activity needed to control thatch. Healthy soils generate large populations of organisms that consume thatch as fast as it is created. Even with organic management, however, the amount of nitrogen typically applied to sports fields often produces more thatch than decay organisms can consume, but the rate of accumulation is significantly slower. The successful management of superfluous thatch can mitigate or eliminate other problems related to the stress it causes.

Endophytes

If reseeding becomes necessary because of damage from arthropods other than root feeders, a longer-lasting solution may be the use of endophytically enhanced grass seed. Endophytes are fungal organisms that live symbiotically within the cells of the grass plants and reproduce during cell division. They create a bitter-tasting toxin that repels most insects and kills many of those that continue to feed. Many varieties of cool-season grass seeds contain endophytes, and the level of infection varies widely. For turf that is effectively resistant to foliar-feeding insects, endophyte infection should be at least 70 percent or higher. Common sense dictates that the level of uninfected seed be relative to the potential amount of damage that can occur. If the seed has only 50 percent infection, then it is possible to lose half of the turf to insect damage.

Varieties of seeds that are bred with endophytes include perennial ryegrass and many types of fescues. Natural varieties of bluegrass and bentgrass that contain endophytes have not been found; however, plant scientists have spliced endophytes into both bluegrass and bentgrass strains. Unfortunately, the strain of endophytes used is causing sterility, and seed production is impossible. As of this writing, endophytically enhanced bluegrass and bentgrass seeds are not commercially available. The use of endophytically enhanced fescues and perennial ryegrass may be appropriate only under certain circumstances. They may be impractical in some areas of the country where foliar-feeding insects are a problem.

If endophytically enhanced seed is stored for an extended period, the endophytes may die. The length of time the seed can be stored depends on the temperature of the storage facility. A refrigerated facility can keep the endophytes viable for many years, but a standard, uninsulated warehouse in New England, for example, can preserve the endophytes for approximately 12 months. Heat is the endophytes' biggest enemy. The longer they are subjected to temperatures above 50°F (10°C), the fewer endophytes will remain viable. Additionally, the higher the temperature, the more quickly endophyte infection diminishes. Once planted and established, endophytes will reproduce with the plant and remain active for as long as the plant lives.

Endophytes stay in the aboveground portion of the plant and do not normally provide protection from root-feeding insects such as white grubs. Researchers at the University of Rhode Island, however, found that freshly germinated seedlings of endophytic varieties are resistant to Japanese beetle grubs (Johnson et al. 1992). This resistance is greatest in tall fescues but also exists in endophytically enhanced perennial ryegrass and other fescues. The size of the grub was also a factor in these findings. Resistance was greatest against small grubs and insignificant against mature grubs. Efficacy was only evident in the first year after germination. Researchers are attempting to isolate the chemical basis of this resistance, which may eventually result in a biological or botanical grub control product (Casagrande and Johnson 1989). The Rhode Island study also found that "grubs are generally incapable of damaging tall fescue turfgrass in this [Rhode Island] area." This finding has been known to many managers for some time; unfortunately, tall fescue is often an inappropriate choice for many sports fields.

Grass seed infected with endophytes shows other benefits, including improved performance.Research suggests that endophytes produce substances similar to plant hormones (Ayad et al. 1997). Introducing plant hormones can also be accomplished by applying seaweed extract.

Biological and Botanical Controls

Another biological control that is often effective is a commercially prepared fungus capable of attacking and destroying white grubs. Products containing the fungus *Beauveria bassiana* are labeled for turf and claim to control white grubs and some other turf insect pests. Under the right conditions, they have the potential to be as effective as chemicals. As with any biological control, environmental conditions play a major role in their efficacy.

The botanical insecticide neem has also been tested as a control for grubs. Neem is an insect growth regulator that interrupts the insect's maturation process, usually during molting. Unfortunately, the product has no effect on turf grubs because it cannot penetrate the soil to the level where the larvae reside. Eventually, producers of the product hope to devise a vehicle to carry the product to greater soil depths. Neem has been tested with success on other turf pests such as chinch bugs, billbugs, sod webworms, and armyworms. Products containing neem compounds, labeled for use against these insects, are commercially available.

A promising new strategy for combating damage from grubs and many other insect groups is to apply a natural repellant to the turf before the adult insects lay their eggs. Most beetles that lay eggs in turf produce only one generation per year. Preventing those adult females from laying eggs in the turf can eliminate grub damage without further treatment. Repellants containing garlic juice, capsaicin (extracts from hot peppers), or other materials that persuade insects to go elsewhere are becoming increasingly more popular with turf managers. One manufacturer (Garlic Research Labs) recommends 13 to 26 ounces of their 100 percent garlic juice concentrate per acre, mixed with enough water to drench the soil, applied every 10 to 30 days depending on soil type and the amount of precipitation. Sandier soils, especially after heavy rains, will need reapplications sooner. For this strategy to be effective, knowledge of the pest's life cycle and timing is crucial.

Bacillus thurengiensis (Bt) is the active ingredient in many biological insecticides that are labeled for sod webworms, armyworms, black cutworms, and other turf-eating caterpillars. Of the many strains of Bt, the one most often labeled for turf pests is the kurstaki strain. Bt is a natural bacterium that is relatively specific to lepidopterous larvae because it only affects larvae with alkaline digestive fluids. When it is applied to the turf canopy, only grazing organisms will ingest the Bt, and organisms with acidic digestive juices will not be infected. There is little danger that nontarget organisms will be harmed.

Insecticidal soaps (IS) are effective against soft-bodied turf pests, but they may be impractical for nocturnal pests. IS's mode of action is to desiccate the insect, and it must make contact with the target organism to be effective—which could prove difficult at night.

Almost all white grubs are susceptible to milky spore disease, caused by the bacteria *Bacillus popilliae* or *Bacillus lentimorbus*. However, a different strain of the bacteria is unique to each species of grub, and unless the grub is infected with the right strain, it probably will not contract milky spore disease. Currently, and for the past four decades, products designed to infect grubs with milky spore disease are commercially available, but they contain only the strain of bacteria that affects Japanese beetle larvae. One manufacturer (St. Gabriel Labs) is attempting to produce the strains necessary to control almost all species of white grubs. At this point, the product is not commercially available, but it may be soon (see Figure 5-17).

When a grub ingests the appropriate strain of *Bacillus popilliae*, the bacteria multiply in the larva's bloodstream and cause death. The bacteria reproduce inside the remains of the grub and increase the inoculation of the area. After two to four years, the spread of the disease is usually sufficient to keep the population of larvae below the tolerance level for turf. Depending on climate and soil conditions, this inoculation can last for more than 15 years. Experiments at Cornell University suggest that the best time to apply milky spore is mid- to late summer, when the new brood of Japanese beetle larvae have hatched and begun to feed (Vittum et al. 1999, Couch 2000). In the Northeast and Pacific Northwest, spring soil temperatures are often not warm enough for milky spores to work. Grubs are coldblooded—that is, their temperature is the same as their environment's. Cold grubs are relatively inactive, and their consumption of spores and everything else is minimal. Spores reproduce inside the grub but do so slowly at lower temperatures. Thus, inoculation of an area in a cool region may take longer than in a warmer locale. The shell of the spores breaks down when it comes in contact with the gastrointestinal juices of the grub. Sometimes, in cold grubs, the

FIGURE 5-17   Milky grub (right) is infected with the bacterium Bacillus popilliae which multiplies inside the host and inoculates the immediate area around where the larva expires (compare with healthy grub, left). Photo courtesy St. Gabriel Laboratories.

spore's shell does not break down enough as it passes through the grub to cause infection. The shell, however, is weakened by its exposure to the grub's gastric juices and
will likely cause infection the next time it is ingested.

The most common cause of failure using milky spore disease is the mistaken identification of the grub. Most white grubs look similar, and the only way to differentiate
between a Japanese beetle larva and other turf grubs is the raster pattern located on the
tail end of their bodies. These patterns have subtle differences that identify the species
of adult the larva will eventually become. Most turfgrass extension agents can provide
illustrations of these patterns, which also can be found in books such as *Destructive
Turfgrass Insects* (Potter 1998) and *Turfgrass Problems* (Gussack and Rossi 2001).

Although evidence is anecdotal, more than one turf manager has noticed that when
the soil's calcium-to-magnesium ratio (Ca:Mg) is adjusted to ~8:1, grub problems
seemed to disappear. A researcher at the University of Massachusetts attempted to
replicate this, but her results were negative (Vittum 1984). This research, however, did
not focus on the Ca:Mg ratio but rather on the influence of lime on Japanese beetle
grub populations. Research specific to the benefits of an ideal Ca:Mg ratio is scant.

Another, often effective treatment for grubs is the application of entomopathogenic
nematodes. These near-microscopic worms enter the bodies of grubs and release bacteria that quickly infect and kill them. Nematodes usually enter the insect larvae through
natural openings, and the bacteria they release produce a toxic enzyme that kills the grub
within 24 hours. The nematodes then use the remains of the grub as a resource for their
breeding activities. Usually, those resources will support the conception of three successive generations of nematodes, after which the nematodes must escape the body of the
host and find new larvae to infect. At soil temperatures around 70°F (20°C), this cycle
takes one to two weeks. The infective stage of the nematode is called the *juvenile stage*.
Juveniles do not eat and can live in the soil for extended periods.

Nematodes need moisture to remain active. If they are introduced into a dry soil,
or if the soil dries out after they are applied, they are likely to be ineffective at controlling grubs. If they are applied in the spring and the soil dries out during the summer,
they may have to be reapplied in the fall if they are to control the newest brood of larvae. It is best to thoroughly moisten the soil before applying nematodes. Nematodes
can migrate into the soil if moisture is adequate. They appear to accumulate after several annual applications and continue to control grubs without reapplication, but it is
not known for how long.

Nematodes function best in loamy soils where porosity is ample, but not so porous
that the soil dries out quickly. Heavy soils inhibit the movement of nematodes, but
grubs are rarely found in these soils, so the point is somewhat moot. Sandy soils, on
the other hand, which can harbor large infestations of grubs, often do not stay moist
enough to sustain active nematodes. Unless irrigated or in a naturally moist climate,
nematodes may not perform well in a sandy soil. If moisture is adequate, most juveniles can exist for about three months in the soil without a host.

There is evidence that nematodes can enter a dormant stage to survive conditions
such as drought or frost. Introducing them as protection from grubs before grub
activity is present is a common practice. Most nematodes can exist in a temperature
range of 32° to 90°F. They are, however, most active in soils between 65° and 85°F. Turf

mowed too low during the hottest part of the season may allow soil temperatures to exceed the upper limits of the nematodes' temperature range. Some strains of nematodes can migrate down into cooler horizons; some cannot.

Nematodes can withstand high pressure—up to 300 pounds per square inch (psi)—which makes it possible to apply them through almost any water-dispensing system. They are best applied in the early morning, in early evening, or on a cloudy day. Exposure to direct sunlight for more than seven minutes can sterilize them. They will still be able to infect and kill grubs, but they will not be able to reproduce.

Many strains of nematodes are entomopathogenic, but only a few are commonly used in commercial offerings. The *Steinernema sp.* is a strain that attaches itself to a soil particle and waits in ambush for a grub. Research suggests this strain is less effective at controlling grubs because the nematodes reside too close to the soil's surface (Gaugler 2000). A strain called *Steinernema glaseri* shows greater promise as an effective, biological grub control. The *Steinernema* nematodes reside near the surface of the soil and attach themselves to hosts that frequent the soil-thatch interface. Webworms, cutworms, armyworms, and woodborers are particularly susceptible to this strain of nematode. Steinernematids are most effective at temperatures between 72° and 82°F (21°–26°C). The *Heterorhabditis sp.* is a hunter that seeks out grubs by following their trail of exudates. Unlike the *Steinernema* strain, it can find and infect larvae several inches below the soil's surface. The *Steinernema* nematodes reproduce via a male and a female entering the grub, whereas the *Heterorhabditis* nematodes are hermaphroditic; only one is needed inside the grub to initiate the reproductive cycle. Each of these strains can be effective under the right conditions, and preparations that include both *Steinernema sp.* and *Heterorhabditis sp.* are available. A long list of suppliers appears in the *Directory of Least Toxic Pest Control Products* (produced by Bio-Integral Resource Center [BIRC]; see "Sources and Resources" for contact information). This directory contains sources of many biological and botanical pest controls.

Managers who have problems with mole crickets may also be able to use entomopathogenic nematodes soon. A new strain, recently discovered in South America—where mole crickets originated—is capable of controlling them on a large scale (Roth 2001). Researchers at the universities of Florida and Nebraska and at Ohio State University have been experimenting with several strains, including *Steinernema riobrava*, *S. scapterisci*, and *Heterorhabditis indica*; they have found that *S. scapterisci* provides the most effective control against mole crickets (Roth 2001). The University of Florida has secured three patents for using them as an insect control, and researchers there expect the nematodes will be commercially available soon. Producers have run into a logistical problem, however. The nematodes must be reared in vivo using mole crickets as hosts—and mole crickets are difficult to breed and even harder to catch.

Pest Nematodes

Entomopathogenic nematodes are different from pest nematodes (phytopathogenic), which attack plant roots, and they cannot change from being insect pathogens to plant pathogens. However, some species of nematodes do not normally feed on roots but will if their preferred source of food is not available. Tylenchus nematodes, for example, normally feed on fungi that may or may not be pathogenic to plants, but the nematode can change from being a beneficial nematode to a pest if soil fungi are not available. In a biologically active soil, Tylenchus would never be a significant pest but might provide many benefits to plants. The Tylenchus might mistakenly consume the Chytrid fungus, which becomes a parasite when ingested by a nematode. Arthobotrys fungi release the same materials as plant roots to attract and trap phytopathogenic nematodes. High populations of organisms living in the rhizosphere, such as mycorrhizae and bacteria, normally offer adequate protection from pest nematodes. The Mononchus nematode feeds primarily on other nematodes, many of which are pests. In a biologically rich soil, pest nematodes are rarely a problem. In view of the fact that the vast majority of nematode species are beneficial—some crucial—to a functioning soil ecosystem, using a nematicide is almost always counterproductive.

Integrated Pest Management

Many turf managers often ignore the simple philosophy that a problem should be found before treatment is applied. Integrated pest management (IPM) has, to some, become just another commercially attractive buzzword like low-spray, no-spray, and natural. In a true IPM program, treatment is usually withheld until both the problem and the problem area are identified. In order to do this properly, monitoring or scouting must be part of the program. The problem with monitoring, according to many professionals, is that it is too time-consuming. Unfortunately, what many managers fail to understand is that monitoring or scouting will, most often, pay for itself (and often result in significant savings).

A great example of this is a project conducted by Cornell University in 1991 at a golf course in upstate New York (Leslie 1994). Workers scouted the entire course for grubs by lifting sections of sod with a cup cutter in a 10-foot by 10-foot grid pattern. The cup cutter removes a plug that measures $\frac{1}{10}$ square foot so an estimated number of grubs per square foot can be calculated. The workers identified all the problem areas on the course for a labor expense of $360 They reduced their normal pesticide application by 75% in the first year, and the course did not sustain any damage from grubs. The scouting program was an immense success. A program like this would net higher profits no matter what type of material—chemical, botanical, or biological—is used to control the grubs.

There are other good examples of how monitoring has not only reduced the number of problems but also reduced the cost of maintenance; however, the grounds crew must be trained to identify pests and tolerable thresholds. This training may lead to higher wages for staff members, but the outcome is better insect control and more savings.

Another Cornell University research project (Grant et al. 1994) monitored grub populations on more than 300 residential lawns in upstate New York and found that even in a bad year (good for the grubs), only 18 percent of the total lawn area monitored needed treatment. They also found that most preventive treatments for grubs were a waste of time and money. If, on average, a manager could cut back the amount of grub controls by 82 percent, the savings would be significant.

Light traps can be a helpful tool to indicate what types of insect pests are visiting the area, especially at night. Early indications of various pests can prepare or alert managers to scout more frequently and apply controls before significant damage occurs.

Finding problems before they become epidemic is always the most prudent practice, for both aesthetic and economic reasons. Treating problems that do not exist can be a waste of time, effort, and money as well as an unnecessary infusion of pollutants into the environment. It can also alter the ecology of the treated area to a point where new problems are created.

Starting Over

If grub damage is severe, renovation may be the only solution. Disturbing the soil with a tiller, Aera-Vator®, Rotadairon®, or other type of cultivating device before seeding has its advantages and its disadvantages. The tiller can act as a physical killer to grubs, literally beating them to death, but it can also introduce excessive oxygen into the soil, which can destroy a good portion of the soil's organic matter component. In a rich soil, the trade may be worth it, but in an already poor soil, the loss of fertility may jeopardize the health of the new seedlings to a point where maladies other than grubs affect the turf.

Tilling in good-quality, mature compost is an effective way to counter this problem. Mature compost, if incorporated into the top 4 to 6 inches of the soil, can be used at doses of 1 to 2 cubic yards per 1,000 square feet. Too much, however, can create a layer of soil that makes too abrupt a change in consistency from the layer beneath it. This condition (called *layering*) can inhibit the movement of water and gases through soil horizons.

Another problem with the tiller is the amount of dormant weed seeds brought to the surface by deep tillage. Shallow tillage brings fewer seeds to the surface. Additionally, if well-made, mature compost is incorporated, the speed at which turf seeds germinate is generally increased and seed mortality usually decreases, especially when seaweed extract is also applied. The turf canopy often establishes quickly enough that weeds don't have the opportunity to become competitive.

Slit overseeding is another alternative that neither disturbs the soil significantly nor causes the destruction of organic matter. This tool physically kills some of the grubs, but it doesn't cut deeply enough to cause significant impact. Core aerating also adversely affects a grub population. Topdressing with a compost and sand mix can replace the oxidized organic matter lost.

Animal Damage

In many cases, the population of grubs is not concentrated enough to damage turf but is adequate to attract skunks, moles, raccoons, crows, and other animals foraging for larvae. The damage caused by these creatures digging through the turf can be significant. The immediate response by many turf managers is to apply an effective larvicide as soon as possible. Unfortunately, this practice is often a waste of time and money. The first problem is that the animals may be foraging for something other than grubs. The second is that by the time the larvicide takes effect, most of the animal damage may be done. A third factor to consider is that when these animals are most actively foraging, the grubs are usually at their most advanced instar stage—a stage at which most larvicides offer little or no control.

Animals are great indicators of problem areas. Notes can be taken or maps drawn indicating hot spots. Over the years, this information may prove extremely valuable. Knowing where problems areas are can increase the success of future treatments or repellant applications.

Skunks, when they are not digging for grubs, are generally beneficial. Other favorites in their diet include grasshoppers, crickets, cutworms, and other fleshy insects such as sod webworms and caterpillars. They also feed on bird eggs, moles, shrews, and small reptiles. Skunks nest in wood or brush piles, hollow logs or trees, or stacks of lumber or firewood. Removal of nesting sites such as these can reduce the amount of skunk activity.

Similarly, raccoons like to nest in abandoned burrows, hollow trees or logs, or other covered and cozy refuges. Elimination of the nesting sites usually results in a reduction of raccoon activity.

Moles are also beneficial animals that can damage turf. It's unlikely that controlling white grubs will have much effect on mole activity because they eat other insect larvae and earthworms. The raised ridges created by moles are unsightly and can cause turf root mortality if left unattended for too long. In spring, mole activity near the surface is typically greater than at other times of the year and is not normally indicative of predation. Male moles dig extensive tunnels just below the surface to hunt for females, not necessarily for food. In fact, during wetter times of the year, moles forage for food deep enough below the surface that evidence of their activity is unnoticeable. Moles are solitary creatures, so there are rarely more than three to four in an affected area.

Trapping is the most effective method of eliminating moles, but this strategy may not be practical on sports fields. None of the folklorish remedies like chewing gum, car exhaust, lye, razor blades, thorns, household chemicals, gasoline, broken glass, human hair, or flooding the tunnels have any significant effect. Flooding can eliminate newborn moles, but adults are good swimmers. Many of these so-called remedies are much more harmful to turf than the moles are. Any type of roller can flatten the unsightly ridges created by moles and, if this is done within several hours of the tunnel's creation, turf usually recovers quickly. The few minutes per day it takes to repair damage from moles is less costly, less time-consuming, and has less ecological impact than applying a larvicide for grubs or setting (and checking) traps.

A few commercially available products containing castor oil as their active ingredient have shown promising results. These products must be watered into the soil to be effective, but drought or heavy rains may reduce their effectiveness. Healthy, well-rooted turf can mask the damage caused by moles. In a thick stand of turf, moles don't always break the surface because turf roots hold it together so well. Additionally, the healthy, thick stand of turf may offer few meals for moles anyway. Moles generally don't inhabit any one area for long unless factors such as poor management encourage high populations of insect larvae. Patience and a roller may be the best remedy.

Treatment for animal damage can consist of a rake, a roller, possibly some seed, and some well-aged compost. In a healthy turf, the evidence of grub hunters should be gone within a few days. Conventional treatment for grubs may stress the biology of the area and inhibit its ability to recover as quickly.

Birds, such as starlings or crows, that appear as pests on the field may be performing a valuable service by foraging for insect larvae or adults. There is no guarantee that what they are eating are, in fact, turf pests, but if insect pests are abundant, a large portion of the bird's diet will likely consist of that insect. In addition, some birds, like starlings, can act like an ultralight, silent-running, microfine aeration machine, pecking tiny holes in the sod where air and water can more easily interface with the soil.

Crows can cause more damage than the four-legged diggers. They rip and tear up turf in large chunks and rarely find enough grubs to justify the amount of damage they cause. Their foraging, however, is a pretty clear signal to the manager that a closer look is advisable. Crows can wreak havoc on an area for as long as plump, tasty grubs are close to the surface, and about the only course of action available is to repair the damage as often as needed. Crows tend to work in the same area, but their schedule is often inconsistent. During some periods, daily repairs will be necessary, and then the crows will take a day or two off. Just when it seems as though they've gone elsewhere, the damage reappears.

Treatments for grubs are ineffective, for the most part, because when crows and other animals are digging for grubs, the larva are usually too mature to control. If grooming, fertility, water, and patience are applied, chances are good that the turf will recover and be stronger than before. If the manager is not willing to tolerate the damage component of this cycle, however, then the bird's target insect must be identified and treated well before the foraging begins. Action requires prior knowledge of the susceptible areas and of the insect pest's life cycle. Larvicides must be used at early instar stages and repellants before eggs are deposited. Eradicating the birds, by whatever means, is counterproductive and, in many regions, illegal. Unfortunately, controlling the insects with pesticides may cause a disruption to the ecology of the immediate environment that may, in the long term, cause further problems. Again, the strategy of repelling the adult females before egg-laying occurs may be just the ticket for eliminating damage from both grubs and grub hunters.

The best winged hunter is probably the robin. It waits patiently and appears to look or listen for activity beneath the soil's surface. When it determines the location and depth of its prey, it plunges its beak into the soil and almost always extracts some food.

If bird populations become a real problem, USDA researchers found, grape flavoring from a food-grade chemical called *methyl anthranilate* effectively repels for many birds. Products containing this ingredient can be diluted and sprayed onto problem areas; the birds generally find it distasteful. A couple of EPA-registered products on the market (ReJex-iT® AG-36 and ReJex-iT® TP-40) contain this active ingredient.

Many managers welcome winged predators and some, in fact, erect bird and bat houses to attract more of these hungry hunters. Although it is inconsistent and difficult to quantify, predation does have a dollar value, and it makes economic as well as ecological sense to exploit it as much as possible.

Beneficial pests such as birds, earthworms, moles, skunks, and other organisms whose activities are largely advantageous to their immediate ecosystem but may cause some aesthetic impact on the landscape. Unfortunately, eliminating these pests can result in infestations of other, far more damaging pests.

CHECK YOUR PERSPECTIVE

The Turf Resource Center and Lawn Institute recently released an article in which pesticides are compared with medicines. Many of the chemicals that kill turf pests are presented as similar, both in structure and purpose, to medicines that kill diseases or parasites in humans. The point of the article was that we (the public) should be no more afraid of pesticides than we are of medicines. To anyone familiar with statistics about medicinally induced injury or death, however, the article inadvertently points out the dangers of both pesticides and many modern medicines. There is no question that more people are sickened, injured, or killed from the side effects of many medicines than from exposure to pesticides—for that matter, exposure to lightning, earthquakes, floods, tornadoes, hurricanes, typhoons, forest fires, volcanic eruptions, avalanches, and some small wars, too. So how does this comparison serve to reduce our fear of pesticides? It depends on how one looks at it. To some, this article seems to indicate that pesticides are as benign as medicines; to others, as dangerous as medicines. In this instance, the same words generate two very different perspectives.

There are many strong arguments for and against the use of pesticides, and, generally, they all make sense to someone. People who are concerned with the environment or human health may be inclined to believe almost anything negative about pesticides. Generally, they are convinced that pesticides pollute the environment, disrupt the ecosystem, and threaten human health. On the other hand, people whose livelihoods are somehow connected to the purchase, sale, or application of pesticides may believe almost any positive statement made about these chemicals. Many of them believe that environmental and human health concerns are nonissues and that there is no hard evidence to substantiate these claims. Over time, the pesticide issue has evolved into a political tug-of-war. Standing between these opposing viewpoints are people who don't understand, don't care, or both. Most athletes, fans, and coaches are probably in this group. If the manager can provide a playing field that looks good and is functionally safe for sports players, coaches, and fans probably don't care how it is maintained.

In science, especially turf science, discussions of tolerance are ubiquitous. The amount of tolerance any manager has for any pest ultimately depends on the decision makers. If acceptable levels of weeds or insect damage is low (they cannot tolerate much), then that becomes the tolerance threshold of the fields. The lower the threshold, the more intense the management regime must be, regardless of how the fields are managed (chemical versus ecological).

The powers that be may not understand ecology, but they can usually understand economics. If it is apparent to them that their higher expectations carry relatively higher costs, they may be inclined to tolerate a more natural-looking playing field. The term *playing field* may also change one's perspective. The term *sports field* often brings to mind an expensive facility where professional sporting events take place, whereas a *playing field* may be envisioned as a place where young people play. Does the tolerance threshold on a *playing field* have to be as low as it is on a *sports field*?

From an ecological perspective, pesticides may alter the balance of soil relationships to the point where the need for more control is perpetuated. The fear that all will spoil as the biocidal tap begins to close is endearing to most pesticide manufacturers, but if turf is growing in a healthy ecosystem, the reality is quite different.

POINTS TO REMEMBER

Disease

- Pest problems can be related either directly or indirectly to plant stress.
- Plants have defense mechanisms, but they are the least exploited approach to pest control.
- A biologically active soil is likely to exhibit natural disease suppression from organisms that compete, antagonize, or parasitize pathogens.
- Well-made, well-aged compost seems to harbor a lot of disease-suppressive organisms. Some of the these organisms have been isolated, identified, and proliferated in special breeding chambers for application through irrigation systems.
- Poor cultural practices such as mowing too short or with dull blades can often add just enough stress to help pathogens succeed.
- The most important problem facing most sports field managers is compaction. Many fields host more athletic activity than they can physically withstand, and soil inevitably becomes compacted.
- Many of the pesticides we use to solve problems may inadvertently cause others if the material being applied stresses predators, plants, or key soil organisms.
- Clippings returned to the soil can be highly beneficial. They provide food for earthworms and other important organisms and return as much as 2 pounds of nitrogen per 1,000 square feet.
- Stress is often related to nutrient deficiencies. By encouraging large and active populations of soil organisms, one can biologically manage many plant nutrients efficiently and effectively.
- Heat and drought can cause more stress and damage than most other natural phenomena.
- Air movement through turf is an important natural action that evaporates the leaf surface moisture, which helps many pathogens to succeed.
- Detecting disease at an early stage is important to turf health. Personnel should be trained to recognize disease symptoms and required to report them at once.

Weeds

- Multiple turf cultivars provide a stable and resilient playing surface. Introducing more than one variety may improve establishment and longevity in areas where a single cultivar won't do well.
- Cutting height has more impact on weeds than any other cultural practice. Research shows that the higher turf is cut, the lower the occurrence of weeds.
- The use of herbicides is more effective, less expensive, and has less impact on the ecosystem if the identity of target weeds is known. Moreover, chronic problems with

specific weeds can reveal physical, chemical, or biological soil problems that are relatively easy to remedy.

- Preemergent herbicides are often overused and may not be necessary every year.
- Returning grass clippings can help maintain a thick and invasive turf canopy that makes weed establishment more difficult. On the other hand, if weeds are already established, collecting clippings during periods when seed heads are being produced can reduce weed proliferation.
- Too little or too much fertilizer can stimulate weed growth by either suppressing a vigorous turf or creating conditions conducive to other pest problems.
- Overseeding is an important management practice that is often overlooked.
- New natural weed controls are commercially available—some of them very effective—but using them without establishing conditions that favor turf is not much different from a chemical program, just more expensive.
- Conditions in the soil that favor weeds include improper pH, imbalanced base saturation, low cation exchange capacity, nutrient imbalance, high temperature, and low moisture, not to mention poor physical conditions and inadequate biological activity. Analysis is often an effective method of determining whether any of these conditions needs attention.

Insects

- Plants have powerful defense systems against insects, but they must be strong and healthy for these systems to work effectively.
- Often defense mechanisms are disabled during hot, dry, and stressful periods. Sometimes, low-volume but high-frequency irrigation can reduce stress enough to make a significant difference.
- Applications of pesticides often eradicate more than just target pests. Predators are abundant in a healthy turf ecosystem but are susceptible to many of the same biocides as their prey.
- Thatch is often home to many pest insects. Earthworms are the most effective biological dethatching machines known, but their populations depend on adequate organic resources and they have a low tolerance for many pesticides.
- Many varieties of ryegrass and fescue contain endophytes, or fungi living within the plants tops that protects the plant from foraging organisms.
- Many biological and botanical controls effectively reduce pest populations to below an acceptable threshold without excessively impacting nontarget organisms.
- Although not an insect, plant-pathogenic nematodes can be an important turf pest. They are, however, effectively controlled in a biologically active system by predators and pathogens.
- Integrated pest management (IPM) is a frequently misconstrued term meaning that a problem should be found before it is treated. Treating problems that do not exist can cause an unnecessary infusion of toxins into the environment and alter the ecology of the treated area to a point where new problems are created.

Chapter 6

CULTURAL PRACTICES

Knowledge is a valuable asset, but realizing more is unknown than known is a humbling and important awakening for most professionals. Most experienced managers realize this. Decades of accumulated experiences and wisdom earned from countless successes and failures register in the confident but humble expression of the veteran turf manager. Knowing the right thing to do and the right time to do it is a product of this experience, an application of skill—an art. This steward has learned to overcome the urge for reckless reaction in favor of thoughtful response. He comprehends the anomalies of his fields and their ever-changing conditions. He recognizes that products and practices that work elsewhere may lack efficacy at home. He understands that research and anecdotal evidence sometimes lead to innovations but often must be customized to fit his unique setting. If he wants to reduce or eliminate pesticide use, however, he also must consider the ecology of his environment and recognize how crucial it is to his decision-making process.

This chapter contains ideas and innovations practiced by turf managers and researchers who favor adjustments in cultural methods over applications of biocides. Some may be practical and successful for the reader, and some may not. Some may have to be adjusted or tuned to fit the circumstances of a particular area. Some may need to be considered and disregarded. If only one idea from this chapter reduces the use of pesticides on a reader's fields, this book will have accomplished its goal.

The practices that cultivate beautiful and healthy turf are not all learned in the classroom or the textbook. Many are learned in the field, usually with the guidance of a master who's spent years honing his skills well beyond what schools and research could offer. His humility is as valuable a skill as any other he's learned. The grounds supervisor is often weighed down with an overwhelming amount of information from multiple sources and must sift and cull until the ideas that make sense pass through his discriminating filters. Even then, there's no guarantee of success and often no surprise if he is humbled yet again. Skepticism becomes an automatic response to the latest and greatest of anything. The experienced manager takes advice, whether it's from a university, another grounds manager, or a salesperson, with an open mind and a grain of salt. He understands that no matter how successful a procedure is elsewhere, it must be tested and probably adjusted before it has real value to him. The innovative steward experiments with methods that make sense, but he doesn't confuse himself by testing too many hypotheses at once.

Successful cultural practices include what the turf manager doesn't do as much as what he does do. If there is intent in an omission, it is a cultural practice. Leaving the clippings on the fields is a cultural practice if it's intentional. Not irrigating or applying fertilizer or skipping a mowing cycle during heat stress periods or disease outbreak is also a cultural practice if it is omitted on purpose.

Good ideas that work are often shared. Managers and researchers who've had success with some cultural practice often write about their experiences, and there's usually a turf, golf, or landscape periodical somewhere that publishes the story. Searching the journals and trade magazines for interesting ideas can easily absorb too much valuable time; luckily, a database at Michigan State University called the Turfgrass Information Center has collected an impressive number of records that pertain to such articles, books, etc. (For contact information, see "Sources and Resources.")

Most modern turf managers have many expensive tools at their disposal that are designed to create better, faster playing surfaces, and accomplish it in less time than ever before. Some of these specialized tools are used every day and others as infrequently as annually, but all are considered essential. Further, the way in which they are used is critical. Every manager worth his salt knows the dangers of poorly adjusted or improperly used mowers, sprayers, spreaders, aerators, or verticutters. Almost every tool has the potential to beautify or to create an unmitigated disaster. Proper use and accurate adjustments are critical but not normally difficult for someone with experience. It is important, however, that the operator of these specialized tools consider their impact on the ecosystem that promotes healthy, disease-resistant, and competitive grass. Many beneficial practices can become counterproductive if executed improperly, too often, or not often enough.

There is probably no place on earth where sports turf conditions exist naturally, so we cannot peek at how nature cultivates a healthy playing field. On the other hand, most living organisms—including plants—have an innate ability to adapt to environmental conditions as long as certain basic needs are met. Grass plants grow in a system that includes the plant, the soil, and the atmosphere. The dependence of each element on the other can be enhanced but cannot be replaced by man-made inputs, especially if the manager is trying to maintain his fields ecologically.

ORGANIC MATTER AND BIOLOGICAL ACTIVITY

Organic matter is home, food, and energy for billions of essential organisms in the turf ecosystem. Inadequate resources for these organisms can result in a reduction of biological activity and an increase in problems that it ordinarily suppresses. Cultural practices that reduce this asset increase the likelihood of problems. Compaction, for example, is a constant problem for most sports field managers. A compacted soil lacks pore space that would otherwise contain roots, atmosphere, and water, constituents that are vital to both healthy plants and beneficial soil organisms. As the volume of air-filled pores in the soil is reduced below 20%, soil biological activity begins to wane. If the air space is reduced to below 10 percent, anaerobic organisms begin to dominate. Anaerobic respiration can produce compounds that are toxic to turf roots. Soil gases are unable to cycle to and from the aboveground atmosphere in compacted conditions, and carbon dioxide can accumulate to toxic levels.

Mowing with heavy equipment—especially when the soil is wet—and collecting clippings (food for earthworms and other decay organisms) can contribute to the natural inclination toward compaction. Overuse of aeration tools can also contribute to long-term problems if the introduction of too much air is oxidizing valuable organic matter that is not being replaced. This is generally less of a concern to most managers because the importance of organic matter is overshadowed by the importance of having a well-drained playing surface. Managers who understand the value of organic matter in the soil usually have less frequent and less severe turf problems.

The creation of soil organic matter is a slow biological process (see Chapter 1, under "Humus"), and many environmental conditions work to control its accumulation and properties. Regions with warmer climates and longer growing seasons naturally have less soil organic matter than colder climates with shorter seasons. Drier regions generally have lower natural levels of soil organic matter also. Set against the natural conditions that influence the accumulation of soil organic matter are cultural practices that can accelerate its demise. Organic matter includes everything from the living biomass to stable humus with thatch, plant residues, and labile humus in between. For the purpose of this discussion, superfluous thatch or plant residues are not considered when soil organic matter is mentioned. The discussion pertains to stable, labile, and other forms of humus.

The first step toward preserving this valuable asset is to understand some of the many benefits it provides (see Chapter 1, under "Biological Contribution"). One of the main objectives of this book is to convince the reader that soil organic matter and the diversity of life it supports are vital components of a healthy and functioning turf ecosystem. A crop that needs as much attention as the turf is the crop of organisms living in the soil. These organisms contribute immeasurably to the health and welfare of turf plants. Their ability to manage nitrogen, for example, makes them indispensable. Applying too little or too much nitrogen is easy for even the most experienced applicator. The factors that influence both the plants' need and their utilization of nitrogen are constantly changing and unpredictable. Soil organisms have the innate ability to regulate the amount of nitrogen available to plants in almost perfect synchrony with plant needs. The same is true with most other soil-borne nutrients. How is it possible that soil organisms can regulate nutrients without knowing, in advance, what plants need? Believe it or not, plant roots release nutrients that foster populations of specific organisms that are best suited to serve plant requirements.

Contrary to what many believe, adequate levels of biologically matured organic matter do not compromise drainage or playability but *do* provide a plethora of benefits, many of which reduce stress or increase the turf's resistance to stress.

Some of the factors that influence the accumulation and characteristics of organic matter include oxygen, water, temperature, pH, and the carbon-to-nitrogen ratio of the soil. These factors also influence plant growth, which is the main source of residues contributing to the formation of soil organic matter. In general, conditions that are optimal for the plants are also best for the accumulation of organic matter. However, *optimal* means *most favorable, desirable,* or *satisfactory.* Excessive levels of anything good for plants can cause problems. Most of us are well aware of problems caused by too much water or fertilizer, but many other materials and cultural practices taken to excess can also cause problems.

Indiscriminate applications of lime, for example, can raise the soil pH to levels that are favorable for decay organisms, but there may not be a corresponding increase in the production of plant residues (i.e., plant growth is not increased). The resulting increase in the population and activity of decay organisms can cause a related decrease in soil organic matter. Managers who lime without the benefit of a soil pH test run the risk of creating this scenario. In Figure 6-1, it is evident that elevated levels of lime increase the evolution of carbon dioxide from the decomposition of soil organic matter. A soil pH test should be the only criterion for applying lime (see Chapter 4, under "pH," "How Much Lime?" and "Too Alkaline?"). Constant and prolonged use of calcareous sand can also raise the soil's pH to above optimum, and correction may be difficult, if not impractical. Regular contributions of well-made, well-aged compost during topdress operations can replace organic matter losses from a higher-than-optimal pH and buffer changes in pH from calcareous sand.

SAND AND DRAINAGE

With so much attention paid to drainage, many sports fields start out with a conspicuous absence of organic matter in the soil, and managers seem to keep it that way, whether intentionally or inadvertently. The natural porosity of sand increases the

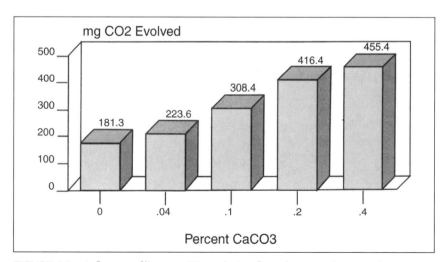

FIGURE 6-1   Influence of lime on CO_2 evolution from decomposing organic matter. Adapted from Waksman, 1936.

volume of air that resides in the soil, reducing the likelihood of humus accumulation. Core aeration, which is often essential to alleviate compaction, increases oxygenation even more. More sand is usually applied during topdressing operations. Many managers use a mixture of sand and a small percentage of topsoil as a topdressing material. Unfortunately, sand contributes no organic matter to the soil, and the quality of the topsoil used in these mixes is rarely tested for organic matter or anything else. It's important to note here that the addition of sand to clay soil can ultimately create more compaction and less drainage than adding nothing. An equal ratio of sand and clay is used to make bricks, and although the brick-making process differs from conditions in the soil, the potential for severe compaction and insignificant drainage remains.

Drainage is an important consideration on sports fields. Damage caused by playing, marching, or driving on wet fields can be severe and protracted. The ultimate remedy for superfluous water is a system whereby it drains rapidly through the soil profile and is then conveyed out of the subsoil into catch basins. Prescription Athletic Turf (PAT) is a system that speeds this process by pumping water from the drainpipes, creating a vacuum that literally sucks excess moisture out of the soil. Native soil fields often cannot be drained with underground drainage systems because water does not move quickly enough through the soil profile. In these cases, crowning becomes the only method of conveying excess water from the field. Crown construction is employed to increase the speed at which water exits the field. The center of many football or soccer fields is built with a crown 1 to 2 feet higher than the sidelines and 2 to 3 feet higher than the drainage ditch that surrounds the field. Both crowning and underground drainage are needed for worst-case scenarios and, albeit infrequently, they do occur.

Managers with limited budgets may not have the luxury of either system; their only recourse is to make do with what they have. Idealistically speaking, the best action a manager can take during extremely wet conditions is to keep players, pedestrians, and vehicles off the turf. This is often impractical. In a situation where the field has neither crowning nor a drainage system, topdressing with sand is not going improve its water-shedding capabilities (see Figure 6-2). A compost/sand topdress mixture will not improve drainage either, but it typically improves the health and vigor of the turf and, over time, may improve the water absorption capacity of the soil. A thicker, healthier turf can tolerate the damage caused by playing on wet ground better than can turf with problems. Crowning can be increased over time by topdressing more heavily in the center of the field. Depending on how much crowning is needed, however, this process could take decades.

Another consideration for dyed-in-the-wool sand users is whether or not correct particle sizes are being applied. Many managers use what is conveniently available, which may be fine for making cement but not necessarily appropriate for topdressing turf (see Figure 6-3). The size of sand particles can range from 0.05 mm to 2 mm. This means that coarse sand particles can be as much as 40 times larger than fine particles. Using sand with a broad range of particle sizes can lead to compaction problems over time. Very coarse sand (almost fine gravel) can make turf roots more prone to drought stress. Ask the sand supplier for a sieve analysis before purchasing. Using sand without compost is not being advocated here, but even with compost, 60 to 80 percent of the sand particles should be between 0.25 and 1.0 mm (medium to coarse).

FIGURE 6-2   Applications of sand do not improve drainage if water cannot percolate through the native soil. Photo courtesy Dartmouth College Maintenance.

Angularity is yet another consideration. Rounded sand particles tend to move under relatively light forces, and surface strength is often significantly reduced. Players, marchers, and maintenance vehicles can easily disrupt the turf's surface. Sharper sand particles tend to lock together and create a firmer surface. On the other hand, sand that is too sharp can stress turf roots.

FIGURE 6-3   Is your source of sand appropriate for turf? This sand is used to make concrete and has a wide range of particle sizes.

Adding compost with sand can, over time, compensate for the lack of firmness inherent in sand with low angularity and buffer the effects of sand that is too sharp. Activities of soil organisms create organic glues that flocculate sand particles, increase surface strength, and preserve porosity. Some sand-based fields are constructed with synthetic subsurface mats. This system works well to increase surface strength, especially where sharper sand is unavailable, but it is not a substitute for the biological resources provided by compost. The mat lies about an inch below the surface, and turf roots grow down through the mat. It is nearly impossible to tear turf out because cleats can't reach any deeper than the surface of the mat. Unfortunately, cultivation through these mats can be problematic. Some managers add topsoil to firm sand particles, but without knowing the texture and other physical attributes of the topsoil, there's little guarantee it will effectively bind sand without causing other problems.

TOPSOIL

Imported topsoil is usually altered between excavation and installation. The digging, scraping, dozing, loading, transporting, dumping, mixing, screening, and spreading of topsoil causes significant changes to its structure, chemistry, and biology. If topsoil sits in a pile for an extended period, more of these changes occur. Unfortunately, none of these changes improves the quality of the topsoil. Organic matter content is reduced, beneficial organisms such as earthworms and mycorrhizae fungi are all but wiped out, and the aggregation of soil particles is significantly diminished. The biological component can recover and eventually repair much of the damage if the topsoil contains optimum levels of organic resources, but the organic matter component is significantly reduced between the time it is excavated and when it is delivered. The only component of topsoil that may remain unaltered is the weed seed content (see Figure 6-4).

COMPOST

A well-made and well-aged compost substituted for topsoil in the topdressing mix can not only arrest the loss of soil organic matter but also provide scores of other benefits—including disease suppression, thatch reduction, stress resistance, and reduced water consumption—without compromising drainage. Indeed, well-made mature compost can spark an explosion in the population of earthworms, whose tunnels significantly improve drainage. A topdressing mix with compost is especially helpful during core aeration; filling core holes with a compost mix can, over time, make soil less prone to compaction. Mixtures as rich as 1:1 (sand:compost) can gradually introduce enough organic matter to resist compaction on a more sustained basis.

Topdressing with any material that is significantly unlike the native soil can eventually cause layering, a condition that suppresses the movement of moisture and gases through soil horizons. Layering can create what is known as a *perched water table*, which limits the amount of both water and gases available to turf roots. Compost significantly reduces the likelihood of this phenomenon because it stimulates earthworm

FIGURE 6-4   Topsoil undergoes some major changes between
excavation and installation, none of which offer improvement.

activity. Earthworms constantly mix materials from different horizons, and their tunnels ensure adequate movement of moisture and gases through the soil profile. Topdressing with compost in conjunction with core aeration is also an appropriate method of interfacing different soil materials (see Figures 6-5a, 6-5b, and 6-5c). (See Chapter 3 for more information about the benefits of compost.)

HOW MUCH ORGANIC MATTER IS ENOUGH?

This discussion of organic matter begs the question of what constitutes an adequate level. The answer, unfortunately, is imprecise. As one begins to make important contributions of organic matter, such as applications of compost/sand topdress mixtures, it usually becomes apparent that levels prior to this action were inadequate. What is excessive is harder to define, but luckily, chances are that that level is economically impractical to attain. Each $1/4$-inch of topdress layer requires almost 34 cubic yards of material per acre. Burying turf with an excessively thick topdress layer is never sensible no matter what kind of material is applied, but the expense of this action would suppress even the most overzealous tendencies.

Architects who build fields in conformity with USGA specifications believe that 0.5 to 2 percent organic matter in a soil is adequate. They also believe that levels in excess of that amount may lead to drainage problems. An analysis of soil extracted from an ecologically maintained golf green in New Hampshire revealed organic matter levels between 3 and 4 percent, and drainage has not been a problem there. This is actually a surprisingly low figure after almost four decades of topdressing with compost, but it represents an extremely functional ecosystem that consumes the energy in these organic

Photo courtesy Dartmouth College Maintenance.

Photo courtesy Earth & Turf Company.

FIGURES 6-5 A, B and C   No matter how it is applied, a well-made, well-aged compost in the topdress mix can provide scores of benefits. Photo above courtesy Earth & Turf Company.

residues to perform essential biological activities. In a root zone study that began in 1997, researchers at Rutgers confirm that compost does not impede drainage. They found that a 20 percent contribution of compost in the root zone mixture outperformed all other combinations. The report added, "Unfortunately, [the compost plots] don't meet USGA specs. because they will only drain at 3" to 6" per hr." But, "Surprisingly they will NOT have standing water even after a heavy rain event" (Rossi 2002[b]).

Anecdotal data from a turf manager in Georgia showed that organic content in the surface layer can exceed 10 percent in less than a year if what he considers to be proper cultivation and topdressing is not carried out. Soils that accumulate that much dead plant matter in a single year must lack adequate levels of essential saprophytic soil organisms and probably receive superfluous nitrogen. Management should focus more on cultivating a healthy and diverse biomass than on putting holes, sand, and nitrogen in or on the soil. Excessive thatch and other undecomposed plant residues are not the kind of organic matter being advocated in this book. Cultivation may still be necessary to remove some of this tough, fibrous material even in a soil with an active biomass, but accumulation of these residues is typically much slower than in a sandy, biologically inactive soil.

To prescribe a precise or ideal amount of soil organic matter for all fields everywhere does not take into consideration all the environmental factors that control its accumulation and its destruction (see Chapter 1). It is unlikely that many managers would have the resources to build organic matter levels far beyond optimum. The exception might be a field that was originally built on bog or muck soil and already has excessively high levels of soil organic matter. If the field has been in operation for some time without drainage problems, these high levels of organic matter may not be cause for concern.

COMPACTION

Plant roots do not grow in soil; they grow in the spaces between soil particles. As the soil becomes compacted, those spaces shrink and root growth is inhibited. In compacted soil, roots tend to grow shorter and thicker, have less surface area, and occupy a shallower horizon of the soil profile. These stunted roots are unable to absorb adequate water and nutrients, resulting in lower shoot density, a reduction in carbohydrate reserves, and less drought resistance. Rhizome development in compacted soils is limited by more than a third, which in turn limits the turf's ability to fill in thin areas. Water trapped in compacted soil has difficulty moving up through soil horizons to the surface where it can evaporate and reduce the soil's temperature. Instead, this soil water can heat from the increased thermal conductivity of a denser soil and begin to poach the turf's roots.

Retarded water infiltration is another side effect of compaction. Just a small increase in bulk soil density can result in a significant reduction of the rate at which rainwater can permeate the soil's surface. Figure 6-6 shows the drop in infiltration rates as soil density increases. These values were measured at different locations and a certain degree of variation can be expected with different soil textures, but the overall

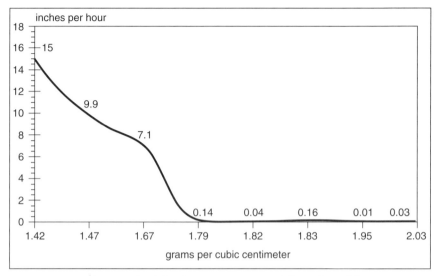

FIGURE 6-6   Influence of soil density on water permeability. Adapted from Ocean County Soil Conservation District (Friedman et al. 2001).

picture shows that the soil's ability to absorb and retain water is significantly reduced as density increases. In these data, there seems to be a critical threshold at ~1.7 grams per cubic centimeter (g/cm^3) soil density (typical of a sandy clay loam). Just a 7 percent increase in density (from 1.67 to 1.79 g/cm^3) results in a 98 percent decrease in the water infiltration rate.

Density values that affect root growth vary in different soils. Values given by the USDA's Natural Resources Conservation Service are shown in Table 6-1. Where attention is paid to the creation and preservation of organic matter, soils are less prone to compaction, but it can still occur.

TABLE 6-1
Soil Density Ranges
Rough guidelines: minimum density for optimum root growth

Texture	Bulk Density (g/cc)
Coarse, medium, and fine sand or loamy sand	1.80
Very fine sand or loamy very fine sand	1.77
Sandy loam	1.75
Loam or sandy clay loam	1.70
Clay loam	1.65
Sandy clay	1.60
Silt or silt loam	1.55
Silty clay loam	1.50
Silty clay	1.45
Clay	1.40

Compaction is most often a result of compression from too much traffic in a given area. Traffic includes players, cheerleaders, fans, marching bands, vehicles, and equipment. It is an unusual playing field that isn't eventually compacted from use. Practice fields can dilute the wear associated with a greater number of activities.

The weight of vehicles can exert excessive pressure on the soil. If fields are used for parking lots during events that draw an overflow of vehicles, compaction will always be a problem, especially if vehicles drive on wet ground. Vehicles driven on soft, wet soil often create ruts that have to be smoothed and reseeded, but this remedy does not repair the compaction underneath the ruts. High-quality turf may be extremely difficult to maintain on fields used as parking lots (see Figures 6-7a and 6-7b).

Another important problem created by compaction is sports injuries. There is a linear relationship between the level of compaction and the number of player injuries. An increase in the reported incidences of shinsplints and other running injuries should be a compelling signal to the turf manager that soil compaction must be relieved. Ignoring these signs may lead to more severe injuries to both the players and the turf plants in the not-too-distant future.

Mowers and other turf maintenance equipment can be heavy vehicles that add to compaction. If a manager has a choice of mowers, especially during wetter periods, the machine that exerts the least pressure on the soil is usually the best choice. This machine may not be lightest of the fleet but has the biggest footprint—that is, the one that exerts the least pressure per square inch. Large flotation tires and lower inflation pressure can significantly reduce soil compression. Tractors that are used for everything from plowing or blowing snow to moving earth may not have appropriate treads, and the tires may be overinflated for mowing turf (see Figure 6-8).

You can calculate the footprint of a mower by measuring the length of contact (front to back) that the tire has on a hard surface and multiplying it by the width of the

FIGURE 6-7A   Vehicles driven on soft wet soil can cause severe compaction that is not easy to fix. Photo courtesy Dartmouth College Maintenance.

FIGURE 6-7B   Vandalism can be as injurious as intentional trespass, but more difficult to control.

tire. For example, if an 8-inch-wide tire has 5 inches of contact, then the footprint of one tire is:

$$8 \times 5 = 40 \text{ inches}^2$$

If the machine has four tires the same size, then its total footprint is:

$$4 \times 40 - 160 \text{ inches}^2.$$

Often, the front tires are a different size and must be calculated separately. The pressure exerted by the machine equals the weight of the machine divided by the total footprint. If the machine weighs 1,200 pounds and has a total footprint of 160 square inches, then:

$$1,200 \div 160 = 7\frac{1}{2} \text{ pounds per inch}^2 \text{ (psi)}$$

FIGURE 6-8   Wide, low-pressure tires diffuse the weight of heavy equipment.

To put this figure in perspective, an average-sized athlete standing on one foot is applying $3\frac{1}{2}$ to 4 psi. This pressure increases if the player is running or jumping. The ideal amount of pressure exerted from a mower is difficult to calculate but would involve measurements of practicalities. A hovering push-mower that exerts nearly 0 psi on the soil would be ideal but impractical on a 2-acre field. On the other hand, using a mower that can cut 15 to 20 acres per hour on the same field while exerting >14 psi may be impractical too.

When the time comes to purchase new (or used) turf equipment, a predetermination of the footprint force may be advisable (see Figures 6-9a, 6-9b, and 6-9c).

The footprint calculation is an important consideration when choosing a machine, but keep in mind that the total weight of the vehicle is still applying relative pressure on the soil. When considering which machine to buy or lease, ask yourself another question: Which would cause the least damage if it ran over your foot?

Equipment that combines operations can also retard compaction. Each phase of renovation or other operations that require multiple trips over the field can contribute to a greater degree of compaction. Machines such as the RotaDairon® (RotaDairon Emrex) can aerate, prepare a seedbed, and plant seed—all in one pass. Multitasking equipment that accomplishes more work with fewer trips over the field usually reduces vehicle-induced compaction (see Figure 6-10).

A recent study from Rutgers (Rossi 2000[c]) suggests that core cultivation gives only temporary relief from compaction, and that within three weeks of aeration,

FIGURES 6-9A and B   Hover mowers exert little if any compression on the soil but may be impractical for large areas of turf.

FIGURE 6-9C   A mower that can cut 10–15 acres per hour may be practical for very large expanses of turf but superfluous for two or three soccer fields. Photo courtesy Land Pride.

compaction often returns to pretreatment levels. Returning clippings to fields that are prone to compaction can encourage populations of earthworms to alleviate compaction on a daily basis. Their tunneling activities create passageways through which air and water can infiltrate. If castings left on the surface of the fields present a problem, they can be easily smoothed each morning with a drag cable. Unfortunately, it may be inappropriate to leave wet clippings on the fields. Wet clippings can create unsightly clumps, especially if more than a third of top growth is cut, and may result in censure from superiors. If problematic fields can be mowed later in the day, the dry clippings left behind are rarely noticed. It is important, however, to consider the stress

FIGURE 6-10   Machines that mutitask with a single pass can reduce the frequency and severity of compaction. Photo courtesy RotaDairon Emrex, Inc.

factor if mowing on a very hot afternoon. During the summer, earthworms are relatively inactive at the surface, and the driest part of the day can also be the hottest and most stressful period. The stress of mowing added to heat and perhaps drought stress might be more damaging than beneficial. If practical, early-evening mowing may be best for recycling clippings on stressed fields.

If dollar spot is a perpetual problem, however, research from the University of Kentucky (Williams and Powell 1995) has shown that mowing early in the morning (especially with reel mowers) reduces the severity of the disease more than any other comparable cultural practice. Depending on how high and how often the turf is cut, returning the clippings may still be possible during early-morning mowing. Mulching mowers are helpful in reducing clumps. These machines recut clippings into small pieces that can move through the canopy more easily and decompose more rapidly. Mulching mowers are sometimes less fuel-efficient, especially if too much grass is being cut in one pass, but if cutting schedules conform to growth rate instead of time, fuel consumption is generally comparable (see Figure 6-11).

Other benefits from recycled clippings include contributions of nitrogen, better water infiltration, improved color, disease suppression, crabgrass suppression, increased root production, and thatch reduction. Over half the nitrogen from the fertilizer we apply resides in the clippings we often remove and discard. This return of organic nitrogen stimulates biological activity that cycles valuable carbon dioxide back to plant leaves for carbohydrate production, which increases root growth. Color improvement and the suppression of disease and crabgrass are secondary side effects. Over 25 percent more root mass is often produced where clippings are returned—which, on a dry basis, can contribute $1/2$ ton to 4 tons of organic matter per acre annually. As the moisture evapo-

FIGURE 6-11   Mulching mowers are designed to re-cut clippings into smaller pieces that can work down throught the canopy more easily.

FIGURE 6-12   Earthworms can maintain aeration better than most
mechanical systems during those periods of the season when they are active.

rates from fresh clippings, the surrounding area is cooled, mitigating heat stress. If recycling clippings on fields is impractical under any circumstances, their value for composting should not be ignored. All the benefits mentioned above are retained and
enhanced in the compost process. Compost can be applied when topdressing.

EARTHWORMS

Biological mitigation of compaction can often be accomplished by cultivating a thriving population of earthworms. Earthworms feed on clippings or compost topdress
applications, and their activities can alleviate compaction on a constant basis. They
may or may not be able to keep up with the amount of traffic, but it is reasonable to
assume that the larger their population and the more resources available to them at or
near the surface, the more tunneling and aeration they will perform. Their castings may
be a nuisance to managers who mow at golf course cutting heights, but they can easily
be smoothed with a drag cable. This process is called *poling* by some golf course superintendents, and not only does it dispatch earthworm castings but also it removes dew
and smoothes anomalies caused by other burrowing organisms. Managers who mow at
or above 1 inch, depending on the thickness of the turf, may never notice earthworm
activity (see Figure 6-12).

Drag (or poling) cables vary in thickness and length. The ideal length sweeps the
field in a single pass. Engage Agro (see "Sources and Resources" for contact information) makes a ³/₄-inch-thick braided nylon cable with a lead-weighted core called a
Fairway Snake. It was specifically manufactured to remove the dew from golf course

fairways and reduce the turf's susceptibility to dollar spot. The cable is towed between two ATVs or other light utility vehicles. Homemade rigs made from steel rope can also be used. Some managers double the cable, enabling a double sweep on each pass. The trailing cable length may need a section of chain or other type of weight to keep it from tangling and twisting with the leading length. Poling is a practice that takes experienced operators very little time per field. It removes dew and mycelium and smoothes earthworm castings, ant mounds, and debris left by green June beetles.

Earthworms can generate as much as 120 tons of castings per acre per year. This material contains valuable nutrients and organisms that promote healthy, stress-resistant plants. Some ancient civilizations revered the earthworm to the extent that it became a protected species. Earthworms borrow down 5 feet or more—far deeper than any mechanical aeration tool—and return valuable minerals from soil depths to the surface. An acre of soil can be home to as many as 500,000 earthworms building as much as 250 miles of tunnels in a week's time. Their activities not only improve the infiltration of oxygen and water to plant roots but also allow plant tops easier access to carbon dioxide they and other decay organisms generate. The resulting decrease in soil compaction at horizons beyond where aeration tools can reach allows roots easier access to deep soil moisture and nutrients.

Earthworm tunnels are coated with a sticky mucous that preserves the passageway longer than those created by tines. Some scientists estimate that these tunnels can stay intact for as long as a year. The mucous is rich in nutrients and thought to contain hormones that stimulate plant growth. Turf roots often occupy these tunnels and can reach greater soil depths using less energy.

EARTHWORMS AND THATCH

When earthworms are active, thatch decomposition is relatively rapid. Earthworms reduce thatch layers more effectively than most other soil organisms combined, with the possible exception of cleated athletes. Thatch accumulation can lead to conditions that stress turf or provide opportunities for pest problems. Under these circumstances, thatch management by earthworms is a welcome phenomenon. Thatch in small quantities, however, can be beneficial—it mitigates compaction and provides athletes a more forgiving surface—and, in rare cases, excessive earthworm activity can reduce thatch below optimum levels. However, periods of this overactivity would likely result in the alleviation of compaction and stimulation of plant growth (contributing to the accumulation of thatch). The system can be somewhat self-sustaining.

Earthworm activity normally subsides during hotter periods of the season, providing an opportunity for some thatch to accumulate. Generally, thatch accumulates only in fields where creeping species of grasses are grown. Kentucky bluegrass, for example, can potentially produce ideal layers of thatch—one reason for its popularity as a sports turf variety. Bluegrass thatch protects its roots from being torn by athletes and can provide a softer landing for players who fall or are tackled. Thatch can also keep players out of the mud when games are played on rainy days. Clump grasses, like fescues, are less likely to produce thatch.

Turf that sees a lot of sports activity, whether games, practices, or marching bands, seldom has ample opportunity to accumulate thatch. Wear associated with frequent use can inadvertently control thatch, but this situation is not necessarily ideal. Wear from athletes is rarely spread evenly over the field. Usually, wear is concentrated in certain areas of the field, and it can be severe, which rarely benefits the welfare of the turf. Once the turf is completely worn away, thatch accumulation is not even a remote concern. Foot traffic has a significant impact on thatch, and if it could be directed evenly throughout the field, thatch would have a more difficult time accumulating. If the marching band, cheerleaders, or both could periodically practice on different sections of a field, effective thatch reduction may occur more evenly.. Thatch accumulation is often seen on the less used portions of the baseball outfield and the corners of football fields, where wear is nominal and infrequent.

Some managers, however, have to deal with excessive thatch on fields even where earthworms are active. An excessive thatch layer is often the result of compaction, too much nitrogen, and pesticides that suppress or eliminate earthworms. Regular core aeration and topdressing during the heavy growth periods of the season can usually keep thatch under control without disrupting play, but every so often a more aggressive approach may be needed. Machines that cut deeply into the sod can remove a substantial amount of material, including vital components of weeds such as chickweed and clover. This practice is often more disruptive to the game than coring and is usually done at the end or the very beginning of the season. Some managers control thatch by frequent topdressing. All of these thatch-reducing practices put together do not adequately replace the activities of earthworms. Their consumption of thatch is only one of their many benefits.

EARTHWORMS AND LOCALIZED DRY SPOTS

Earthworm activity can also reduce the likelihood of a condition know as *localized dry spot* (LDS), where the soil in small areas becomes extremely dry and resists rewetting. LDS is often associated with extremely sandy soil, excessive thatch, or compaction, all of which can be mitigated, directly or indirectly, by earthworms. The conventionally prescribed method of treating LDS is with wetting agents. Many wetting agents, such as yucca extracts, are natural and innocuous, but, like pesticides, they often don't address the problem, just the symptom. Often, wetting agents work well for a time and then begin to fail because the severity of the problem has increased beyond the capability of the product. Another popular—but temporary—method of dealing with LDS is to perforate the soil's surface with a thin tine pitchfork or a water fork (which forces water through its tines) and then flood the area with water and wetting agents.

Generally, the cause of LDS is the deposition of organic hydrophobic substances on soil particles. Biological activity in an average soil absorbs most of these substances, but in extremely sandy conditions, bioremediation is often inadequate. Compost, clippings, and organic fertilizers stimulate the activities of earthworms as well as many other beneficial soil organisms that protect the soil from LDS. Sometimes LDS is a result of topographical phenomena such as high spots. The USGA recommends that high spots be hand-watered periodically to avoid LDS. It is possible to lower high spots by coring, removing the cores, and then rolling (without filling in the core holes with a topdress material). The space inside the holes often allows the ground to be compressed without actually causing compaction. These practices should not replace earthworm management but rather used in conjunction with cultural methods that preserve this valuable resource.

Pesticides that kill earthworms may inadvertently contribute to compaction and the loss of other benefits these organisms provide. Products that contain phorate, bendiocarb, carbaryl, chloropicrin, and benomyl are extremely toxic to earthworms. Other active ingredients that are less lethal but still toxic to earthworms include ethoprophos, isazophos, methiocarb, propoxur, carbendazim, thiabendazole, and thiophanate-methyl (Ernst 1995). The direct and indirect contributions earthworms offer to plant health are sacrificed when these materials are applied.

Using mature compost in the topdress mix is important not only for earthworms but also for most other beneficial soil organisms. The constant replenishment of composted residues feeds and reinoculates the valuable life forces in the soil, increases the water reserve, improves porosity (reducing compaction), promotes finer turf root hairs, reduces thermal conductivity, suppresses disease, regulates nutrient availability, and reduces stress. Topdressing with mature compost is one of the most consequential practices an ecological turf manager can perform.

AERATION

If topdressing is normally performed in conjunction with core cultivation, the compost or compost/sand mix can be applied whether cores are harvested or not. The amount of topdress material applied should be adjusted if cores are reincorporated. A ratio of 1:1 (sand:compost) is a good beginning. The mix can be adjusted over time to better suit the uniqueness of the field—its regional characteristics, topography, soil—and the availability of compost. It is extremely important that well-made, well-aged compost is used (see Chapter 3). The compost may need to be screened and thoroughly mixed with sand before use. If screening and mixing equipment is beyond the institution's resources to own and unavailable to rent, conventional sources of topdress mixtures will likely have the necessary equipment. Once the mix is made, it can be applied with most topdressing machines like most other topdress mixes.

Care should be taken not to topdress during periods of severe stress. This precaution is advisable no matter what type of material is being applied. The abrasiveness of sand being worked into the canopy of a stressed turf (not to mention the weight of the equipment) may create problems. Liquid applications of seaweed extract, humates, compost tea, or any combination of the three can be used to mitigate stressed turf. If the cores are to be reincorporated, less topdress material is normally applied to prevent smothering the canopy.

Cores can be broken apart with a drag mat, verticutter, or power brushes after the topdress material is applied. Many managers choose to apply the topdressing mixture before coring because the weight of the topdressing apparatus, especially when filled, can reduce the effectiveness of coring. Coring after topdressing often improves the overall aeration of the field. Many managers incorporate seed whenever they core and topdress. If new seed is planted, existing turf may need to be mowed lower so it won't shade out new seedlings. Lower the height of cut sooner for varieties like perennial ryegrass that germinate quickly and later for slower varieties like Kentucky bluegrass.

Experiments at Rutgers suggest that the larger the diameter of the core extracted, the greater degree of compaction relief and the greater number of complaints (Hartwiger 2001, Rossi 2000c). They arrived at a core diameter of ⅝ inch as a good compromise. However, this may be too large and lift the turf on sand fields and too small on heavier native soil fields. Other researchers believe that the diameter of the core has less to do with adequate compaction relief than the percentage of surface area impacted. Statistically, fields where 15 to 20 percent of the surface is impacted, regardless of the tine size, fare the best. To calculate the percentage of surface impacted, multiply the tine diameter by ½ to determine the radius, then use this formula:

$$r^2 \times \pi \ (r = \text{radius}, \pi = 3.1416)$$

to find the surface area impacted by a single core hole. Then multiply the surface area of one core hole by the number of cores per square foot and divide by 1.44. The answer equals the percentage of surface area impacted. If, for example, a manager uses a ⅝ (0.625) -inch hollow tine spaced 2 inches apart (36 holes per square foot), then:

$$(0.625 \times 0.5)^2 \times 3.1416 \times 36 \div 1.44 \approx 7.67\%$$

To impact between 15 and 20 percent of the field's surface area, the aerator would have to pass over it twice. This formula may be excessive for some fields and inadequate for others, depending on the amount of wear and the soil's resistance to compaction. Large-diameter hollow tines may be impractical on some sand-based fields because they may lift and tear the sod instead of extracting a clean core. Some machines are built with a skid plate, through which the coring tines operate, to prevent the sod from being lifted or torn, but widely spaced narrow tines may be more appropriate.

Experiments with solid tines or Hydrojecting® (Toro) showed more ephemeral relief but suggest that they may be a prudent choice for midseason cultivation. Some managers avoid using solid tines because they can glaze the walls of the hole, preventing penetration by roots, water, and air. This is less likely to occur in a soil that is mostly sand. There are almost as many kinds of tines available for aeration as there are spoken languages on earth. In addition to all the different length and diameter hollow and solid tines, there are also many shapes. Some have unusual tapers. Some have bullet-shaped tips. Cross tines are made to provide gentler cultivation where the turf's surface strength is questionable. Bayonet tines are designed for deep, longer-lasting aeration (see Figure 6-13). Most tines are made from case-hardened steel or carbide, but they still wear out relatively quickly. One manufacturer (JRM) coined a new name for the steel it uses—Dellennium© described as "carbide with an attitude." The Hydroject tool causes less surface disruption than the solid tine, penetrates deeper, and does not glaze the walls of the hole it creates, but it does not replace the practice of core removal.

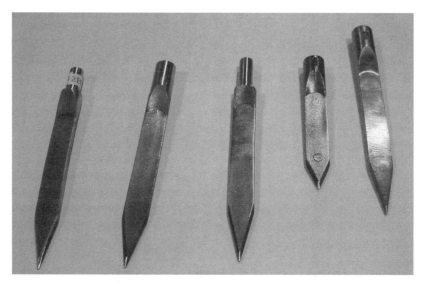

FIGURE 6-13   There are almost as many different available tines for aeration as there are spoken languages on earth.

Like mowing, core cultivation is difficult to avoid on a sports field. Some managers topdress lightly and frequently as a substitute for coring, but In high-traffic areas, this procedure may only postpone the inevitable. Unlike mowing, coring can disrupt the playing and practice schedule. The appropriate time for coring—in terms of what is best for the turf—may be inappropriate for the coaches. Like most maintenance procedures designed to pamper turf, cultivation causes stress, and the ideal time for stressful operations is when the turf is growing most vigorously. This generally is in the spring and fall for cool-season grasses and in the summer for warm-season grasses. Unfortunately, these may not be ideal times for players. Compromises often must be made—but stressing already stressed turf is not usually a good idea. If coring must be done during stressful periods, practices that mitigate stress, such as irrigation and applications of seaweed extract, should also be employed.

Some managers believe aeration can cause compaction beneath the depth of the tine's penetration and recommend that coring depth be altered from time to time. The drill-and-fill aerators penetrate deeply through the soil, but they work slowly. They do a good job of relieving compaction and can refill the holes they create with porous ceramics or other amendments designed to relieve compaction and improve drainage. They can penetrate more deeply than the typical tine but may be impractical on large fields (see Figure 6-14).

There are other types of aeration machines, each with strengths and weaknesses. Deep slitting tines, for example, rotate on a horizontal shaft, and some models can cut through the sod and soil to a depth of 20 inches. The skid plate, through which the tines cut, prevents the sod from lifting or tearing. This type of aerator is relatively fast and clean, but in some soil types the effect may be ephemeral (see Figures 6-15a and 6-15b).

FIGURE 6-14   Drill and fill aerators penetrate deeply but work slowly. They do a good job of relieving compaction and can fill the holes they create with amendments designed to relieve compaction and improve drainage.

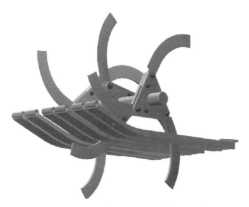

FIGURES 6-15A and B   Deep slitting tines rotate on a horizontal shaft and some models can penetrate the soil as deep as 20 inches. Photos courtesy Imants USA.

The shatter tine type of aerator provides shallow cultivation and can be run in a passive (with the power take-off, or PTO, off) or active (with the PTO on) mode. In the passive mode, there is less surface disruption and shallow aeration. The roller behind the tines leaves a smooth surface. In the active mode, the soil's surface is severely disrupted, but the machine prepares an excellent seedbed. In fact, some manufacturers offer optional seed hopper attachments. Shatter tine aerators are more effective on moderately dry soil. The tines, $3\frac{1}{4}$ inches long, are solid, and wear loss can be as much as $1\frac{1}{4}$ inch per season under heavy use (see Figures 6-16a and 6-16b).

Deep tine aerators like the Vertidrain® provide long-lasting aeration, but they are relatively slow and expensive to run. The deep tine aerator can reach down far enough to relieve some subsoil compaction, but its brutal nature requires a relatively high level of maintenance, and some models require a monster tractor to pull them. Deep tine aerators are most appropriate for severely compacted soil. In a fraternity of aerators, its brothers might consider this machine the animal (see Figure 6-17).

No matter what tool one chooses, it is often a good idea to apply some seed when cultivating. Typically, aeration opens up the canopy (unless it is already open), and what is better to fill the open spots with than new turf plants?

Some managers like to measure compaction before treating it. Several methods such as water infiltration, indicator weeds, knifing, and penetrometers can be employed. The water infiltration method can be as simple as observing how fast water soaks in during irrigation or by using the tin can method, whereby both ends of a can are removed and one edge sharpened with a grinder so it can penetrate into the soil more easily. The can is pushed ~2 to 3 inches into the soil and a predetermined amount of water poured into it. Then the time it takes the soil to absorb the water is

FIGURE 6-16A   The shatter tine type aerator provides shallow cultivation and can be run in a passive or active mode.

FIGURE 6-16B   This picture shows the difference in surface disruption between passive (left) and active (right) mode. Photo courtesy Dartmouth College Maintenance.

measured. It is important to perform this test soon after aeration so that a basis measurement can be determined.

Weeds that indicate compaction are listed in Table 5-2. This method is most appropriate for managers who are intimately familiar with the subtle changes that occur on their fields. The incidence of a single weed that tolerates compaction may be a false alarm.

FIGURE 6-17   Deep tine aerators are best for severely compacted soil. In the brotherhood of aerators, this machine would be considered the animal.

Knifing is the simple procedure of stabbing the ground with a pocketknife or screwdriver and observing the amount of force required to penetrate the soil. This method relies on a good memory, as one must compare the required force soon after aeration to the resistance felt in subsequent tests. On the other hand, if it is difficult to penetrate more than 1 or 2 inches with a knife, there is little doubt that the soil is severely compacted.

FIGURE 6-18   A penetrometer gives a measurement of compaction (usually in pascals or pounds per square area) that can be recorded and compared. Photo courtesy Spectrum Technologies, Inc.

A penetrometer gives a numeric pressure reading (usually in newtons, pascals, or pounds) that can be recorded and compared. Digital penetrometers, like the SC900 (Spectrum Technologies), measure compaction at different depths and record the data in an internal memory bank, which can later be downloaded to a computer (see Figure 6-18). The resulting information can be revealing, but in most cases, comparison data are needed. Generally speaking, values above 300 to 400 psi (2.07 to 2.76 megapascals) are too compacted for vigorous turf root growth and adequate water infiltration, but this threshold varies with soil type. Readings taken right after aeration can serve as a basis for comparison. If those aren't available, readings from a less used area—where turf is growing vigorously—can be used. Comparative readings should come from similar soil types. Several measurements should be taken and averaged to get a sense of the field's overall condition.

The meter can also be used to identify compacted areas of the field. It may be advisable to draw a map of the field and record where each measurement is taken on the map. The SC900 will identify the measurement number of each series. The informa-

TABLE 6-2
SC960 Data

Name: Paul Sachs
Serial #: 121
Datum: WGS 84

Soil Compaction in PSI

Longitude Latitude Number Logger Started	0 in.	1 in.	2 in.	3 in.	4 in.	5 in.	6 in.	7 in.
N = 1	31	66	71	87	97	71	127	173
N = 2	20	71	97	107	117	107	71	87
N = 3	36	46	71	71	97	102	61	61
N = 4	15	15	76	92	71	71	66	56
N = 5	76	76	76	76	87	66	71	97
N = 6	36	92	102	112	117	107	127	112

tion downloaded onto the computer will label each measurement and give values at different depths (see Table 6-2). The information can easily be visualized in a bar or line chart.

Identifying compaction with a digital penetrometer is easy and usually indisputable. Monitoring compaction whenever possible is a good idea, but of course it is likely that the soil will become compacted after a prolonged period of heavy use. Aeration at the end of the sport season may give the turf more of a respite than if it is done at the beginning, depending on the season, the type of sport, and the length of time before the field is used heavily again.

Some managers believe it is important to completely fill core holes, especially in the spring, to prevent insects such as sod webworm or cutworm adults from laying eggs in the partially filled holes. Once the topdress material is worked into the canopy, a small amount of irrigation ($\sim\frac{1}{10}$ inch) can be used to wash the remaining material through the canopy and reduce the stress of the operation. The use of liquid seaweed extracts or humates is often helpful at this stage. The manager should notice that the turf makes a much quicker recovery with compost in the topdress material than it would with just sand or sand mixed with topsoil. He may also notice that it takes a longer time than usual for the field to become compacted again.

Aeration technology for sports fields has recently advanced to an innovative and very different methodology. A new type of machine, TopAerator, developed in Switzerland (Bartschi Fobro) is making its debut, and the entire concept of coring has been discarded. This aerator has an 8-foot-wide thrusting—in a shallow digging motion—horizontal knife blade that works like a sod cutter but cuts as deep as 8 inches under the surface. It lifts and bends the sod in one direction while a roller behind the knife bends it in the other direction. A third roller follows to smooth out the disruption. The bending action loosens every cubic inch of soil above and slightly below the knife. The knife cuts at a slight downward angle to lift the sod and to avoid compaction of the subsoil. When the operation is completed, there is no cleanup—and, best of all, the field can be used almost immediately (depending on how deep the knife was set).

The knife also has liquid dispensing ports positioned every 6 to 8 inches along its tailing edge that can deliver fertilizer or biostimulants, such as seaweed or humates, underneath the roots. Seaweed extract delivered through these dispensing ports should ensure quick recovery from the operation. The knife has a replaceable cutting edge with an estimated lifespan of ~100 acres. This new machine is a large attachment and requires a relatively large tractor with at least 100 horsepower to operate, but it can aerate 3 to 4 acres per hour. Compost topdress mixtures can still be used but may incorporate more easily if applied before aeration. As the sod bends upward and cracks open slightly, some of the material can be absorbed into the surface (see Figures 6-19a and 6-19b).

Zeolite (clinoptilolite) is another product that can be mixed in with topdress materials to reduce compaction, improve water retention, and increase cation exchange capacity (CEC). The stable structure of this natural material provides permanent pores that can retain as well as drain water. Research has shown significant benefits from using zeolite, including greater porosity, increased resistance to compaction, bet-

FIGURE 6-19A   The TerraForce has an eight-foot wide horizontal knife
blade that works like a sod-cutter but cuts as deep as eight inches under
the surface. Photo courtesy Bartschi Fobro.

ter fertilizer efficiency, water conservation, reduced leaching, increased nitrogen efficiency, decreased localized dry spots, and improved nutrient utilization (Schmaderer
2000, Bigelow et al. 2001). Some machines will dispense and incorporate clinoptilolite
or other amendments into the soil. The drill aerator has a hopper for such amendments
and can dispense them into the freshly drilled holes. The Water Wick can dispense

FIGURE 6-19B   When the operation is completed, there is no clean up
and the field can be used almost immediately Photo courtesy Bartschi
Fobro.

FIGURE 6-20 The Water Wick can dispense bands of soil amendments 8-10 inches under the surface.

bands of amendments 8 to 10 inches under the surface (see Figure 6-20). Theoretically, these bands (if porous material is used) can also drain excess water from the field. Some researchers, however, have found that some of these products can hold water too tightly, making it less available to plants. Zeolite products are marketed under brand names including Clino-lite™, Eco-Sand™, Agricolite™, Zeoclere-30™, Z-Plus™, and ZeoTech®, to name a few. All can be found on the World Wide Web.

Crumb rubber is also used as a topdress material. It has characteristics that can protect the crown of the plant from harsh sport activities and retard compaction. Repeated applications of crumb rubber, however, may build up to a point where the surface soil horizon is no longer soil, and plants may be unable to thrive growing in a rubber medium. Most managers who have tried and compared crumb rubber and zeolite with mature compost prefer the organic material (see Figure 6-21).

FIGURE 6-21 Most managers who have tried and compared other soil amendments with mature compost prefer the organic material better.

Once the soil is compacted, plants become stressed and weakened, giving greater opportunity to weeds, insects, and disease pathogens. Compaction, however, is not the only cause of stress. Plants experience stress from many sources, some of which are completely natural.

Excessive heat, drought, cold, or precipitation can stress plants. Many of the plant's own functions, such as germination and flowering, are also sources of stress. These natural events do not always overwhelm plants by themselves, but when they are coupled with the stress of players running, jumping, and making abrupt turns and sudden stops, the plant's stress management becomes a bit more difficult. Add to all of this the stress of maintenance. Almost everything we do to pamper turf causes stress. Turf stress is not difficult to mitigate but nearly impossible to avoid on a sports field.

MOWING

Mowing—that is, the not-so-surgical removal of plant tops—is, without a doubt, a stressful practice, and one that must occur regularly. Turf plants probably do not feel pain from their extremities being amputated, but mowing is nevertheless a type of injury. We all know how important it is to mow with sharp blades and bed knives because they minimize the injury and reduce stress. If reel mowers are used, the wear on bed knives is particularly severe after topdressing, especially if the topdress material is mostly sand. The more often topdressing is done, the more frequently backlapping or grinding must be performed. Rotary mower blades should also be kept sharp. Damage to grass from dull rotary blades is unsightly and can lead to disease or other problems that may spread elsewhere on the field. These blades can lose their edge after only six hours of mowing (see Chapter 5, under "Cultural Practices").

There is talk of new mower technology that uses laser beams instead of blades to cut the grass. Not only is the cutting height extremely accurate but the wound is immediately cauterized by the beam, and the clippings are dried and pulverized on the spot. A prototype of this machine, seen at a German equipment show in the fall of 2000, also had leather seats, mobile Internet access, and a CD player. It has not yet been determined if this new laser technology does, in fact, reduce turf stress, but it certainly reduces fuel consumption, noise, and pollution. Unfortunately, at $30,000, many managers may find it stressful to their budget (White, April 2001).

It has been said that we should not remove much more that one-third of the turf canopy when we mow. It is well documented that turf recovers just fine if more than a third is cut, but photosynthesis can be temporarily halted while reserve energy stored in the plant roots is used to grow new shoots. This causes stress too. Removing more than a third of the plants' tops can arrest root growth for as long as a month. If too much of the canopy is removed, photosynthesis slows to the point where plants must use nutrient reserves in their root systems to sustain themselves. When new top growth is exposed to the sun, photosynthesis again begins to produce nutrients for the roots, but the nutritional needs of the shoots come first. Then the plant must replenish the reserves depleted during the period when leaves were too short before the roots can continue growing again. The energy needed for normal functions plus the restocking of reserves can stop the growth of turf roots for almost a month. Loss of root growth during crucial times of the season can make the difference between turf with problems and turf that is relatively trouble-free, in both the short and the long term. The degree of root growth is relative to how a plant fares through many types of stress such as heat, cold, and drought. In addition, the root's production of organic matter in the soil is a long-term asset that can benefit many future generations of turf plants.

HEIGHT OF CUT

Height of cut (HOC) also has a profound effect on the production and accumulation of organic matter. Root mass is directly affected by the height a manager chooses to cut his fields. Roots grow from the sustenance they get from photosynthates produced in the leaves. The greater the leaf surface area exposed to the sun, the more photosynthesis can occur and the more nutrients become available to roots. Figure 6-22 shows that for each ⅛ inch the mower is raised there is a 30 percent increase in the amount of leaf surface area exposed to the sun. Deeper and more diffusive root systems allow better, more efficient transport of water and nutrients through the plant. Improvements here also increase resistance to drought, increase internal cooling in hot weather, and reduce the root loss that is typical during summer months. The resulting mitigation of stress decreases the plant's susceptibility to opportunistic pests and maintains the production of valuable organic residues at optimum levels.

Coaches often pressure managers to cut turf lower. Higher grass can slow ball speed in sports like soccer where it rolls over the ground, but tests have determined that running speed is not influenced significantly unless the grass is cut unreasonably high. Many coaches would like to see golf course cutting heights on their fields, but they have no idea how difficult it is to maintain healthy turf at an extremely low height of cut. Sometimes it's best to mow at the (turf's) ideal height and wait to see if the coach (or players) object. If they do, lower the height of cut a little, but don't mention the actual cutting height. The coach will likely notice the lower cut, but chances are he or she won't notice it is still higher than average. What he or she may notice is the improved stress resistance and appearance.

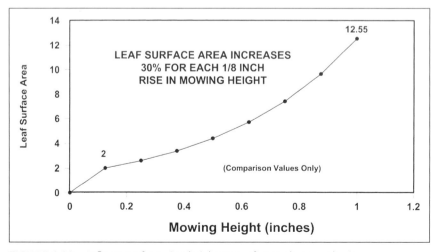

FIGURE 6-22   Influence of mowing height on turfgrass photosynthesis.

The lower the cut on high-speed, high-performance fields, the greater the need for well-aged compost because little organic matter (with the exception of thatch) is produced by these extremely stressed plants (see Chapter 3).

School fields that are not used during the summer can be cut at maximum height. A high, dense turf canopy shades the soil and produces a dense, deep root system. The cutting height can be gradually lowered as the playing/practice season approaches. The process of lowering the height of cut should begin 3 to 4 weeks before the field is scheduled for use. Avoid cutting off more than a third of the top growth at a time. A cutting schedule can be calculated based on maximum turf height, growth rate, and finished height of cut. Generally speaking, cool-season turf will grow from $1/10$ to $3/10$ inch per day. The lower rate of growth might be used if the climate is hot and dry or dwarf varieties of grasses are in use. The higher rate would be used under ideal growing conditions and optimum fertility. If, for example, turf is growing at a rate of $1/5$ inch per day and we want to lower the height of cut from $3\frac{1}{2}$ inches to 2 inches *and* avoid cutting more than a third off at a time, then a suggested cutting schedule might be:

Last Cutting Height	Days Between Cuts	Height Before Cut	New Cutting Height
$3\frac{1}{2}$ inches	5	$4\frac{1}{2}$ inches	3 inches
3 inches	5	4 inches	$2\frac{3}{4}$ inches
$2\frac{3}{4}$ inches	5	$3\frac{3}{4}$ inches	$2\frac{1}{2}$ inches
$2\frac{1}{2}$ inches	5	$3\frac{1}{2}$ inches	$2\frac{1}{4}$ inches
$2\frac{1}{4}$ inches	5	$3\frac{1}{4}$ inches	2 inches

In this example, there is 1 inch of regrowth before each cutting and it takes 25 days to lower the cutting height from $3\frac{1}{2}$ inches to 2 inches. The cutting frequency can be increased to gain a greater change in a shorter period, but cutting more often while lowering the height of cut each time may stress the turf and create problems. The slower the cutting height transition, the less stressful it will be for the turf.

Soil temperature can have a profound effect on the fate of soil organic matter. As illustrated in Figure 1-5, at a soil temperature of 88°F (~31°C), with adequate air and moisture, soil organic matter is destroyed faster than it can accumulate. This is a common condition in tropical and subtropical soils, where high temperature, moisture from tropical rains, and the abundance of air in extremely porous soil are all at an optimum level for decay activity. There is a direct correlation between the average annual temperature of a given region and the native levels of soil organic matter. As one moves closer to the equator, it is evident that the natural existence of soil organic matter lessens (see Figure 1-11). Even in a tropical rain forest, where prolific plant growth produces an abundance of organic residues, little organic matter accumulates in the soil. At lower cutting heights, the soil has less protection from the sun's heat. Elevated soil temperatures not only stimulate biological activity but also stress plants and reduce growth that contributes to the creation of soil organic matter.

Shade can mitigate the effects of high temperatures on soil organic matter, but shading turf is not being suggested. Living mulches, such as turf, can protect the soil from absorbing too much of the sun's energy. Turf stands mowed at maximum height during the hottest part of the year can shade the soil and reduce its temperature. This practice is not always practical on all sports fields. Allowing turf to stand a little taller, however, not only provides a natural shade for the soil but also encourages greater production of organic matter because more photosynthesized food is produced for root growth. Root systems can contribute from $\frac{1}{2}$ ton to 4 tons of organic residues (on a dry basis) per acre per year. Syringing during the hottest part of the day can also help lower soil surface temperatures and reduce plant stress. Recent research indicates, however, that nighttime syringing is more effective at mitigating stress (Huang 2002). On fields where the Prescription Athletic Turf (PAT) system (see "Sand and Drainage," above) is installed, air can be pumped through the underground lines at night to lower soil temperature. Fans or blowers have also been used successfully to lower soil and leaf surface temperature, especially in the early part of the day when there is dew. As air movement evaporates this moisture, the temperature drops significantly.

Research has discovered that high soil temperatures are much more stressful to plants than high air temperatures are (Huang 2000, Xu 2000, Xu 2001). As the soil temperature rises, plants begin to consume a greater portion of the energy they photosynthesize. This phenomenon can reach the point where more energy is consumed than produced. At this stage, plants can deplete much of their energy reserves and become extremely stressed. Adequate amounts of soil organic matter can slow the progress of this syndrome. Soil organic matter holds more moisture than the soil's mineral component, and plants tend to grow finer root hairs in soil enriched with humus. Finer root hairs have a greater amount of surface area and can absorb more water than coarse root hairs in the same period. The plant's ability to transpire is its mechanism to cool itself. Plants that are better able to regulate their temperature mitigate the effects of heat stress and consume less of their own energy. Net gains in energy result in greater production and contributions of organic residues for soil saprophytes, more carbon dioxide for plants, and more humus.

Adequate potassium is important for the plants' ability to tolerate heat, cold, and drought stress. Applying potassium in advance of predictable stress periods increases the plants' high and low temperature tolerance and helps them regulate transpiration. Turf growing in sandy conditions is particularly susceptible to potassium deficiencies, especially after prolonged heavy rain.

WEATHER

Weather is often a source of stress and a major contributor to turfgrass decline, and it is completely beyond anyone's control. An experienced manager, however, can predict and prevent many weather-related problems before those conditions prevail. To do this, however, a certain degree of monitoring is necessary to compile and correlate necessary information. Some managers have their own weather monitoring equipment and keep track of growing degree-days, evapotranspiration (ET), humidity, etc. (Spectrum, Onset, Agronometrical Centre of Excellence [ACE], AnythingWeather,

RainWise), while others get daily reports from DTN online (requires membership) or local meteorologists.

All of this information is meaningless, of course, unless it correlates to impending problems. Researchers have found relationships between the accumulation of growing degree-days, for example, and certain insect or disease problems (Vittum et al. 1999, Potter 1998). Many of these maladies may not plague every turf manager everywhere, but it's good to know the conditions under which the persistent problems exist. Books and articles written about turfgrass pests often contain information that matches the accumulation of certain weather conditions with the onset of certain pests (Schumann et al. 1998).

New high-tech computer systems link to weather monitoring devices and contain software that automatically warns the user of possible impending problems based on weather data it has collected and accumulated. Although these new systems show a great deal of promise, it is important that managers still keep vigil. Commercial airlines have onboard computers that can literally fly the plane without assistance, but they still hire and know the value of their pilots (see Figure 6-23).

Sometimes the onset of a pest is ahead of the forecasted schedule because conditions on the field have accelerated susceptibility. Poor air movement, for example, can foster problems associated with leaf wetness well before overall moisture, humidity, or heat levels reach a critical threshold. Increasing air movement, either by thinning obstacles or providing mechanical assistance with blowers, can decrease susceptibility associated with certain weather conditions.

Among the most difficult weather conditions for turf to deal with are heat and drought. Oppressively hot weather is a challenge for all living things, but to face it without water is often a death-knell. The practice of syringing turf (i.e., briefly applying water) during periods of extreme heat may help prevent turfgrass decline. Many managers attempt to apply a specific amount of water (e.g., ~$\frac{1}{10}$ inch) during the hottest part of the day, while others go out with a hose equipped with a shower-type nozzle and lightly water stressed areas by hand. Recent research suggests that syringing at night may be more effective in lowering soil and leaf temperatures than daytime treatment (Huang 2002). The effect of syringing is similar to what one might feel if, after sitting or working in the hot sun for a prolonged period, one were showered with cool water. This would not only provide instant relief because of the significantly lower water temperature but also a sustained cooling effect from evaporation.

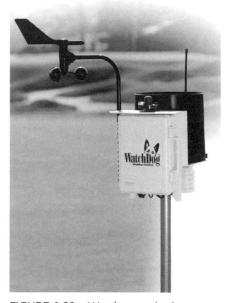

FIGURE 6-23 Weather monitoring equipment can help forecast some pest problems, especially when linked to special computer software. Photo courtesy Spectrum Technologies, Inc.

It's important to note that most of the water applied from syringing evaporates and does not significantly quench the plants' thirst. Normal irrigation schedules may have to be adjusted slightly, but syringing should not be a substitute for replacing ET loss.

Extreme weather conditions cannot be controlled, but they can be tolerated by some varieties better than by others. Seed choices are important for many other reasons too. First and foremost is the suitability of the playing surface, but a close second is the survivability of the selection. Bermuda grass is the popular choice for fields growing in warmer climates, and Kentucky bluegrass seems to be the ideal for cooler regions. Perennial ryegrass is also popular—in the cooler regions as a nurse crop and for filling in, and in warmer regions to provide cover during the winter when Bermuda grass is dormant.

There are, however, a lot of varieties from which to choose. A tremendous amount of research has been done to determine the resilience of different varieties to disease, drought, traffic, low height of cut, heat, cold, salt, insects, and excessive precipitation. This information is useful to a point, but the savvy turf manager understands that just because a variety performs well in a university test plot doesn't always mean it will be the ideal choice for his field. Subtle differences in the climate, topography, and soil conditions may be just enough to negate most of what was learned by research. Additionally, irrigation, fertilization, and cultivation may also change conditions enough to render the test data relatively meaningless. The information gathered by scientists is important and a good starting point, but the turf manager should probably conduct trials of his own before committing to specific varieties of seed.

IRRIGATION

Water can be both friend and enemy to turf and its production of organic matter. Organisms that decompose organic residues are as dependent on moisture as are plants or any other living thing. Common sense dictates that moisture conditions that are ideal for plants are most often ideal for the accumulation of organic matter, simply because the production of organic residues is at an optimum level. If water is supplied through an irrigation system, it is important to monitor soil moisture levels carefully and to practice moderate watering techniques that encourage root growth. Some research suggests that low-volume, high-frequency watering techniques can improve plant and soil health while using water more efficiently (Vargas 1994). Other experts disagree and suggest that deep and infrequent watering is best for most plants (Jordan et al. 2003, Richie et al. 2002).

Deep watering may be difficult to quantify without actually sampling the soil profile and measuring the depth an irrigation application has reached. You can use a soil sampling tube that reaches a depth of 12 inches or more to look at a profile of the soil. Differences in soil texture might allow a given volume of water to permeate below the root zone in one soil but just wet the surface of another. Measuring the amount of water applied to the surface won't translate to an equal infiltration depth in every soil. An inch of water, for example, may permeate through 15 inches of a light, sandy soil but less than 5 inches of a heavy clay soil.

The water-holding capacity of soils also influences irrigation frequency. A light, sandy soil may require only $\frac{3}{4}$ inch of water to percolate through the root zone but could need recharging every 2 to 5 days. On the other hand, a heavy soil may require as much as $2\frac{1}{2}$ inches of water to permeate the entire root zone but may only need it once every 9 to 10 days. In terms of actual water used, an inch of water applied to an acre of turf is equivalent to 27,225 gallons. A $1\frac{1}{2}$-acre soccer field growing on a heavy soil may require almost 100,000 gallons of water for it to percolate through the root zone.

Irrigating too deeply may cause saturation in heavier soils, and water in excess of what is optimal for plants can be counterproductive. Saturated soil has little room for oxygen, which is essential for healthy roots. Stress resulting from overwet soil can reduce plant vigor and the rate at which it produces organic residues. It can also contribute to severe compaction if games are played, bands march, or vehicles drive on saturated fields. It is sometimes a good idea to keep fields a little on the dry side before games. Sudden rains added to regular irrigation just before a big game can create big problems. Disease is more likely on turf that is overwatered than on turf that is underwatered (see Figure 6-24).

If watering restrictions are imposed on irrigating turf and a manager is forced to let fields go dormant, $\frac{1}{4}$ inch of water every 4 to 6 weeks can keep crowns hydrated enough to survive a prolonged drought. It is likely that even in a severe drought, $\frac{1}{4}$ inch or more of rain would fall in a 4- to 6-week period. When watering restrictions are lifted, it is a good idea to water dormant turf deeply. If water use is no longer regulated, however, chances are that nature has already done that.

Over the years, different methods of determining soil moisture, such as moisture blocks, tensiometers, soil psychrometers, infrared thermometers, and time-domain reflectometry, have been developed. Dissolved salts in the soil solution can affect some of these devices, resulting in false readings. Some are expensive, while others are simply

FIGURE 6-24   The water cannon is a relatively inexpensive alternative to a built-in, computerized irrigation system but, like any system, must be used judiciously. Photo courtesy Dartmouth College Maintenance.

impractical. The infrared thermometer, for example, doesn't measure soil moisture per se; rather, it takes the temperature of plant leaves, which can be an indicator of moisture deficiency. A leaf that is hotter than normal means that not enough moisture is being transpired through the plant. The operator of this device must scan a number of areas to determine average moisture needs (see Figure 6-25).

A more precise method of calculating irrigation involves evapotranspiration data, and it shows promising results in terms of plant response and the reduction of stress-related problems. The application of water in amounts that replace approximately what is lost from both evaporation and transpiration seems to create optimal conditions for plant growth and, hence, production of organic residues. Most modern irrigation equipment comes with computer software that calculates the amount of irrigation needed to replace ET loss. Factors that influence ET, such as temperature, humidity, wind, and solar radiation, are either manually entered into the computer or automatically recorded from weather monitoring equipment. The software can calculate water loss from ET and automatically govern the irrigation system to replace it.

If a computer or ET software is unavailable, ET data can be obtained at local meteorological recording stations or your local turfgrass extension service (see also DTN in "Sources and Resources"). ET calculations can also be done manually. Meteorologists have a special pan they use to monitor evaporation. This equipment can be a little expensive, but is available to anyone and can be set up in areas that mimic the average conditions on the field. A homemade system consisting of a shallow pan and a ruler is not as accurate or as easy to monitor, but it is certainly more affordable. More pans can be used if ET data from specific fields must be monitored. The loss (or gain) of water from the pan is measured and multiplied by a crop coefficient to determine ET. Crop coefficients for turf usually range from 0.63 to 0.78 for warm-season grasses and from 0.79 to 0.82 for cool-season grasses (Christians 1998). A more precise coefficient can usually be obtained from a local meteorologist or turfgrass extension agent. If, for example, water loss from the pan is $\frac{1}{4}$ inch on a particular day and the crop coefficient for the species of grass on the field is 0.81, then:

$$0.25 \times 0.81 \approx 0.2 \text{ inch of water}$$

In this case, about $\frac{2}{10}$ inch of irrigation will replace ET loss. Typical ET loss rates are between $\frac{1}{10}$ and $\frac{1}{3}$ inch of water per day. Each $\frac{1}{10}$ inch of ET water loss is roughly equivalent to 2,700 gallons per acre. The schedule at which ET loss is replaced should depend on soil texture, climate, environmental stress levels, and the manager's discretion. If rain is in

FIGURE 6-25   The infrared thermometer takes the temperature of plant leaves, which can be an indicator of moisture deficiency. Photo courtesy Spectrum Technologies, Inc.

the forecast, ET replacement may not be required. During certain periods of the season, it may be appropriate to replace ET loss daily or only once per week. ET calculations don't take into account surface, soil drainage, or other factors that influence the decision of when, how often, and how much to irrigate.

The ECS System, created by Evaporative Control Systems (see "Sources and Resources" for contact information), operates on a completely different mechanism than conventional irrigation. No ET calculations, weather stations, computers, or soil moisture monitors are ever necessary, and the system typically uses only 42 percent of the water needed for an aboveground system. In fact, the ECS system can operate from collected rainwater or even gray water from septic systems. There are far fewer parts that can fail and, in some cases, not even electricity is needed.

Water begins moving through the ECS system in underground pans and is naturally wicked up through the soil as sun and wind evaporate moisture from the surface. When it rains, the movement of water is reversed and the underground pans are refilled. During periods of prolonged drought, the pans are automatically recharged from an external water supply. Plant roots always have an adequate supply of moisture but, because of the natural capillary movement, they are never drowning in excess water (see Figures 6-26a, 6-26b, and 6-26c).

Sound too good to be true? ECS is a reality and, over the long term, not a terribly expensive one, but it is probably not practical for established fields, as completely new construction is required. The pans are installed under 12 to 15 inches of washed medium (0.25 to 0.50 mm particle size) sand. Topsoil or compost can be used in the top 2 inches of the soil, but in order for water to be conveyed to the surface effectively by natural capillary movement, medium sand with less than 3 percent silt or clay must be used. The system is ideal for fields that are soon to be constructed (especially fields being built to USGA specifications), but it may not be practical on an old, native soil field unless starting over is already imminent.

FIGURE 6-26B   Three months of root growth from sod grown in the ECS system. Photos courtesy (ECS) Evaporative Control Systems, Inc.

FIGURE 6-26A   The ECS system wicks water through the soil from underground pans as sun and wind evaporate moisture from the surface. Photos courtesy (ECS) Evaporative Control Systems, Inc.

FIGURE 6-26C   Third year of turf growth irrigated by ECS at the University of Nevada, Reno. Photos courtesy (ECS) Evaporative Control Systems, Inc.

The balance of air and water in the soil naturally regulates the accumulation of soil organic matter. Periods of excess water deplete the amount of air, inhibiting the activities of aerobic decay organisms. Saturated conditions for extended periods eventually suffocate roots, which stresses the plant and reduces the production of their organic residues. During drier periods, air is abundant, but moisture becomes the limiting factor. Maintaining adequate levels of soil organic matter can buffer the effects of too much or too little water.

GRASS VARIETIES

Finding the right varieties is a huge step toward the reduction or elimination of pesticides. Species that thrive in a given area are often more competitive than most weeds and can be relatively resilient to damage from insect pests and disease pathogens. If poor soil conditions prevail, however, few varieties may be able to thrive. If a cultivar is found that performs relatively well in poor soil conditions and soil improvement becomes an objective at some point, that variety may no longer be the best choice. Changes in other conditions such as weather trends or exposure (e.g., shade reduction or expansion) may also make the original choice of seed inappropriate. Sometimes, native, unnamed varieties may serve the turf manager best. Seed varieties are always changing, and new ones seem to appear every year. Seashore paspalum, for example, has become a popular warm-season alternative in the littoral regions of the country. Seed choices for different latitudes or altitudes; proximity to fresh or salt water; arid, semiarid, temperate, tropical, or subtropical zones; and different soil conditions are inappropriate to discuss here. Not only would it take hundreds of pages, but the information is quite ephemeral. What is new as of this writing may be old news by the time the book is printed.

The new kids on the block are transgenic varieties of bluegrass and perennial ryegrass engineered to tolerate glyphosate herbicide applications. These Roundup®

Ready grasses are the missing link in the chemical industry's strategy to provide ease and perfection with wall-to-wall applications of (their brand) herbicide. Unfortunately, these Frankensteinian grasses may not resist insects or disease any better than genetically unmodified varieties. They probably won't grow any better in poor soil conditions either. But neither will anything else. Substituting chemical warfare for good soil stewardship has never been and will never be a good idea.

The turfgrass extension system of the local land grant university is usually a good source of information on new seed varieties and the conditions under which they thrive. Many large universities conduct annual trials and publish their results. These data usually describe performance based on many criteria, including disease resistance, drought, heat, shade, and wear tolerance, thatch, sod strength, performance at different cutting heights, ball speed, response to environmental stresses, and appearance. Another source of information is the National Turfgrass Evaluation Program (NTEP). NTEP collects data from local, regional, and national sources and stores them on a database.

Choosing the most appropriate time to plant seed is also an important consideration. In northern climates, fall is generally the best time to plant seed. The weather is typically cooler, precipitation is more consistent, and competition from weeds is waning. Spring is usually the best time for warm-season grasses, which are more susceptible to winter kill if planted in the fall. Cool-season grasses are also susceptible to winter kill if they germinate or even swell just before a hard frost. Seeds contain only a small amount of moisture (~2 percent), which protects them from freezing temperatures. If seeds absorb significant amounts of moisture just before a killing frost, they are unlikely to produce plants. Many managers employ dormant seeding as a means of improving turf stands for the following growing season, but the seed must remain dormant until the growing season begins again.

Unfortunately, planting times that are optimal for the seed may not be ideal for manager, coaches, or players. Additionally, overseeding is often necessary during the playing season. Using mature compost, seaweed extract, or both can give seedlings a competitive edge and increase the success of a new seeding.

NATURAL AREAS

If space and terrain permit, natural areas may or may not be an appropriate implantation. Areas adjacent to fields but are not in use by anyone for any purpose may be ideally suited for intentional neglect. The addition of natural areas can contribute not only to the beauty of the sports complex and the reduction of maintenance but also provide habitat for beneficial insects, arthropods, birds, mammals, and soil organisms (see Chapter 5, under "Predators"). Natural areas can contain wildflowers, ornamental grasses, perennials, or simply the indigenous species of plants that thrive when the area is undisturbed. Natural areas are ideal in perpetually wet spots where irises, cattails, and other wetland plants can thrive. Turf growing in wet areas is usually prone to problems and requires more intensive management. Some managers believe that natural areas can contribute to the proliferation and spread of noxious weed seeds, but most plants that thrive in natural areas don't compete well at normal cutting heights. Some managers like to burn natural areas in the late fall or early spring to refresh the area and kill weed seed, pathogens, and dormant insects. Unfortunately, there's no guarantee that what is being incinerated is in any way harmful or troublesome. More often than not, securing the necessary permits from the fire department is more trouble than it is worth. If tall plant residues pose a visual problem, they can easily be dispatched with a string trimmer or brush cutter, and the detritus can be added to a compost heap. Natural areas are generally mowed down at least once per year to prevent the establishment of unwanted trees or shrubs.

Some managers like to remove the leftover debris after mowing down natural areas, but that removal is like harvesting a crop. The nutrients extracted from the soil by those plants are not being returned and ultimately must be replaced. The same is true for leaves that fall from the trees scattered around the area. To avoid obstruction of the game during the fall, leaves sometimes must be blown off or collected from the fields; like clippings, they often can be shredded with a mower and left to replenish the soil.

HERESY

Although the subject is blasphemous, if the manager's objective is the elimination of pesticides, a discussion of artificial turf is appropriate. Advancements in synthetic turf technology have reached a point where playing surfaces are comparable to natural turf that has been managed to the nth degree (White, August 2001). In fact, some manufacturers (Players Turf International, Field Turf, Edel Grass) boast play-

FIGURE 6-27   Advancements in synthetic turf technology have reached a point where playing surfaces are comparable to natural turf that has been managed to the nth degree.

ing fields that are safer and more durable than natural turf. Their technology combines a thick mat of green synthetic shag and special topdressing materials that, in varying amounts, create different surfaces. The conditions of these simulated surfaces range from athletic fields, tennis courts, and golf course greens and tees to simple maintenance-free lawns. These playing surfaces never need mowing, aeration, or pest control and can last 20 years or longer. Unlike natural turf, however, artificial turf is unable to mitigate ground temperature. Turf plants are constantly transpiring water, which evaporates and cools the plants and surrounding area. A study done in 1985 at Texas A&M University showed a 70°F temperature difference between Bermuda grass and artificial turf in the same area (Beard and Johns 1985). The heat potential of artificial turf may have health consequences for athletes exerting themselves during extremely hot weather. If pesticide elimination becomes mandatory, however, and few, if any, of the alternatives or practices mentioned in this book are practical, it might be worth considering artificial turf (even if it's used only in places like sidelines where wear is high but the area is not used as part of the game). It isn't a lot less natural than some of the management techniques we currently use (see Figures 6-27 and 6-28).

FIGURE 6-28   The artificial turf field at Dartmouth College looks good all the time and requires very little maintenance.

POINTS TO REMEMBER

- Successful ecological turf maintenance must include managing stress and resources for soil organisms.
- Sand cannot improve the rate at which water drains through most native soils unless the sand component of the soil mixture exceeds 80 percent.

- Aside from adding valuable resources for soil organisms, compost can suppress disease, reduce thatch, increase the turf's stress resistance, and reduce water use—all to a significant degree—without compromising drainage.
- Aeration is an important maintenance routine in reducing compaction, and managing the biological component of the soil can reduce the number of times per season aeration is needed.
- Earthworms relieve compaction, increase water infiltration and the exchange of gases with the atmosphere, reduce thatch, and increase nutrient availability.
- Aeration tools come in many shapes and sizes, each of which addresses a different need or problem, but extracting cores seems to be the most effective method of abating compaction.
- Mowing can be made less stressful by keeping blades sharp and cutting a third or less of the plant's height at a time.
- Many stress-related problems are triggered by unfavorable weather conditions. Monitoring weather conditions often enables turf managers to predict problems and take precautionary action.
- Regardless of the method used to manage sports fields, high-quality turf is not easy to maintain in high-traffic areas.
- If learning ecological methods is mandatory but still an objectionable endeavor, then perhaps the manager should consider artificial turf, which requires little care and always looks good. You'll be the envy of all your colleagues—or will you?

Chapter 7

SIMPLICITY VERSUS STABILITY

In the late 1980s, a group of ambitious people designed and built a structure to contain a separate and independent ecosystem that—aside from the sunlight, electricity, and water that went in and the information that came out—was completely segregated from the rest of the planet. They called it Biosphere II, an eponym from the only other known biosphere in the universe: Earth. The $200 million project was built to test the possibility of establishing Earthlike colonies on other planets and to learn more about the earth's ecosystem. The builders attempted to replicate seven distinct environments in a glass structure that covered nearly 140,000 square feet of the Sonoran desert in Oracle, Arizona. The structure was completely sealed from the outside world. Even the soil was sealed with a stainless-steel tray buried 25 feet below the surface.

Each environment was carefully built with attention paid to the models from which they were taken, but it was impossible to include the complex diversity of organisms that naturally complemented each ecological community. The designers tried to create as much abiotic as biotic diversity, knowing that life's link to the inanimate is crucial. Ecologists knew that biological complexity and diversity were the keys to environmental stability, but the questions involved how many and which groups of organisms were necessary to sustain the environment and how many links could be missing before the system collapsed. Scrupulous planning went into the balance of soil organisms, arthropods, reptiles, birds, plants, and mammals in each food web. The main focus was insects and pollinators; pests were also introduced to provide for important predators. Extinctions were expected, but designers hoped they had enough diversity to provide backup. Some planners felt that if they had time to gradually introduce more and more organisms, equilibrium would eventually be established, but the luxury of so much time was unavailable. Over 4,000 different plants and animals were introduced into Biosphere II (not including the countless organisms inadvertently carried in with soil, compost, plants, water, and on the soles of shoes). Unfortunately, some of the species that were inadvertently introduced thrived, while

215

many organisms that were intentionally seeded either struggled or perished. Of the 25 introduced vertebrates, only six survived the two-year test period.

Food was grown under a biointensive gardening system. Growing sufficient vegetable protein proved problematic, but grains and fodder grew well and could sustain livestock for the production of animal protein. The garden air had to be cooled and dehumidified for optimum food-growing conditions, and the human inhabitants had to spend four to six hours per day to plant, cultivate, harvest, clean, process, and prepare food, not to mention the time they spent recycling wastes. Everything was recycled, including garden, animal, and human wastes.

The swamp in Biosphere II replicated a 90-mile stretch of the Florida Everglades—compressed to 90-feet—that gradually changed from a freshwater to a saltwater environment. The swamp was introduced in sections, each containing plants and other organisms that had a greater need or tolerance for salt than the previous section. The swamp was an essential habitat for protein-producing fish and organisms that cleansed recycled water. The ocean, with almost 1 million gallons of water, was home to a coral reef, fish, and a broad diversity of sea organisms. A giant pump was installed to replicate waves, tides, and other turbulence essential for coral and other sea organisms.

The entire infrastructure was filled with sensors relaying information to a main computer that constantly monitored environmental conditions and made automatic adjustments when necessary. Compounds in the air, water, and soil were checked constantly. Atmospheric temperature and moisture levels were kept constant despite the daytime desert heat and freezing nights. Unfortunately, the energy needed to maintain this climatic stability could not be generated biologically. Energy from the sun was not an option either, as 25 acres of solar panels would have been necessary to provide enough power. A 3.7-megawatt natural gas–powered generator produced electricity, and the air-conditioning cooling towers used 10 million gallons of well water per year.

It seemed the designers had planned for every possibility, but problems began almost immediately after the experiment started. The first disturbing occurrence was the buildup of carbon dioxide and the relatively rapid reduction of oxygen. This phenomenon was probably due to bringing too much immature compost into the facility. The bloom of microorganisms supported by resources in the compost generated huge amounts of carbon dioxide. The vast array of plants inside the terra-aquarium should have been able to assimilate the excess carbon dioxide and produce enough oxygen to eventually stabilize the balance of gases in the atmosphere. Unfortunately, the designers and builders hadn't realized that the still-curing concrete in the structure would react chemically with the excess carbon dioxide, creating calcium carbonate (lime) and water. Plants didn't have access to enough of the carbon dioxide to produce sufficient oxygen. Eventually, oxygen had to be pumped in for the inhabitants' safety.

Problems with the atmosphere actually had a greater impact on life in the ocean than elsewhere in the enclosure. But extinction, both in water and on land, was a major problem too. Some percentage of extinction was expected, but the rate was much higher than anyone anticipated. Tropical birds perished after the first frost, eliminating an entire group of pollinators. Frogs—sensitive barometers of ecological disruption—all died. What was also surprising was that even though the structure was built airtight, many species of plants and arthropods found their way into the facility. Ants, cockroaches, and katydids somehow gained access and proliferated. In fact, a species of Arizona ant became the ecosystem's most abundant organism and eradicated many introduced species, especially soft-bodied insects; even snakes would hide from them. Many of the introduced plants, whose environment was thought to be ideal, struggled or died while alien vines and other invasive plants quickly encroached. These uninvited plants could have easily choked out introduced varieties had humans not intervened.

The architects who designed Biosphere II—like most architects—put more importance on aesthetics than functionality, and nearly half of the available sunlight was blocked. Flat spots on the roof proved an ideal habitat for algae and ice, which blocked more light. Additionally, the glass used for construction blocked some of the wavelengths needed for photosynthesis.

Pollution also became a problem. The inhabitants knew they couldn't use pesticides or chemical fertilizers in such a small ecosystem because they would quickly pollute their own air and drinking water, but contaminants from unexpected sources entered the water and atmosphere anyway. Levels of nutrients, probably from the gardens, began to appear in the water supply. They were able to cleanse the water—to a point—by running it over mats of algae. Heavy metals from the materials used to construct Biosphere II, however, also began to contaminate both the air and water. The bionauts learned they could clean their air by pumping it through soil. The organisms in the soil gobbled up most of the pollutants.

To say that the experiment was a failure doesn't truly embrace the concept of science or the acquisition of knowledge. If the objective of Biosphere II was to prove that human life could be sustained in an Earthlike environment on other planets, then confirmation was not forthcoming. However, if the objective was to learn about the earth's ecosystem, then the experiment was successful.

Discoveries were abundant in Biosphere II. The designers learned that if a biological system can do the job, it will be powers of ten more dependable than any technological or mechanical system. The designers and inhabitants found out that some of the simple things we take for granted, such as wind and waves, are crucial for life and expensive to replicate. It was evident that, even with careful planning, establishing biological balance in one environment, let alone seven, cannot be accomplished overnight. The delicate balance on Earth took millions of years to achieve, and it's still evolving. Even with careful consideration, the rapid infusion of species designed to promote a sustainable system was probably as arbitrary and random as a shotgun blast in the dark.

Presumably, the most important lessons learned from Biosphere II is that we don't know nearly enough to replicate and govern an ecosystem as complex as Earth's and that changes we make to the ecosystem may have consequences that span both distance and time. If nothing else, Biosphere II should give us pause: If the earth's ecosystem should fail in a similar fashion, we have nowhere to go.

Said one of the principal designers of Biosphere II, "Designing a biome is an opportunity to think like God." The remark was made with a smile and a wink, and no one really thought of it as hubris, but it takes a bit of confidence to believe one could think like God. The designer may not have been able to think like God but, to his credit, at least he was thinking. It's unfortunate, but few of us really think about our ecosystem at all. Few of us give much consideration to simple regularities like the rain, sun, and wind. We appreciate them for our own comfort but not for fueling the ecosystem that sustains us. Perhaps we should all try to think like God—and to the inevitable revelation that we can't. But, if we could take it upon ourselves to care for our biosphere as if we created it, it might be better able to mediate the impact of our existence.

The biggest challenge turf managers face may not be pestilence or complaints from coaches; it may be our own arrogance. Some of us operate on the presumption that if we can't manage a site ecologically, then it can't be done. Thomas Edison failed 10,000 times while attempting to invent the light bulb. Each failure, he reasoned, was a discovery in of itself and a step closer to success. The only reason he eventually succeeded was that he wanted to. Likewise, if we are to succeed in reducing or eliminating pesticides on the turf we manage, we must hunger for it. It's not enough to just think it's a good idea.

Frank Rossi, the New York State Extension turfgrass specialist at Cornell University, points out that when a conventional control fails, we tend to blame other factors such as weather or disease pressure, but when a biological product fails, we are often quick to condemn the entire technology. He states, "Chemical pesticide technology has alleviated the burden of understanding the dynamic ecological and biological processes in turf systems…there is little motivation for determining ways of preventing the problem, when such simple curative measures are available" (Rossi 2002[a]).

Perhaps, some day, humanity will be able to recreate the earth's ecosystem on a small scale, but our current understanding of its complexity, diversity, and interactivity is insufficient—and, in light of our need to simplify everything into a three- or four-step program, it seems unlikely we will understand this system anytime in the foreseeable future. Perhaps all we really need to recognize is that it runs on biological fuel and it can only absorb a finite amount of contaminants before beginning to fail. Just like ourselves. If we look carefully at what is necessary for our own health and vitality—good diet, exercise, and minimal exposure to toxins—we may begin to understand the best way to help our ecosystem function properly.

SOURCES AND RESOURCES

Abernathy, S.D., R.H. White, P.F. Colbaugh, M.C. Engelke, G.R. Taylor, and T.C. Hale. 2001. Dollar Spot Resistance Among Blends of Creeping Bentgrass Cultivars. *Crop Science* 41: 806–809. Madison, WI: Crop Science Society of America.

Abu-Hamdeh, Nidal H., and Randall C. Reeder. 2000. Soil Thermal Conductivity: Effects of Density, Moisture, Salt Concentration, and Organic Matter. *Soil Science Society of America Journal* 64: 1285–1290. Madison, WI: Soil Science Society of America.

Acadian Seaplants Limited, 30 Brown Avenue, Dartmouth, Nova Scotia, Canada B3B 1X8; phone: 902.468.2840; fax: 902.468.3474; customerservice@acadian.ca; www.acadianseaplants.com.

Adams, Jean, ed. 1992. *Insect Potpourri: Adventures in Entomology.* Gainesville, FL: Sandhill Crane Press.

Adams, W.A., and R.J. Gibbs. 1994. *Natural Turf for Sport and Amenity: Science and Practice.* Wallingford, UK: CAB International.

Agrometeorological Centre of Excellence (ACE), Box 68, 40 Second Street NE, Carman, Manitoba, Canada R0G 0J0; phone: 204.745.2320; fax: 204.745.6299; info@aceweather.ca; www.aceweather.ca.

Albrecht, W.A. 1938. *Loss of Organic Matter and Its Restoration*, U.S. Dept. of Agriculture Yearbook 1938, 347–376.

Alm, Steven R. 1994. Oriental Beetles in New England. *Turf Notes* 4 (5). Worcester: University of Massachusetts Extension.

———. 1995. Annual Bluegrass Weevil, Hyperodes (Listronotus), *Turf Notes* 5 (2). Worcester: University of Massachusetts Extension.

———. 1999. Turfgrass Insect IPM: Present Status and Future Opportunities, *Turf Notes* 8 (2). Worcester: University of Massachusetts Extension.

American Association for Laboratory Accreditation (A2LA), 5301 Buckeystown Pike, Route 350, Frederick, MD 21704; phone: 301.644.3248; fax: 301.662.2974.

American Society of Agronomy. 1979. Publication #47: *Microbial-Plant Interactions.* Madison, WI: American Society of Agronomy

AMS, Inc., 105 Harrison, American Falls, ID 83211-1230; phone: 800.635.7330 or 208.226.2017; fax: 208.226.7280; ams@ams-samplers.com; www.ams-samplers.com.

Anderson, Arden B. 2000. Science in Agriculture: Advanced Methods for Sustainable Farming. Austin, TX: Acres USA.

AnythingWeather Communications, Inc., 2350 N. Rocky View Road, Castle Rock, CO 80104; phone: 800.845.0383; fax: 978.594.5674; gregg@anythingweather.com; www.anythingweather.com.

Appropriate Technology Transfer for Rural Areas (ATTRA), PO Box 3657, Fayetteville, AR 72702; phone: 800.346.9140; www.attra.org.

Arshad, M.A., and G.M. Coen. 1992. Characterization of Soil Quality: Physical and Chemical Criteria. *American Journal of Alternative Agriculture* 7 (1, 2): 25–31. Greenbelt, MD: Institute for Alternative Agriculture.

Ash, Steven A. 1998. Golf Course IPM for English Daisy. *IPM Practitioner* 20 (9). Berkeley, CA: Bio-Integral Resource Center.

Autrusa Compost Consulting (George Leidig), 941 Perkiomonville Road, Perkiomonville, PA 18074-9607; phone: 610.754.1110; autrusa@aol.com; www.autrusa.com.

Ayad, J.Y., J.E. Maham, V.G. Allen, and C.P. Brown. 1997. Effect of Seaweed Extract and the Endophyte in Tall Fescue on Superoxide Dismutase, Glutathione Reductase, and Ascorbate Peroxidase Under Varying Levels of Moisture Stress. T4.11.1 & EF4.5.1. Lubbock, TX: Texas Tech University, Department of Plant and Soil Science.

Backman, P.A., E.D. Miltner, G.K. Stahnke, and T.W. Cook. July-August 2002. Worming Your Way Out of a Turf Situation: Development of an Integrated Pest Management System to Reduce Earthworm Casts. *USGA Green Section Record* 40 (4). Far Hills, NJ: U.S. Golf Association.

Baker, R.R., and P.E. Dunn, eds. 1990. *New Directions in Biological Control.* New York: Alan R. Liss.

Balogh, James C., and William J. Walker. 1992. *Golf Course Management & Construction.* Boca Raton, FL: Lewis Publishers.

Barbosa, P., and D.K. Letourneau, eds. 1988. *Novel Aspects of Insect-Plant Interactions.* Hoboken, NJ: John Wiley & Sons.

Barbosa, P., V.A. Krischik, and C.G. Jones, eds. 1991. *Microbial Mediation of Plant-Herbivore Interactions.* Hoboken, NJ: John Wiley & Sons.

Bartschi Fobro, 1715 Airpark Drive, Grand Haven, MI 49417; phone: 616.847.0300;, fax: 616.842.1768; info@fobro.com; www.fobro.com.

BBC Laboratories, Inc., 1217 North Stadem Drive, Tempe, AZ 85281; phone: 480.967.5931; fax: 480.967.5036; www.bbc-labs.com.

Beard, J.B. January 1995. Mowing Practices for Conserving Water. *Grounds Maintenance.* Overland Park, KS: Intertec Publishing.

———— 2002. *Turf Management for Golf Courses.* Hoboken, NJ: John Wiley & Sons, Inc.

Beard, J.B., and D. Johns, 1985. The Comparative Heat Dissipation from Three Typical Urban Surfaces: Asphalt, Concrete and a Bermudagrass Turf. In *Texas Turfgrass Res— 1985.* Texas Agric. Exp. Stn. PR 4329. College Station. 125–133.

Beck, Malcolm. 1997. *The Secret Life of Compost.* Austin, TX: Acres USA.

————. February 2000. More Secrets of Compost. *Acres USA.* Austin, TX

Bhowmik, P.C., R.J. Cooper, M.C. Owen, G. Schumann, P. Vittum, and R. Wick. 1994. *Professional Turfgrass Management Guide.* Amherst: University of Massachusetts Cooperative Extension System.

Bhowmik, Prasanta C., Gail Schumann, Patricia J. Vittum, Scott Ebdon, Mary Owen, and Jason Lanier. 2002. *Turf IPM Facts.* Amherst: University of Massachusetts Cooperative Extension System.

Bigelow, Cale A., Daniel C. Bowman, D. Keith Cassel, and Thomas W. Rufty Jr. 2001. Creeping Bentgrass Response to Inorganic Soil Amendments and Mechanically Induced Subsurface Drainage and Aeration. *Crop Science* 41: 797–805. Madison, WI: Crop Science Society of America.

BioSafe Systems, PO Box 936, Glastonbury, CT 06033; phone: 888.273.3088; www.BioSafeSystems.com.

Bio-Integral Resource Centre (BIRC), PO Box 7414, Berkeley, CA 94707; phone: 510.524.2567; birc@igc.org. Produces *Directory of Least Toxic Pest Control Products.*

Bormann, F.H., D. Balmori, and G.T. Geballe. 1993. *Redesigning the American Lawn: A Search for Environmental Harmony.* New Haven, CT: Yale University Press.

Bosworth, Sid. 1998. *Using Plants as Indicators for Diagnosing Soil and Turf Problems.* Unpublished. Available from Department of Plant and Soil Science, University of Vermont, Burlington, VT.

Brady, Nyle C. 1974. *The Nature and Properties of Soils.* New York: Macmillan.

Brame, Bob. 1996. Ergonomic Tee Divot Filling. *USGA Green Section Record* 34 (3). Far Hills, NJ: U.S. Golf Association.

Brede, Doug. 2000. Turfgrass Maintenance Reduction Handbook: Sports, Lawns, and Golf. Hoboken, NJ: John Wiley & Sons, Inc..

Briggs, S.A., and N. Erwin. 1991. *Pesticides and Lawns.* Chevy Chase, MD: Rachel Carson Council.

Brookside Laboratories, Inc., 308 Main Street, New Knoxville, OH 45871; phone: 419.753.2448; fax: 419.753.2949; shaner@blinc.com (lab manager).

Buhler, Douglas D., ed. 1999. *Expanding the Context or Weed Management.* New York: Haworth Press.

Bunce, R.G.H., L. Ryszkowski, and M.G. Paoletti. 1993. *Landscape Ecology and Agroecosystems.* Boca Raton, FL: Lewis Publishers.

Callahan, P.S. 1975. Tuning In to Nature: Solar Energy, Infrared Radiation, and the Insect Communication System. Old Greenwich, CT: The Devin-Adair Co.

Caron, Céline. 2000. Regenerating Soils with Ramial Chipped Wood. *Ecological Landscaper* 7 (1). Framingham, MA: Ecological Landscaping Association.

Carpenter-Boggs, L., A.C. Kennedy, and J.P. Reganold. 2000. Organic and Biodynamic Management: Effects on Soil Biology, *Soil Science Society of America Journal* 64: 1651–1659. Madison, WI: Soil Science Society of America.

Carrow, R.N. May 1994. Understanding and Using Canopy Temperatures. *Grounds Maintenance.* Overland Park, KS: Intertec Publishing.

Carrow, R.N., D.B. Waddington, and P.E. Rieke. 2001. *Turfgrass Soil Fertility and Chemical Problems: Assessment and Management.* Hoboken, NJ: John Wiley & Sons, Inc..

Casagrande, R.A. 1993. *Sustainable Sod Production for the Northeast.* Kingston: University of Rhode Island, Department of Plant Sciences.

Casagrande, R.A., and Cicalese J. Johnson. 1989. 1989 Fieldplots: Tall Fescue/Endophyte Study. *59th Rhode Island Turfgrass Field Day 1990.* p. 3. University of Rhode Island.

Chenu, C., Y. Le Bissonnais, and D. Arrouays. 2000. Organic Matter Influence on Clay Wettability and Soil Aggregate Stability. *Soil Science Society of America Journal* 64: 1479–1486. Madison, WI: Soil Science Society of America.

Cherim, Michael S. June-July 1994. The General Principles of Biological Pest Control. *The Plantsman.* Durham: New Hampshire Plant Growers Association, c/o University of New Hampshire.

———. 1998. *The Green Methods Manual: The Original Bio-control Primer,* 4th ed. Nottingham, NH: The Green Spot Ltd., Publishing Division.

Chet, I., ed. 1987. *Innovative Approaches to Plant Disease Control.* Hoboken, NJ: John Wiley & Sons.

Christians, Nick. 1998. *Fundamentals of Turfgrass Management.* Hoboken, NJ: John Wiley & Sons, Inc..

Cinque, Maria. January 2002. The Next Best Thing: Former NY Jets Football Star Selling New Synthetic Turf Option. *Turf.* St. Johnsbury, VT: Moose River Publishing.

Cockfield, Stephen D., and Daniel A. Potter. 1984. Predation of Sod Webworm (*Lepidoptera: Pryralidae*) Eggs as Affected by Chlorpyrifos Application to Kentucky Bluegrass Turf. *Journal of Economic Entomology* 77 (6).

Coelho, R.W., J.H. Fike, R.E. Schmidt, X. Zhang, V.G. Allen, and J.P. Fontenot. 1996. *Influ-*

ence of Seaweed Extract on Growth, Chemical Composition, and Superoxide Dismutase Activity in Tall Fescue. Blacksburg: Virginia Polytechnic Institute and State University, Department of Crop and Soil Environmental Sciences.

Colbaugh, P.F. May 1994. Dealing with Algae. *Grounds Maintenance*. Overland Park, KS: Intertec Publishing.

Colinas, C., E. Ingham, and R. Molina. 1994. Population Responses of Target and Non-Target Forest-Soil Organisms to Selected Biocides. *Soil Biol. Biochem.* 26:41–48.

Connellan, William. 1921. Compost and the Construction of Compost Heaps. *USGA Green Section Record* 1 (4). Far Hills, NJ: U.S. Golf Association.

Couch, Gary. March 2000. Black Cutworm IPM. *Turf*. St. Johnsbury, VT: Moose River Publishing.

———. 2000. Does Milky Spore Disease Work? *Cornell University Turfgrass Times* 11 (3). Ithaca, NY: Cornell University.

Couillard, A., A.J. Turgreon, and P.E. Rieke. 1997. New Insights into Thatch Biodegradation. *International Turfgrass Society Research Journal (ITRJ)* 8: 427–435.

Craul P.J. 1992. *Urban Soil in Landscape Design*. Hoboken, NJ: John Wiley & Sons.

Cummings, J.L., J.R. Mason, D.L. Otis, and J.F. Heisterberg. 1991. Evaluation of Dimethyl and Methyl Anthranilate as a Canada Goose Repellent on Grass. *Wildlife Society Bulletin* 19: 184–190.

Dalthorp, D., J. Nyrop, and M.G. Villani. 2000[a]. Foundations of Spatial Ecology: The Reification of Patches Through Quantitative Description of Patterns and Pattern Repetition. *Entomologia Experimentalis et Applicata* 96: 119–127. Netherlands: Kluwer Academic Publishers.

———. 2000[b]. Spatial Ecology of the Japanese Beetle, Popillia japonica. *Entomologia Experimentalis et Applicata* 96: 129–139. Netherlands: Kluwer Academic Publishers.

Danneberger, Karl. 2000. Thermal Tolerance: The Role of Heat Shock Proteins. *Turfgrass Trends* 8 (7). Washington, DC.

Davidson, R.H., and W.F. Lyon. 1987. *Insect Pests of Farm, Garden and Orchard*, 8th ed. Hoboken, NJ: John Wiley & Sons.

Davis, J. Graham, and Peter H. Dernoeden. 2002. Dollar Spot Severity, Tissue Nitrogen, and Soil Microbial Activity in Bentgrass as Influenced by Nitrogen Source. *Crop Science* 42: 480–488. Madison, WI: Crop Science Society of America.

Deal, E.E. November 1967. Mowing Heights for Kentucky Bluegrass Turf. *Agronomy Abstracts* 59: 150. Madison, WI: American Society of Agronomy.

De Ceuster, Tom J.J., and Harry A.J. Hoitink. 1999[a]. Prospects for Composts and Biocontrol Agents as Substitutes for Methyl Bromide in Biological Control of Plant Diseases. *Compost Science and Utilization* 7 (3).

———. 1999[b]. Using Compost to Control Plant Diseases. *Biocycle* 40 (6). Emmaus, PA.

Dernoeden, Peter H. 2000. Creeping Bentgrass Management: Summer Stresses, Weeds, and Selected Maladies. Hoboken, NJ: John Wiley & Sons, Inc..

Dernoeden, P.H., M.J. Carroll, and J.M. Krouse. 1993. Weed Management and Tall Fescue Quality as Influenced by Mowing, Nitrogen, and Herbicides. *Crop Science* 33: 1055–1061. Madison, WI: Crop Science Society of America.

Derridj, S., V. Gregoire, J.P. Boutin, and V. Fiala. 1989. Plant Growth Stages in the Interspecific Oviposition Preference of the European Corn Borer and Relations with Chemicals Present on the Leaf Surfaces. Entomologia Experimentalis et Applicata 53: 267–276.

Dest, W.M. 1995. Turfgrass Clipping Management. *Turf Notes* 5 (2). Worcester: University of Massachusetts Extension.

Dest, W.M., S.C. Albin, and K. Guillard. 1992. Turfgrass Clipping Management. *Rutgers Turfgrass Proceedings 1992*. New Brunswick, NJ: Rutgers University.

DiMascio, J.A., P.M. Sweeney, T.K. Dannegerger, and J.C. Kamalay. 1994. Analysis of Heat Shock Response in Perennial Ryegrass Using Maize Heat Shock Protein Clones. *Crop Science* 34: 798–804. Madison, WI: Crop Science Society of America.

Dinelli, Dan F. 1997. IPM on Golf Courses. *IPM Practitioner* 19 (4). Berkeley, CA: Bio-Integral Resource Center.

———. July-August 1999. Using Composts to Improve Turf Ecology. *USGA Green Section Record*. Far Hills, NJ: U.S. Golf Association.

———. 2000. Composts to Improve Turf Ecology. *IPM Practitioner* 22 (10). Berkeley, CA: Bio-Integral Resource Center.

Dodson, Ron. 1996. Integrated Pest Management for Land Managers. *USGA Green Section Record* 34 (5). Far Hills, NJ: U.S. Golf Association.

DTN Weather Center, 11400 Rupp Drive, Burnsville, MN 55337; phone: 952.882.4337; fax: 952.882.4500; www.dtnonline.com.

Duncan, R.R., and R.N. Carrow. 2000. *Seashore Paspalum: The Environmental Turfgrass*. Hoboken, NJ: John Wiley & Sons, Inc..

Earth and Turf Products, 112 South Railroad Avenue, New Holland, PA 17557; phone: 717.355.2276; fax: 717.355.2879; www.earthandturf.com.

Earth Tea Brewer (EPM, Inc.), PO Box 1295, Cottage Grove, OR 97424; phone: 541.767.2747; fax: 541.767.2744; sales@fishworld.com; www.composttea.com.

EarthWorks, PO Box 278K, Martins Creek, PA 18063; phone: 800.732.8873 or 610.250.9560; fax: 610.250.7840; eworks@soilfirst.com; www.soilfirst.com.

EcoSoil Systems, Inc., 10740 Thornmint Road, San Diego, CA 92127; phone: 800.331.8773 or 858.675.1660; fax: 858.676.8345; ccarter@ecosoil.com; www.ecosoil.com.

Edel Grass (The Lantek Group), 235 County Line Road, Amityville, NY 11701; phone: 631.691.2381, ext. 32; email: mlyons@landtekgroup.com.

Edwards, C.A., and P.J. Bohlen. 1996. *Biology and Ecology of Earthworms*, 3rd ed. London: Chapman & Hall.

Elam, P. July 1994. Earthworms: We Need Attitude Adjustment. *Landscape Management*. Cleveland, OH: Advanstar Communications.

Elliott, Monica L. 2000. Black Box Research: Seeking Answers to the Effectiveness of Bacterial Inoculants. *USGA Green Section Record* 38 (6). Far Hills, NJ: U.S. Golf Association.

Engage Agro Corporation, 315 Woodlawn Road West, Guelph, Ontario, Canada N1H 7K8; phone: 800.900.5487; www.engageagro.com.

EPM, Inc., PO Box 1295, Cottage Grove, OR 97424; phone: 541-767-2747; fax: 541-767-2744; sales@composttea.com; www.composttea.com.

Ernst, David. 1995. *The Farmer's Earthworm Handbook*. Brookfield, WI: Lessiter Publications.

Esnard, Joseph, 2000. Why Turf Needs Good Nematodes. *Cornell University Turfgrass Times* 11 (2). Ithaca, NY: Cornell University.

European Turfgrass Laboratories Ltd., Unit 58, Stirling Enterprise Park, Stirling FK7 7RP Scotland; phone: 44.1786.449195; fax: 44.1786.449688.

Evaporative Control Systems, Inc.(ECS), 12955 Mahogany Drive, Reno, NV 89511-6217; phone: 775.852.2973; fax: 775.852.1340; info@ecsgreen.com; www.ecsgreen.com.

Fagerness, Matthew J., and Fred H. Yelverton. 2001. Plant Growth Regulator and Mowing Height Effects on Seasonal Root Growth of Penncross Creeping Bentgrass. *Crop Science* 41: 1901–1905. Madison, WI: Crop Science Society of America.

Field Turf, Inc., 5050 Pare Street, Suite 280, Montreal, Quebec, Canada H4P 1P3; phone: 800.724.2969 or 514.340.9311; fax: 514.340.9374; www.fieldturf.com.

Foth, Henry D., and Boyd G. Ellis. 1988. *Soil Fertility*. Hoboken, NJ: John Wiley & Sons.

Frank, Jeff. 2000. Quantum Physics and Horticulture. Keynote Address, Long Island Organic Horticulture (LIOHA) Conference, Massapequa, NY.

Franklin, S. 1988. *Building a Healthy Lawn: A Safe and Natural Approach.* Pownal, VT: Storey Communications.

Fream, Ronald W. 2001. Do You Have Green Creep? *USGA Green Section Record* 39 (1). Far Hills, NJ: U.S. Golf Association.

Fresh Aire Implements (Duke Merrion), 2283 South Road 300, East Danville, IN 46122; phone: 765.498.1070.

Friedman, David, Carl Montana, Paul Welle, Chris Smith, and David Lamm. 2001. *Impact of Soil Disturbance During Construction on Bulk Density and Infiltration in Ocean County, New Jersey.* USDA Natural Resource Conservation Service. http://ocscd .org/soil.pdf.

Friendly Robotics, 8336 Sterling Street, Irving, TX 75063; phone: 888.404.7626 or 214.260.1600; fax: 214.277.8181; friendly@friendlyrobotics.com; www.friendlyrobotics .com.

Garlic Research Labs, 624 Ruberta Avenue, Glendale, CA 91201; phone: 800.424.7990; garlik@earthlink.net.

Gaugler, Randy. 2000. Matching Nematodes to Target Pests. *IPM Practitioner* 22 (2). Berkeley, CA: Bio-Integral Resource Center.

Gaugler, Randy, and Harry K. Kaya. 1990. *Entomopathogenic Nematodes in Biological Control.* Boca Raton, FL: CRC Press.

Gempler's, 100 Countryside Drive, PO Box 270, Belleville, WI 53508; phone: 800.382.8473 or 608.424.1544; fax: 608.424.1661; www.gemplers.com.

Giesler, Loren J., Gary Y. Yuen, and Garald L. Horst. 2000. Canopy Microenvironments and Applied Bacteria Population Dynamics in Shaded Tall Fescue. *Crop Science* 40: 1325–1331. Madison, WI: Crop Science Society of America.

Gobran, George R., Walter W. Wenzel, and Enzo Lombi. 2001. *Trace Elements in the Rhizosphere.* Boca Raton, FL: CRC Press.

Grainge, M., and S. Ahmed. 1988. *Handbook of Plants with Pest Control Properties.* Hoboken, NJ: John Wiley & Sons.

Grant, J., M. Villani, and J. Nyrop. 1994. Predicting Grub Populations in Home Lawns. *Cornell University Turf Times* 5 (2). Ithaca, NY: Cornell University.

Grant, Jennifer A. 1995. What Does It Really Mean? *TurfGrass TRENDS* 4 (8): 1–2. Washington D.C. turfgrasstrends@advanstar.com.

Grissell, Eric. 2001. *Insects and Gardens.* Portland, OR: Timber Press.

Grossman, Joel. 2000. Compost Cures: Microbial-Powered Composts and Compost Teas Are Becoming Respected Weapons in the War Against Pests. *Growing Edge* 11 (3). Corvallis, OR.

Ground UP, LLC, 6515 W. Marginal Way SW, Seattle, WA 98106; phone: 206.571.4671; fax: 206.767.2026; Rno9616@aol.com.

Growing Solutions, Inc., 160 Madison Street, Eugene, OR 97402; phone: 541.343.8727; fax: 541.343.8374; info@growingsolutions.com; www.growingsolutions.com.

Gussack, Eva, and Frank S. Rossi. 2001. *Turfgrass Problems: Picture Clues and Management Options.* Ithaca, NY: Natural Resource, Agriculture, and Engineering Service (NRAES).

Hach Company, Products for Analysis, PO Box 389, Loveland, CO 80539; phone: 800.227.4224; fax: 970.669.2932; orders@hach.com; www.hach.com.

Hale, Maynard G., and David M. Orcutt. 1987. *The Physiology of Plants Under Stress.* Hoboken, NJ: John Wiley & Sons.

Hall, R. October 1994. Turf Pros Respond to Biostimulants. *Landscape Management.* Duluth, MN: Advanstar Communications.

Hanna Instruments, Inc., 584 Park East Drive, Woonsocket, RI 02895-0849; phone: 800.426.6287 or 401.765.7500; fax: 401.765.7575; sales@hannainst.com; www .hannainst.com.

Harban, Walter S. 1921. Winter Work on the Golf Course. *USGA Green Section Record* 1 (2). Far Hills, NJ: U.S. Golf Association.

Harper, John C., II. April 2001. Growing Turf Under Shaded Conditions. *Turf.* St. Johnsbury, VT: Moose River Publishing.

Hartwiger, Chris, and Patrick O'Brien. 2001. Core Aeration by the Numbers. *USGA Green Section Record* 39 (4). Far Hills, NJ: U.S. Golf Association.

Hartwiger, Christopher E., Charles H. Peacock, Joseph M. DiPaola, and D. Keith Cassel. 2001. Impact of Light-Weight Rolling on Putting Green Performance. *Crop Science* 41: 1179–1184. Madison, WI: Crop Science Society of America.

Heinrichs, E.A., ed. 1988. *Plant Stress–Insect Interactions.* Hoboken, NJ: John Wiley & Sons.

Hendricks, C.W., M.T. Holmes, and E.R. Ingham. 1998. Foodweb Methodology to Assess Ecological Effects of Anthropogenic Stressors in Soil. *Trends in Soil Science* 2:181–189.

Hendrix, Paul F. 1995. *Earthworm Ecology and Biogeography.* Boca Raton, FL: CRC Press.

Herbert Ranch, Inc. (Pat Herbert), PO Box 65, Hollister, CA 95024-0065; phone: 831.637.5515; fax: 831.637.0139; patti@herbertranch.com; www.herbertranch.com.

Hill, W., B.B. Clarke, and J.A. Murphy. 1999. Take-all Patch Suppression in Creeping Bentgrass with Manganese and Copper. *HortScience* 34: 891–892. American Society for Horticultural Science.

Hoitink, Harry A.J., and Marcella E. Grebus. 1994. Nurseries Find New Value in Composted Products. *Biocycle* 35: 51–52. Emmaus, PA.

Hoitink, Harry A.J,. and A.G. Stone. 1995. Factors Affecting Suppressiveness of Composts to Plant Disease. *HortScience* 30 (4). American Society for Horticultural Science.

Hoitink, Harry A.J., A.G. Stone, and D.Y. Han. 1997. Suppression of Plant Diseases by Composts. *HortScience* 32 (2). American Society for Horticultural Science.

Huang, Bingru. 2000. Summer Decline of Cool Season Turfgrasses: Heat Stress and Cultural Management. *Turfgrass Trends* 8 (6). Washington, DC.

———. July-August 2002. Getting to the Root of Summer Bentgrass Decline: How Summer Heat Affects Creeping Bentgrass Roots. *USGA Green Section Record* 40 (4). Far Hills, NJ: U.S. Golf Association.

Huang, Bingru, and Hongwen Gao. 2000. Growth and Carbohydrate Metabolism of Creeping Bentgrass Cultivars in Response to Increasing Temperatures. *Crop Science* 40: 1115–1120. Madison, WI: Crop Science Society of America.

Huang, P.M. and M. Schnitzer. 1986. *Interactions of Soil Minerals with Natural Organics and Microbes.* Madison, WI: Soil Science Society of America.

Huffaker, Carl B., and Robert L. Rabb. 1984 *Ecological Entomology.* Hoboken, NJ: John Wiley & Sons.

Hull, Richard J. 1996. Nitrogen Usage by Turfgrass. *Turfgrass Trends* 5 (11). Washington, DC.

Hull, Richard J., and John T. Bushoven. 2001. A Metabolic Approach: Improving Nitrogen Use Efficiency in Turfgrasses. *USGA Green Section Record* 39 (4). Hills, NJ: U.S. Golf Association.

Hummel, Norman W., Jr. 1993. Annual Bluegrass Biology and Control. *Cornell University Turfgrass Times* 4 (1). Ithaca, NY: Cornell University.

Imants USA, 941 Perkiomonville Road, Perkiomonville, PA 18074-9607; phone: 610.754.1110; fax: 610.754.1112; sales@imantsusa.com; www.imants.com.

Ingham, E.R. 1985. Review of the Effects of Twelve Selected Biocides on Target and Non-Target Soil Organisms. *Crop Protection* 4: 3032.

Ingham, E.R. 1998. Soil Organisms and Their Role in Healthy Turf. *Turf Grass Trends* 7:1–6.

Ingham, E.R. 2003. *Compost Tea Manual: Latest Recipes, Methods, and Research*, 4th ed. Corvallis, OR: Soil Food Web.

Ingham, E.R., and D.C. Coleman. 1984. Effects of Streptomycin, Cycloheximide, Fungizone, Captan, Carbofuran, Cygon and PCNB on Soil Microbe Populations and Nutrient Cycling. *Microbial Ecology* 10:345–358.

Ingham, E.R., and W.G. Thies. 1996. Soil Foodweb Responses in the First Year Following Clearcutting and Chloropicrin Application to a Mature Douglas-Fir Forest to Control Laminated Root Rot. *Applied Soil Ecol.* 3:35–47.

Ingham, E.R., and W. Thies. 1997. Changes in Rhizosphere Microflora and Microfauna 10 Years Following Douglas-Fir Live Tree Injection with Chloropicrin or Methylisothiocyanate. *Can. Jr. For Res.* 27:724–731.

Ingham, E.R., D.C. Coleman, and D.A. Crossley, Jr. 1994. Use of Sulfamethoxazole-Penicillin, Oxytetracycline, Carbofuran, Carbaryl, Napthalene and Temik to Remove Key Organism Groups in Soil in a Corn Agroecosystem. J. Sustain. *Agric.* 4(3):7–30.

Ingham, E.R., D.C. Coleman and J.C. Moore. 1989. Analysis of Food-Web Structure and Function in a Shortgrass Prairie, a Mountain Meadow and Lodgepole Pine Forest. *Biol. Fertil. Soils* 8:29–37.

Ingham, E.R., D.C. Coleman, R. Parmelee and D.A. Crossley. 1991. Reduction of Microbial and Faunal Groups Following Application of Streptomycin and Captan in Georgia No-Till Agroecosystems. *Pedobiologia* 35:297–304.

Ingham, E.R., J.A. Trofymow, R.N. Ames, H.W. Hunt, C.R. Morley, J.C. Moore and D.C. Coleman. 1986. Trophic Interactions and Nitrogen Cycling in a Semiarid Grassland Soil. Part II. System Responses to Removal of Different Groups of Soil Microbes or Fauna. *J. Applied Ecology* 23:615–630.

ISTRC New Mix Lab LLC, 1530 Kansas City Road, Suite 110, Olathe, KS 66061; phone: 800.362.8873; fax: 913.829.8873.

Jackson, N. November-December 1994. Winter Turf Problems. *Turf Notes*. Reprinted from *The Yankee Nursery Quarterly* 4 (4). Worcester: New England Cooperative Extension Systems, University of Massachusetts.

Jenny, H. 1941. *Factors of Soil Formation*. New York: McGraw-Hill.

Jiang, Yiwei, and Bingru Huang. 2000. Effects of Drought on Heat Stress Alone and in Combination on Kentucky Bluegrass. *Crop Science* 40: 1358–1362. Madison, WI: Crop Science Society of America.

———. 2001. Osmotic Adjustment and Root Growth Associated with Drought Preconditioning-Enhanced Heat Tolerance in Kentucky Bluegrass. *Crop Science* 41: 1168–1173. Madison, WI: Crop Science Society of America.

———. 2002. Protein Alterations in Tall Fescue in Response to Drought Stress and Abscisic Acid. *Crop Science* 42: 202–207. Madison, WI: Crop Science Society of America.

Johnson, Cicalese J., R. Casagrande, and H. Faubert. 1992. Effects of Acremonium Endophytes on Japanese Beetle Grubs (Popillia japonica). *Agronomy Abstracts 1992* p. 171. Madison, WI: American Society of Agronomy.

Jones, J. Benton, Jr. 1998. *Plant Nutrition Manual*. Boca Raton, FL: CRC Press.

Jordan, J.E., R.H. White, D.M. Victor, T.C. Hale, J.C. Thomas, and M.C. Engelke. 2003. Effect of Irrigation Frequency on Turf Quality, Shoot Density, and Root Length Density of Five Bentgrass Cultivars. *Crop Science* 43: 282–287. Madison, WI: Crop Science Society of America.

Josephine Porter Institute of Applied Biodynamics, PO Box 133, Woolwine, VA 24185; phone: 540. 930.2463; http://igg.com/bdnow/jpi/.

JRM, Inc., PO Box 15678, Wilmington, NC 28408; phone: 910.793.8328; fax: 910.793.9543; www.jrmonline.com; customersupport@jrmonline.com.

Kauffman, Scott. 2000. Pesticide Use Rises Slightly. *Golf Week's Superintendent News* 2 (9). Orlando, FL.

Keefer, Robert F. 2000. *Handbook of Soils for Landscape Architects*. New York: Oxford University Press.

Kenna, Mike. 2001. Nature Will Find a Way: Common Myths about Soil Microbiology. *USGA Green Section Record* 39 (3). Far Hills, NJ: U.S. Golf Association.

Kim, Tae-Joon, Frank Rossi, and Joseph Neal. 1997. Ecological Aspects of Crabgrass Infestation in Cool-Season Turf. *Cornell University Turfgrass Times* 8 (2). Ithaca, NY: Cornell University

Kinkead, Scott. May-June 2002. Topdressing 101: A Look at How Far It's Come, and Where It's Going. *Superintendent*. St. Johnsbury, VT: Moose River Publishing.

Koch, George W., and Harold A. Mooney, eds. 1996. *Carbon Dioxide and Terrestrial Ecosystems*. San Diego, CA: Academic Press.

Kopp, Kelly L., and Karl Guillard. 2002. Clipping Management and Nitrogen Fertilization of Turfgrass: Growth, Nitrogen Utilization, and Quality. *Crop Science* 42: 1225–1231. Madison, WI: Crop Science Society of America.

Kuo, Y., T.W. Fermanian, and D.J. Wehner. 2000. Nitrogen Utilization in Creeping Bentgrass *Journal of Turfgrass Management* 3 (2). Binghamton, NY: Haworth Press.

Labbance, Bob. April 2002. Water, Water. *Turf*. St. Johnsbury, VT: Moose River Publishing.

Lamboy, Jana. February 2000. Humus and Turf: Its Mysterious Role and Composition. *Turf*. St. Johnsbury, VT: Moose River Publishing.

LaMotte Company, PO Box 329, Chestertown, MD 21620; phone: 800.344.3100 or 410.778.3100; fax: 410.778.6394; mkt@lamotte.com; www.lamotte.com.

Land Pride, Division of Great Plains Mfg., PO Box 5060, Salina, KS 67402-5060; phone: 888.987.7433 or 785.823.3276; fax: 800.382.2349 or 785.822.5601; www.landpride.com.

Lawn Institute. 2002. Leaves of Grass: Environmental Benefits of a Well-Maintained Lawn. *Acres USA* 32 (3). Austin, TX.

Lee, Kenneth E. 1985. *Earthworms: Their Ecology and Relationships with Soils and Land Use*. Orlando, FL: Academic Press.

Leius, K. 1967. Influence of Wildflowers on Parasitism of Tent Caterpillar and Codling Moth. *Canadian Entomology*. 99: 444–446.

Lennert, Larry. 1990. The Role of Iron in Turfgrass Management in Wisconsin. US Golf Association Turfgrass Information (Center) http://www.lib.msu.edu/tgif #:17611.

Leslie, A.R., ed. 1994. *Handbook of Integrated Pest Management for Turf and Ornamentals*. Boca Raton, FL: Lewis Publishers.

Li, Deying, Young K. Joo, Nick E. Christians, and David D. Minner. 2000. Inorganic Soil Amendment Effects on Sand-Based Sports Turf Media. *Crop Science* 40: 1121–1125. Madison, WI: Crop Science Society of America.

Lilly, Sharon. 1999. *Golf Course Tree Management*. Hoboken, NJ: John Wiley & Sons, Inc..

Links Analytical, 22170 S. Saling Road, Estacada, OR 97023; phone: 503.630.7769; fax: 503.630.7764; links@europa.com.

Liu, Xiaozhong, and Bingru Huang. 2002. Mowing Effects on Root Production, Growth, and Mortality of Creeping Bentgrass. *Crop Science* 42: 1241–1250. Madison, WI: Crop Science Society of America.

Liu, Xiaozhong, Bingru Huang, and Gary Banowetz. 2002[a]. Cytokinin Effects on Creeping Bentgrass Responses to Heat Stress: I. Shoot and Root Growth. *Crop Science* 42: 457–465. Madison, WI: Crop Science Society of America.

———. 2002[b]. Cytokinin Effects on Creeping Bentgrass Responses to Heat Stress: II. Leaf Senescence and Antioxidant Metabolism. *Crop Science* 42: 466–472. Madison, WI: Crop Science Society of America.

Lizzi, Yves, Claude Coulomb, Claude Polian, Philippe Jean Coulomb, and Philippe Olivier Coulomb. September 1998. Seaweed and Mildew: What Does the Future Hold? *Phytoma: The Defense of Plants* 508: 29–30.

Lloyd, J., ed. 1997. *Plant Health Care for Woody Ornamentals.* Savoy, IL: International Society of Arboriculture.

Lucas, R.E., and M.L. Vitosh. November 1978. *Soil Organic Matter Dynamics.* Michigan State University Research Report 32.91. East Lansing, MI.

Lyceum, PO Box 254, 18 Fairview Street (Westhampton Beach), Westhampton, NY 11977; phone: 631.288.2834; jtf4647@aol.com; www.greenguerrilla.com.

Makarov, I.B. 1986. Seasonal Dynamics of Soil Humus Content. *Moscow University Soil Science Bulletin* 41 (3): 19–26.

Martens, Mary-Howell R. 2000. The Soil Food Web: Tuning In to the World Beneath Our Feet. *Acres USA* 30 (4). Austin, TX.

Magdoff, Fred, and Harold van Es. 2000. *Building Soils for Better Crops*, 2nd ed. Beltsville, MD: Sustainable Agriculture Network.

Maske, C. 2000. Personal Communication. *Maske's Organic Gardening.* Decatur, IL.

Mason, J.R., L. Clark, and T.P. Miller. *Evaluation of a Pelleted Bait Containing Methyl Anthranilate as a Bird Repellent.* U.S. Department of Agriculture, Animal and Plant Health Inspection Service, Denver Wildlife Research Center, c/o Monell Chemical Senses Center, Philadelphia, PA.

McCarty, L.B., John W. Everest, David W. Hall, Tim R. Murphy, and Fred Yelverton. 2000. *Color Atlas of Turfgrass Weeds.* Hoboken, NJ: John Wiley & Sons, Inc..

McKewon, Marty. May 2001. Why Are Forecasts Always Wrong? *Turf.* St. Johnsbury, VT: Moose River Publishing.

McMullen, Eric. May-June 2002. Lightweight Water: The Ratio of Bicarbonate to TDS Is as Important as the Specific Numbers. *Superintendent.* St. Johnsbury, VT: Moose River Publishing.

Mellor, David R. 2001. *Picture Perfect: Mowing Techniques for Lawns, Landscapes, and Sports.* Hoboken, NJ: John Wiley & Sons, Inc.

Methods of Soil Analysis. American Society of Agronomy. Madison, WI.

MicrobBrewer, 182 Capital Lane, Roseburg, OR 97470; phone: 541.673.0500; fax: 541.673.1395; info@microbbrewer.com; www.microbbrewer.com

Midwest Bio-Systems, 28933-35E Street, Tampico, IL 61283; phone: 800-335-8501; fax: 815-438-7028.

Morningstar Minerals, PO Box 9, #22 CR 3957, Farmington, New Mexico 87499; phone 866.898.4467 or 505.564.4391; www.msminerals.com.

Musser, H. Burton. 1962. *Turf Management.* New York: McGraw-Hill.

Mycogen Corporation, 5501 Oberlin Drive, San Diego, CA 92121; phone: 800.745.7476; fax: 619.552.0459; www.mycogen.com.

Nakasaki, Kiyohiko, Sachiko Hiraoka, and Hiroyuki Nagata. 1998. A New Operation for Producing Disease-Suppressive Compost from Grass Clippings. *Applied and Environmental Microbiology* 64 (10): 4015–4020. American Society for Microbiology.

National Turfgrass Evaluation Program (NTEP). 10300 Baltimore Ave. Bldg. 003, Rm. 218, Beltsville Agricultural Resource Center, West Beltsville, MD 20705. Pone: 301-504-5125; fax: 301-504-5167; http://www.nept.org; kmorris@netp.org.

Natural Resource, Agriculture, and Engineering Service. 1992. *On-Farm Composting Handbook.* Northeast Regional Engineering Service #54. Ithaca, NY: Cornell Cooperative Extension.

Neal, J.C. 1990. Waging War on Crabgrass. *Cornell University Turfgrass Times* 1 (1). Ithaca, NY: Cornell University.

———. July 1992. Plan Before You Plant. *WeedFacts.* Ithaca, NY: Cornell University.

———. August 1993. Turfgrass Weed Management: An IPM Approach. *WeedFacts.* Ithaca, NY: Cornell University.

Nektarios, P.A., T.S. Steenhuis, A.M. Petrovic, and J.-Y. Parlange. 1999. Fingered Flow in Laboratory Golf Putting Greens. *Journal of Turfgrass Management* 3 (1): 53. Binghamton, NY: Haworth Press.

Nelson, Eric B. Impacts of Conventional Turfgrass Pesticides on the Efficacy of Composted Amendments Used for the Biological Control of Turfgrass Diseases. 1997. Unpublished. Available through Cornell University, Ithaca, NY.

———. 2002. *Biological Control of Turfgrass Diseases.* Unpublished. available through Cornell University, Ithaca, NY.

———. 1994. More Than Meets the Eye: The Microbiology of Turfgrass Soils. *Turf Grass Trends* 3 (2). Washington, DC.

———. 1995. The Microbiology of Turfgrass Soils. *Cornell University Turfgrass Times* 5 (4). Ithaca, NY: Cornell University.

———. July 1997. Biological Control of Turfgrass Diseases. *Golf Course Management.* Lawrence, KS.

———. 2001. What Are Those Microbes? *Cornell University Turfgrass Times* 12 (1). Ithaca, NY: Cornell University.

Nelson, Eric B., and Frank S. Rossi. 2001. Creeping Bentgrass Cultivar Influences Biocontrol. *Cornell University Turfgrass Times* 12 (2). Ithaca, NY: Cornell University.

Nelson, Matt. 1997. Natural Areas: Establishing Natural Areas on the Golf Course. *USGA Green Section Record* 35 (6). Far Hills, NJ: U.S. Golf Association.

Neumann, S., and G.J. Boland. 1999. Influence of Selected Adjuvants on Disease Severity by Phoma Herbarium on Dandelion. *Weed Technology* 13: 675–679.

Norrie, J., and D.A. Hiltz. March-April 1999. Seaweed Extract Research and Applications in Agriculture. *Agro-Food Industry Hi-Tech.*

North American Kelp, 41 Cross Street, Waldoboro, ME 04572; phone: 888.662.5357 or 207.832.7506; fax: 207.832.6905; nak@noamkelp.com; www.noamkelp.com.

Northwest Irrigation, 30373 Highway 34, Albany, OR 97321; phone: 866.4.BREWER or 541.928.0114; fax: 541.928.0307; info@microbbrewer.com; www.microbbrewer.com.

N.W. Hummel & Co., 35 King Street, PO Box 606, Trumansburg, NY 14886; phone: 607.387.5694; fax: 607.387.9499; SOILDR1@Epix.net; www.turfdoctor.com.

O'Brien, Patrick M. 1996. The Magic of Sulfur. *USGA Green Section Record* 34 (3). Far Hills, NJ: U.S. Golf Association.

———. 1996. Optimizing the Turfgrass Canopy Environment with Fans. *USGA Green Section Record* 34 (4). Far Hills, NJ: U.S. Golf Association.

Olkowski, William, Sheila Daar, and Helga Olkowski. 1991. *Common-Sense Pest Control.* Newtown, CT: Taunton Press.

Onset Computer Corporation, PO Box 3450, Pocasset, MA 02559-3450; phone: 800.LOGGERS or 508.759.9500; fax: 508.759.9100; sales@onsetcomp.com; www.onsetcomp.com.

Peak Minerals (Azomite, Inc.), PO Box 6588, Branson, MO 65615; phone: 877.296.6483 or 417.334.8500; fax: 417.334.8825; azomite@aol.com; www.azomite.com.

Petrik Laboratories, 109 Harter Avenue, Woodland, CA 95776; phone: 530.666.1157; fax: 530.661.0489; mike@petriklabs.com; www.petrik.com.

Petrovic, Martin A. 1997. The Art and Science of Turfgrass Soil Management. *Cornell University Turfgrass Times* 8 (3). Ithaca, NY: Cornell University.

———. 2000. Oxygen Injection and Bentgrass Rooting. *Cornell University Turfgrass Times* 11 (3). Ithaca, NY: Cornell University.

———. 2001. Understanding the Exchange: Turfgrass Nutrient Management and Cation Exchange Capacity. *Cornell University Turfgrass Times* 12 (1). Ithaca, NY: Cornell University.

Petrovic, Martin A., C.A. Sanchiroco, D.J. Lisk, R.G. Young, and P. Larrson-Kovach. 1993. Pesticide Leaching from Simulated Golf Course Fairways. *Cornell University Turfgrass Times* 4 (2). Ithaca, NY: Cornell University.

Pfeiffer, E.E. 1970. *Weeds and What They Tell.* Reprinted by Bio-Dynamic Literature, Wyoming, RI.

Phelan, P.L. 1997. Soil-Management History and the Role of Plant Mineral Balance as a Determinant of Maize Susceptibility to the European Corn Borer. *Biological Agriculture and Horticulture* 15 (1-4) 25–34.

Phelan, P.L., J.F. Mason, and B.R. Stinner. 1995. Soil-Fertility Management and Host Preference by European Corn Borer, *Ostrinia nubilalis* (Hübner), on *Zeo mays* L.: A Comparison of Organic and Conventional Chemical Farming. *Agriculture, Ecosystems and Environment* 56: 1–8. New York: Elsevier Science.

Phelan, P.L., K.H. Norris, and J.F. Mason. 1996. Soil-Management History and Host Preference by *Ostrinia nubilalis*: Evidence for Plant Mineral Balance Mediating insect-Plant Interactions. *Environmental Entomology* 25(6): 1329–1336. Entomological Society of America.

Pierzynski, Gary M., J. Thomas Sims, and George F. Vance. 1994. *Soils and Environmental Quality.* Boca Raton, FL: Lewis Publishers.

Pike Lab Supplies (Bob Pike), RFD#2, Box 92, Strong, ME 04983; phone: 207.684.5131; pike@inetme.com; www.maine.com/tse/pals/welcome.html

Piper, C.V,. and R.A. Oakley. 1921[a]. Humus Producing Materials and the Making and Use of Compost. *USGA Green Section Record* 1 (4). Far Hills, NJ: U.S. Golf Association.

———. 1921[b]. Some Suggestions for Fall Treatment of Putting Greens. *USGA Green Section Record* 1 (8). Far Hills, NJ: U.S. Golf Association.

Players Turf International LLC, 809 W. Detweiller Drive, Peoria, IL 61615; phone: 877.307.5530; fax: 309.693.0354; www.playersturf.com; contact: Ray Sever.

Potter, Daniel A. 1991. Earthworms, Thatch, and Pesticides. *USGA Green Section Record* 29 (5). Far Hills, NJ: U.S. Golf Association.

———. 1992. Natural Enemies Reduce Pest Populations in Turf. *USGA Green Section Record* 30 (6). Far Hills, NJ: U.S. Golf Association.

———. 1998. *Destructive Turfgrass Insects: Biology, Diagnosis, and Control.* Hoboken, NJ: John Wiley & Sons, Inc..

———. 2001. Conserve Beneficial Insects on Your Golf Course. *USGA Green Section Record* 39 (6). Far Hills, NJ: U.S. Golf Association.

Prakash, Anand, and Jagadiswari Rao. 1997. *Botanical Pesticides in Agriculture.* Boca Raton, FL: CRC Press.

Price, P.W., T.M. Lewinsohn, G.W. Fernandes, and W.W. Benson, eds. 1991. *Plan-Animal Interactions.* Hoboken, NJ: John Wiley & Sons.

Prostak, Randall G. 2002[a]. Managing Crabgrass Without Herbicides: What Changes in Management and Budget Need to Be Considered? (Part 1). *Horticultural Notes* 13 (1). Amherst: University of Massachusetts Extension.

———. 2002[b]. Managing Crabgrass Without Herbicides: What Changes in Management and Budget Need to Be Considered? (Part 2). *Horticultural Notes* 13 (2). Amherst: University of Massachusetts Extension.

Qian, Yaling, and Ronald F. Follett. 2002. Assessing Soil Carbon Sequestration in Turfgrass Systems Using Long-Term Soil Testing Data. *Agronomy Journal* 94: 930–935. Madison, WI: American Society of Agronomy.

Quarles, W. 1996. New Microbial Pesticides for IPM. *IPM Practitioner* 18 (8). Berkeley, CA.

Quarles, W., ed. 2001[a]. Golf Course Pests. *IPM Practitioner* 23 (5/6). Berkeley, CA.

———. 2001[b]. Black Cutworm IPM. *IPM Practitioner* 23 (5/6). Berkeley, CA.

————. 2001[c]. Compost Tea for Organic Farming and Gardening. *IPM Practitioner* 23 (9). Berkeley, CA.

————. 2002[a]. Mountains or Molehills? *Common Sense Pest Control Quarterly* 17 (4). Berkeley, CA.

————. 2002[b]. Insectary Plants, Intercropping, and Biological Control. *IPM Practitioner* 24 (3). Berkeley, CA.

RainWise, Inc., PO Box 443, Bar Harbor, ME 04609; phone: 800.762.5723 or 207.288.5169; fax: 207.288.3477; sales@rainwise.com; www.rainwise.com.

Rechcigl, Jack E., ed. 1995. *Soil Amendments: Impacts on Biotic Systems.* Boca Raton, FL: Lewis Publishers.

Richie, W.E., R.L. Green, G.J. Klein, and J.S. Hartin. 2002. Tall Fescue Performance Influences by Irrigation Scheduling, Cultivar, and Mowing Height. *Crop Science* 42: 2011–2017. Madison, WI: Crop Science Society of America.

Ridzon, Leonard, and Charles Walters, Jr. 1990. *The Carbon Connection.* Austin, TX: Acres USA.

Rieke, P.E., M.T. Saffel, and J.A. Murphy. 1991. Turfgrass Soil Management Research Report—1990 [VI. Wetting Agent Studies]. *Proceedings of the 61st Annual Michigan Turfgrass* 20 44–49. East Lansing, MI: Michigan State University.

Roberts, Eliot C. 1992. Private communication. The Lawn Institute, Pleasant Hill, TN.

————. 2002. What Lies Beneath: Realizing Soil's Potential for Water Conservation. July 2002. *Turf.* St. Johnsbury, VT: Moose River Publishing.

Roberts, J. February 1995. *Spring Fertilization Jump Starts Turf, Landscape Management.* Cleveland, OH: Advanstar Communications.

Rossi, Frank S. 1999. Everything You Ever Wanted to Know About Crabgrass…But Didn't Know Who to Ask. *Cornell University Turfgrass Times* 10 (4): Ithaca, NY: Cornell University.

————. 2000[a]. Wondering About Golf Course Ecology. *Cornell University Turfgrass Times* 10 (3): Ithaca, NY: Cornell University.

————. 2000[b]. Does Bentgrass Overseeding Work? *Cornell University Turfgrass Times* 10 (4): Ithaca, NY: Cornell University.

————. 2000[c]. Core Cultivation: A Necessary Evil? *Cornell University Turfgrass Times* 11 (3): Ithaca, NY: Cornell University.

————. 2001. Lessons from the Lorax: The Golf Industry Would Do Well to Pay Attention to Sage Advice from Dr. Seuss. *USGA Green Section Record* 39 (3): Far Hills, NJ.

————. 2002[a]. Subtle Aspects of Microbes Determine Performance, *Cornell University Turfgrass Times* 12 (4): Ithaca, NY: Cornell University.

————. July 4, 2002[b]. Update on Rootzone Amendment Work, Year 5. Week 15. *Short-CUTT.* Ithaca, NY: Cornell University.

RotaDairon Emrex, Inc., 458 Wyoming Avenue, Kingston, PA 18704; phone: 800.554.4863 or 570.602.3050; fax: 570.602.3053; rotadaironemrex@aol.com; www.mge-dairon.com.

Roth, Steve. March 2001. A New Nematode Joins the Fight: Biological Control for Mole Crickets. *Turf.* St. Johnsbury, VT: Moose River Publishing.

Sachs, Paul D. 1996. *Handbook of Successful Ecological Lawn Care.* Newbury, VT: Edaphic Press.

————. 1999. *Edaphos: Dynamics of a Natural Soil System.* 2nd ed. Newbury, VT: Edaphic Press.

Sachs, Paul D., and Richard T. Luff. September-October 2001. Compost on Your Course: Tips and Advice for Better Use. Part 1. *Superintendent.* St. Johnsbury, VT: Moose River Publishing.

————. November-December 2001. Compost on Your Course: Tips and Advice for Better Use. Part 2. *Superintendent.* St. Johnsbury, VT: Moose River Publishing.

———. 2002. *Ecological Golf Course Management*. Hoboken, NJ: John Wiley & Sons, Inc..

St. Gabriel Labs, 14044 Litchfield Drive, Orange, VA 22960; phone: 540.672.0866; fax: 540.672.0052; sales@milkyspore.com; www.milkyspore.com.

Senesac, A. 1992. Fall Weed Control. *Cornell University Turfgrass Times* 3 (3). Ithaca, NY: Cornell University.

Schmaderer, Jason. June 2000. Rethinking the Rootzone: The Agronomic Benefits of Porous Ceramic Amendments. *Turf*. St. Johnsbury, VT: Moose River Publishing.

Schmidt, R.E., and X. Zhang. 1997. *Influence of Seaweed on Growth and Stress Tolerance of Grasses*. T.4.6.1. Fort Worth, TX: Proceedings of American Forage and Grassland Council. 158–162.

———. 1998a. How Humic Substances Help Turfgrass Grow: Research Reveals Diverse Roles for Some Little-Known Products. *Golf Course Management* 66 (7): 65–67. Lawrence, KS: Golf Course Superintendents Association of America.

———. 1998[b]. Manipulation of Mineral Nutrition with Organic Growth Regulators on Turfgrass Antioxidant Activity and Tolerance to Environmental Stress. Blacksburg: Virginia Polytechnic Institute and State University, Department of Crop and Soil Environmental Sciences.

———. 1998[c]. Manipulation of Mineral Nutrition with Organic Growth Regulators on Creeping Bentgrass Turf and Tolerance to Environmental Stress. Blacksburg: Virginia Polytechnic Institute and State University, Department of Crop and Soil Environmental Sciences.

Schriefer, Donald L. 2000[a]. *Agriculture in Transition*. Austin, TX: Acres USA.

———. 2000[b]. *From the Soil Up*. Austin, TX: Acres USA.

Schultz, W. 1989. *The Chemical Free Lawn*. Emmaus, PA: Rodale Press.

Schumann, Gail L. 1994. Predicting Rhizoctonia Blight (Hot-Weather Brown Patch). *Turf Notes* 4 (5). Worcester: University of Massachusetts Extension.

———. May 1994. Disease Control in Cool-Season Grasses. *Landscape Management*. Cleveland, OH: Advanstar Communications

———. 1995. Remember Last Summer. *Turf Notes* 5 (3). Worcester, University of Massachusetts Extension.

Schumann, Gail L., Patricia J. Vittum, Monica L. Elliott, and Patricia P. Cobb. 1998. *IPM Handbook for Golf Courses*. Hoboken, NJ: John Wiley & Sons, Inc..

Senn, T.L. 1987. *Seaweed and Plant Growth*. No publisher noted. Clemson, SC: Clemson University, Department of Horticulture.

Senn, T.L,. and A.R. Kingman. March 1, 1973. A Review of Humus and Humic Acids. *Clemson University Research Series* 145. Clemson, SC.

SFI. 2000[a]. Soil Food Web, Inc., 1128 NE 2nd Street, Suite 120, Corvallis, OR 97330; www.soilfoodweb.com; and Soil Food Web New York, 555-7 Hallock Avenue, Port Jefferson Station, NY 11776; phone: 631.474.8848; fax: 631.474.8847; soilfoodwebny@aol.com.

SFI. 2000[b]. online at http://www.soilfoodweb.com/products/bacterialresources.html.

Simpson, T.C. 1931. *The Game of Golf: The Upkeep of a Golf Course*. Philadelphia: J.B. Lippincott, 197–218.

Smigocki, Ann, Sunggi Heu, Iris McCanna, Chris Wozniak, and George Buta. 1997. Insecticidal Compounds Induced by Regulated Overproduction of Cytokinins in Transgenic Plants. In *Advances in Insect Control*, ed. N. Carozzi and M. Koziel. Washington, DC: Taylor & Francis, 225–236.

Smith, C.M. 1989. *Plant Resistance to Insects: A Fundamental Approach*. Hoboken, NJ: John Wiley & Sons.

Spectrum Technologies, Inc., 23839 W. Andrew Road, Plainfield, Illinois 60544; phone: 815.436.4440; fax: 815.436.4460; specmeters@aol.com; www.specmeters.com.

Soil Fertility and Organic Matter as Critical Components of Production Systems. 1987. SSSA 19. Madison, WI: Soil Science Society of America.

Staub, Theodor. 2001. Induced Disease Resistance in Crop Health Management. *Plant Health Progress*. Online. http://www.planthealthprogress.org. Riehen, Switzerland: Plant Health Progress, doi:10.1094/PHP-2001-0913-01-PS.

Stevenson, F.J. 1986. *Cycles of Soil: C, N, P, S, Micronutrients*. Hoboken, NJ: John Wiley & Sons.

———. 1994. *Humus Chemistry: Genesis, Composition, Reactions*. 2nd ed. Hoboken, NJ: John Wiley & Sons.

Stoton, Michael. 2002. Plant-Stress Detection: Old Problem, New Solution. *Acres USA* 32 (3). Austin, TX.

Stuart, K. Spring 1992. A Life with the Soil. *Orion* 11 (2): 17–29. New York: Myrin Institute.

Sullivan, D.M., A.I. Bary, D.R. Thomas, S.C. Fransen, and C.G. Cogger. 2002. Food Waste Compost Effects on Fertilizer Nitrogen Efficiency, Available Nitrogen, and Tall Fescue Yield. *Soil Science Society of America Journal* 66: 154–161. Madison, WI: Soil Science Society of America.

Sullivan, W. Michael, Zhongchun Jiang, and Richard J. Hull. 2000. Root Morphology and Its Relationship with Nitrate Uptake in Kentucky Bluegrass. *Crop Science* 40 (3). Madison, WI: Crop Science Society of America.

Summa Minerals, 2310 Sherman Place, Las Vegas, NV 89102; phone: 702.256.2990; summaminerals@mail.com.

Sumner, Malcolm E., ed. 2000. *Handbook of Soil Science*. Boca Raton, FL: CRC Press.

Tani, Toshikazu, and James B. Beard. 1997. *Color Atlas of Turfgrass Diseases: Disease Characteristics and Control*. Hoboken, NJ: John Wiley & Sons, Inc..

Terry, Lee A., Daniel A. Potter, and Patricia G. Spicer. 1993. Insecticides Affect Predatory Arthropods and Predation of Japanese Beetle (Coleoptera: Scrabaeidae) Eggs and Fall Armyworm (Lepidoptera: Noctuidae) Pupae in Turfgrass. *Journal of Economic Entomology* 86 (3).

Thomas Turf Services, Inc., 2151 Harvey Mitchell Parkway South, Suite 302, College Station, TX 77840-5247; phone: 979.764.2050; fax: 979.764.2151; soiltest@thomasturf.com.

Thurn, Mary. 1995. Composts as Soil Amendments. *Cornell University Turfgrass Times* 5 (4). Ithaca, NY: Cornell University.

Tifton Physical Soil Testing Loboratory, Inc., 1412 Murray Avenue, Tifton, GA 31794; phone: 912.382.7292; fax: 912.382.7992; pgaines@surfsouth.com.

Torello, W.A., Haim Gunner, and Ming Coler. 1998. Microbial Population Dynamics in Sand Green Profiles: The Effects Of Vesicular-Arbuscular Mycorrhiza Fungi on Turfgrass Vigor, Disease/Insect Activity, Environmental Stress Resistance, and Fertilizer Efficiency. *1998 Turfgrass Field Day*, 47–48. Amherst: University of Massachusetts.

———. 1999. Biological Disease Control in Golf Turf: A Unique Approach Utilizing Newly Developed Carrier Technology for a New Anti-Pathogenic Activity Bacterium. *1999 Turfgrass Field Day*, 25. Amherst: University of Massachusetts.

Toro Company, Commercial Division, 8111 Lyndale Avenue S, Bloomington, MN 55420; phone: 952.888.8801; www.toro.com.

Trenholm, L.E., R.N. Carrow, and R.R. Duncan. 2000. Mechanisms of Wear Tolerance in Seashore Paspalum and Bermudagrass. *Crop Science* 40: 1350–1357. Madison, WI: Crop Science Society of America.

Trusty, Steve and Suz. September 2001. Solutions to High-Tech Demands: Sharing Sports Turf Knowledge and Experience Is Key. *Turf*. St. Johnsbury, VI: Moose River Publishing.

Turf Diagnostics and Design, Inc., 310A N. Winchester Street, Olathe, KS 66062; phone: 913.780.6725; fax: 913.789.6759; sferro@turfdiag.com.

Turf Resource Center and Lawn Institute, 1855-A Hicks Road, Rolling Meadows, IL 60008; phone: 800.405.TURF or 847.705.9898; fax: 847.705.8347; www.TurfGrassSod.org or www.LawnInstitute.com.

Turfgrass Information Center, Michigan State University Libraries, 100 Library, East Lansing, MI 48828-1048; phone: (517) 353-7209; fax: 517.353.1975; tgif@msu.edu.

Turgeon, Alfred J., ed. 1994. *Turf weeds and Their Control.* Madison, WI: Crop Science Society of America.

Unruh, J.B., N.E. Christians, and H.T. Horner. 1997. Herbicidal Effects of the Dipeptide Alaninyl-Alanine on Perennial Rygrass (*Lolium perenne L.*) Seedlings. *Crop Science* 37: 201–212. Madison, WI: Crop Science Society of America.

U.S. Composting Council, PO Box 407, Amherst, OH 44001-0407; phone: 440.989.2748; www.compostingcouncil.org.

U.S. Environmental Protection Agency. http://www.epa.gov/pesticides/biopesticides/.

Uva, Richard H., Joseph C. Neal, and Joseph M. DiTomaso. 1997. *Weeds of the Northeast.* Ithaca, NY: Cornell University Press.

van Veen, A., and P.J. Kuikman. December 1990. Soil Structural Aspects of Decomposition of Organic Matter by Micro-organisms. *Biogeochemistry* 11 (3): 213–233.

Vargas, J.M., Jr. 1994. *Management of Turfgrass Diseases.* 2nd ed. Boca Raton, FL: Lewis Publishers.

Vavrek, R.C. November-December 1990. Beneficial Turfgrass Invertebrates. *USGA Green Section Record* 28 (6). Far Hills, NJ: U.S. Golf Assocation.

———. July-August 2002. Traffic: How Much Can You Bare? Wear and Compaction Can Leave You with Unsightly Bare Spots. *USGA Green Section Record* 40 (4). Far Hills, NJ: U.S. Golf Assocation.

Vermeulen, Paul H. 1997. Know When to Over-Irrigate: An Easy Way to Monitor Soil Salinity. *USGA Green Section Record* 35 (5). Far Hills, NJ: U.S. Golf Assocation.

Villani, Mike. 1998. Moisture Effects on Entomopathogenic Nematodes. *Cornell University Turfgrass Times* 9 (1). Ithaca, NY: Cornell University.

Vilter, H. 1983. Peroxidases from Phaeophyceae: Catalysis of Halogenation by Peroxidases from *Ascophyllum nodosum. Botanica Marina* 26: 429–435.

Vilter, H., K.-W. Glombitza, and A. Grawe. 1983. Peroxidases from Phaeophyceae: Extraction and Detection of the Peroxidases. *Botanica Marina* 26: 331–340.

Vittum, Patricia J. 1984. Effect of Lime Applications on Japanese Beetle (*Coleoptera: Scarabaeidae*) Grub Populations in Massachusetts Soils. *Journal of Economic Entomology* 77: 687–690.

———. 1994. Hyperodes Update. *Turf Notes* 4 (5). Worcester: University of Massachusetts Extension.

———. 1995. Black Turfgrass Ataenius Update. *Turf Notes* 5 (2). Worcester: University of Massachusetts Extension.

———. 1999. Identifying and Managing White Grubs in New England. *Turf Notes* 8 (2). Worcester: University of Massachusetts Extension.

Vittum, Patricia J., Michael G. Villani, and Haruo Tashiro, 1999. *Turfgrass Insects of the United States and Canada.* 2nd ed. Ithaca, NY: Cornell University Press.

Waisel, Yoav, Amram Eshel, and Uzi Kafkafi, eds. 1996. *Plant Roots: The Hidden Half,* 2nd ed. New York: Marcel Dekker.

Wallace, Arthur, and Richard E. Terry, eds. 1998. *Handbook of Soil Conditioners: Substances That Enhance the Physical Properties of Soil.* New York: Marcel Dekker.

Walters, C., Jr. 1991. *Weeds: Control Without Poisons.* Kansas City, MO: Acres USA.

Waksman, S.A. 1936. *Humus.* Baltimore: Williams and Wilkins.

Water Wick. 491 North Main St., Southampton, NY 11968. Phone: 888-287-1644; www.waterwick.com; info@waterwick.com.

Watkins, John E. 1996. Nitrogen Fertilization's Effect on Turfgrass Disease Injury. *Turfgrass Trends* 5 (11). Washington, DC.

Watschke, Thomas L., Peter H. Dernoeden, and David J. Shetlar. 1995. *Managing Turfgrass Pests*. Boca Raton, FL: Lewis Publishers.

Weston, Leslie. 2002. Weed-Suppressive Groundcovers: A More Attractive and Effective Way to Manage Weeds. *Cornell University Turfgrass Times* 12 (4). Ithaca, NY: Cornell University.

White, Patrick. September 2000. Leave 'Em Lie. *Turf*. St. Johnsbury, VT: Moose River Publishing.

———. April 2001. Beam Me Up: The Future Is Now for One Company's New Mower. *Turf*. St. Johnsbury, VT: Moose River Publishing.

———. August 2001. Artificial Flavors: A Number of New Products Have Put Artificial Turf Back in the Game, and Even on Some Lawns. *Turf*. St. Johnsbury, VT: Moose River Publishing.

White, W.C., and D.N. Collins, eds. 1982. *The Fertilizer Handbook*. Washington, DC: Fertilizer Institute.

Wilkinson, Robert E., ed. 1994. *Plant-Environment Interactions*. New York: Marcel Dekker.

Williams, David W., and A.J. Powell, Jr. 1995. Dew Removal and Dollar Spot on Creeping Bentgrass. *Golf Course Management* 63 (8): 49–52. Lawrence, KS: Golf Course Superintendents Association of America.

Williams, Nancy D., and Joseph C. Neal. 1993. Annual Bluegrass Biology and Control. *Cornell University Turfgrass Times* 4 (1). Ithaca, NY: Cornell University.

Wiseman, B.R., and R.R. Duncan. 1996. Resistance of *Paspalum spp.* to *Spodoptera frugiperda* (J.E. Smith) (*Lepidoptera: Noctuidae*) Larvae. *Journal of Turfgrass Management* 1 (4): 23. Binghamton, NY: Haworth Press.

Witteveen, Gordon, and Michael Bavier. 1998. *Practical Golf Course Maintenance*. Hoboken, NJ: John Wiley & Sons, Inc..

Woods End Research, POB 297, 1850 Old Rome Road, Mt. Vernon, ME 04352; phone: 207.293.2457; fax: 207.293.2488; solvita@woodsend.org; www.woodsend.org.

Xu, Qingzhang, and Bingru Huang. 2000[a]. Growth and Physiological Responses of Creeping Bentgrass to Changes in Air and Soil Temperatures. *Crop Science* 40: 1363–1367. Madison, WI: Crop Science Society of America.

———. 2000[b]. Effects of Differential Air and Soil Temperature on Carbohydrate Metabolism in Creeping Bentgrass. *Crop Science* 40: 1368–1374. Madison, WI: Crop Science Society of America.

———. 2001. Lowering Soil Temperatures Improves Creeping Bentgrass Growth Under Heat Stress. *Crop Science* 41: 1878–1883. Madison, WI: Crop Science Society of America.

Yuen, G.Y., C.C. Jochum, L.J. Giesler, M.D. Shulski, E.A. Walter-Shea, K.G. Hubbard, and G.L. Horst. 2002. UV-B Biodosimetry in Turfgrass Canopies. *Crop Science* 42: 859–868. Madison, WI: Crop Science Society of America.

Zhang, W., W.A. Dick, and H.A.J. Hoitink. 1996. Compost-Induced Systemic Acquired Resistance in Cucumber to Pythium Root Rot and Anthracnose. *Journal of the American Phytopathological Society* 86: 1066–1070. St. Paul, MN.

Zhang, Xunzhong and R.E. Schmidt. 1999. Biostimulating Turfgrasses. *Grounds Maintenance*. 11: 14–32. Overland Park, KS: Intertec Publishing.

———. 2000. Hormone-Containing Products' Impact on Antioxidant Status of Tall Fescue and Creeping Bentgrass Subjected to Drought. *Crop Science* 40: 1344–1349. Madison, WI: Crop Science Society of America.

Zontek, Stanley. May-June 2000. Using Compost to Improve Poor Soils. *USGA Green Section Record*. 38 (3). Far Hills, NJ: U.S. Golf Association.

GLOSSARY

This glossary provides definitions for terms used in this book and some of the terms used in many of the sources listed under "Sources and Resources."

Abiotic—Not living.

Acid—Any substance that can release hydrogen ions in a solution.

Actinomycete—Decay microorganism with a fungus-like appearance but, like bacteria, no well-defined nucleus.

Adsorb—See Adsorption.

Adsorption—The adherence of one material to the surface of another via electro-magnetic forces (e.g., dust to a television screen).

Adventitious rooting—Roots emanating from aboveground plant parts.

Aegis—Protection.

Aerobic—Needing oxygen to live.

Alkaline—Refers to substances with a pH greater than 7.

Allelopathic—Usually refers to the negative influence a plant has on other plants or microorganisms.

Allelochemicals (or Allelopathic chemicals)—Substances produced by one plant that have a negative effect on another.

Amorphous—Without consistency in its structure or form.

Anaerobic—Refers to an environment with little or no oxygen or organisms that require little or no oxygen to live.

Anaerobiosis—Life in the absence of oxygen.

Antagonist—An organism that works against the action of another.

Anthropogenic—Caused by human action.

Apatite—A natural phosphate material.

Aragonite—Calcium carbonate (lime) formed by shellfish.

Arthropod—An animal with a segmented body and exoskeletal structure (e.g., insects, spiders, and crustaceans).

Assimilation—Digestion and diffusion of nutrients by an organism for growth and/or sustenance.

ATM—Atmosphere; a measurement of pressure of a gas.

Atmosphere—The naturally existing gases of any given environment. Also a measurement of pressure (see ATM).

Autoclave—A machine that, with heat and pressure, can react gases with other materials. It is also used to sterilize tools and equipment.

Autotroph—Organism that can synthesize organic carbon compounds from atmospheric carbon dioxide, using energy from light or chemical reactions.

Bases—See Base cation.

Base cation—A positively charged ion historically belonging to the earth metal family (potassium, magnesium, calcium, etc.).

Biomass—The cumulative mass of all living things in a given environment.

Biota—Biomass.

Biotic—Pertaining to life or living organisms.

Botany—The study of plants.

Calcite—Calcium carbonate (lime)

Carbon-to-Nitrogen ratio—A ratio measured by weight of the number of parts carbon to each part nitrogen (e.g., 10:1, 50:1).

Carbohydrates—A group of organic compounds that includes sugars, starch, and cellulose.

Carnivores—Organisms that consume animals or insects for sustenance.

Cation—An ion of an element or compound with a positive electromagnetic charge.

Cation exchange capacity—The total amount of exchangeable cations that a given soil can adsorb.

Cellulose—The most abundant organic compound on earth, found mostly in the cell walls of plants.

Chelation—The combination of metal (inorganic) and organic ions into a stable compound sometimes referred to as a *chelate*.

Chlorosis—Loss of normal green color in plants.

Colloids—Very small soil particles with a negative electromagnetic charge that are capable of attracting, holding, and exchanging cations.

Consumer—See Heterotroph.

Cultivar—A specific plant variety.

Detritus—The detached fragments of any structure, biotic or abiotic, that are decomposing or weathering.

Dolomite—Calcium, magnesium carbonate (magnesium lime).

Edaphic—Refers to factors or conditions in the soil such as soil structure, atmosphere, fertility, and biological diversity, that influence the growth of plants.

Edaphology—The study of edaphic factors.

Entomo—Prefix pertaining to insects.

Enzymes—A group of proteins that hasten biochemical reactions in both living and dead organisms.

Eutrophy—The excessive nutrient enrichment of ponds or lakes, causing the accelerated growth of plants and microorganism and depletion of oxygen.

Evapotranspiration—Water loss from the soil from both evaporation and transpiration through plants.

Exude—The release of substances from cells or organs of an organisms.

Faunal—Pertaining to microscopic or visible animals.

Fecundity—The reproductive capabilities of an organism.

Floral—Pertaining to plants or bacteria, fungi, actinomycetes, etc.

Free oxygen—Gaseous oxygen not bound to other elements.

Furrow slice—Plow depth of approximately 6 to 7 inches.

Geoponic—Pertaining to agriculture or the growing of plants on land.

Gustation—An organism's sense of taste.

Guttation—The release of nutrient-rich liquid from plant leaves.

Hemicellulose—A carbohydrate resembling cellulose but more soluble; found in the cell walls of plants.

Herbivore—Organism that consumes plants for sustenance.

Heterotroph—Organism that derives nutrients for growth and sustenance from organic carbon compounds but is incapable of synthesizing carbon compounds from atmospheric carbon dioxide.

Humification—The biological process of converting organic matter into humic substances.

Humology—The study of humus.

Hydrolysis—The reaction of hydrogen (H) or hydroxyl (OH) ions from water with other molecules, usually resulting in simpler molecules more easily assimilated by organisms.

Hypha—A microscopic tube that is a basic component of most fungi in their growth phase.

In situ—Refers to natural or original position. (Example: Organisms in situ may respond differently to a stimulus than they would in a laboratory.)

Ion—Any atom or molecule with either a positive or negative electromagnetic charge.

Kairomone—A chemical substance produced by organisms (e.g., plants or insects) that attracts another species or the opposite gender to it. (Examples: 1. Fruit produces kairomones that attract certain insects. 2. Many insects produce kairomones called *pheromones* that attract the opposite sex.)

Kame—A ridge, hill, or mound deposited by glacial meltwater.

Kettle—A hollow formed by glacial drift.

Labile—Undergoing chemical, physical, or biological change.

Ligand—A compound, molecule, or ion bonded to a central compound, molecule, or atom.

Lignin—A biologically resistant fibrous organic compound deposited in the cell walls of cellulose whose purpose is to strengthen and support stems, branches, roots, etc.

Lodging—When plants become too topheavy to stand upright and instead lie over on the ground.

Macro—A prefix meaning "large."

Meso—A prefix meaning "middle."

Metabolism—The biological and chemical changes that occur in living organisms or the changes that occur to organic compounds during assimilation by another organism.

Metabolite—A product of metabolism, or a substance involved in metabolism.

Meteorology—The study or science of the earth's atmosphere.

Methodology—A system, or the study of methods.

Micelle—Microcell; a negatively charged (colloidal) soil particle most commonly found in either a mineral form (clay) or organic form (humus).

Micro—A prefix meaning "small"; usually, microscopic.

Mineralization—The biological process of transforming organic compounds into inorganic compounds (minerals) (e.g., mineralization of protein into ammonium).

Mineralogy—The study or science of minerals.

Mitigate—Lessen or reduce severity.

Mmho or Millimho—A thousandth of a mho, which is a measure of a material's ability to conduct electricity. Usually used in soil tests to determine salt levels.

Molecule—The smallest particle of a compound that can exist independently without changing its original chemical properties.

Monoculture—The cultural practice of growing only one variety of crop in a specific area every season without variance.

Morphology—The study or science of the form or structure of living organisms.

Mucilage—Compounds synthesized by plants and microbes that swell in water, taking on a gelatinous consistency, that function to maintain a moist environment and bind soil particles together to form an aggregation.

Myco—A prefix that refers to fungi.

Nitrification—A process performed by soil bacteria that transforms ammonium nitrogen into nitrite and, finally, nitrate nitrogen. Nitrate is the form of nitrogen most often used by plants.

OM—Abbreviation for organic matter.

Oxidation—Usually refers to the addition of oxygen to or combination of oxygen with other elements or compounds, but can also refer to an increase of positive valence.

Oxidize—Add oxygen or increase positive valence. See Oxidation.

Parent material—The original rock from which a soil is derived.

Pedology—The study or science of soils.

Pedosphere—The top layer of the earth's crust, where soils exist.

Phenology—The study or science of biological phenomena and their relationship to environmental factors.

Pheromone—A chemical produced by an insect or other animal that attracts another member of the same species, usually of the opposite sex.

Phyllosphere—Leaf surfaces.

Physiology—The study or science of the biological functions and/or activities of living organisms.

Phyto—A prefix referring to plants.

Phytopathogen—A plant parasite.

Phytotoxic—A substance that is toxic to plants.

Porosity—The spaces between soil particles.

Producer—See Autotroph.

Rhizosphere—The area of soil in immediate proximity to roots or root hairs of living plants.

Saprophyte—An organism that can absorb nutrient from dead organic matter.

Senescence—The aging process.

SOM—Abbreviation for soil organic matter.

Steward—A person who manages or cares for property of another. In agriculture, the term can refer to someone who cares for his own land but believes that ownership does not entitle one to dispose of the soil's resources for personal gain.

Substrate—Material used by organisms for food.

Superfluity—Oversupply.

Symbiosis—A relationship between two organisms, usually obligatory and often of mutual benefit.

Synergy—Where the activities or reactions of two or more organisms or substances are greater than the sum of the agents acting separately.

Taxonomy—The science of classification.

Tectonic—Pertaining to the structure and form of the earth's crust.

Texture analysis—An analysis of soil particles determining the percentages of sand, silt, and clay.

Throughfall—Moisture or precipitation that drips from aboveground plants, such as trees, to the ground. Throughfall is thought to contain some substances leached from leaf surfaces.

Topography—Pertaining to the surface characteristics of a given landscape.

Trophic levels—Levels of consumers within a food chain in relation to producers of organic nutrients, such as plants. (For example, producers–primary consumers–secondary consumers–tertiary consumers–decay organisms.)

Valence—A measurement of how many electrons an atom or molecule can share in a chemical combination. A negative valence indicates electrons offered in a chemical bond, whereas a positive valence is the number of electrons that can be accepted.

Volatile—Refers to substances that can easily change, often into a gas.

INDEX